The Last Corpsman

The Last Corpsman

THE STORY OF
JOHN I. UNGER
CHIEF HOSPITAL CORPSMAN, U.S. NAVY,
AND FORMER WORLD WAR II PRISONER OF WAR IN THE PACIFIC

JUAN CARLOS MARCOS

The Last Corpsman: The Story of John I. Unger, Chief Hospital Corpsman, U.S. Navy, and Former World War II Prisoner of War in the Pacific

For information about this title or to order other books and/or electronic media, contact the publisher:

Elie Press, LLC
Evergreen, Colorado
E-mail: Eliepress317@gmail.com

ISBNs:
978-0-9960838-2-9 Hardcover
978-0-9960838-3-6 Softcover
978-0-9960838-4-3 eBook
978-0-9960838-5-0 Audio book

Printed in the United States of America

Cover and Interior design: 1106 Design

Publisher's Cataloging-In-Publication Data
(Prepared by The Donohue Group, Inc.)

Names: Marcos, Juan Carlos, author.
Title: The last corpsman : the story of John I. Unger, Chief Hospital Corpsman, U.S. Navy, and former World War II prisoner of war in the Pacific / Juan Carlos Marcos.
Description: Evergreen, Colorado : Elie Press, LLC, [2018] | Includes bibliographical references.
Identifiers: ISBN 9780996083829 (hardcover) | ISBN 9780996083836 (softcover) | ISBN 9780996083843 (ebook)
Subjects: LCSH: Unger, John I., 1920- | World War, 1939-1945--Prisoners and prisons--Biography. | United States. Navy--Hospital corpsmen--Biography. | Wake Island, Battle of, Wake Island, 1941. | Man-woman relationships--United States. | Soldiers--United States--Correspondence. | LCGFT: Biographies.
Classification: LCC D811.U45 M37 2018 (print) | LCC D811.U45 (ebook) | DDC 940.548173--dc23

★　　★　　★

*To all American Prisoners of War throughout our history who have
served with courage and distinction*

★　　★　　★

CONTENTS

★   ★   ★

AUTHOR'S NOTE

This is my second book. My first book, *Warriors at the Helm: A Leader's Guide to Success in Business*, was about several colleagues and me sharing our experiences regarding what we believe are key behaviors that work or don't work in the corporate environment. The bottom line about that book is that it was about things we directly experienced. Writing *Warriors at the Helm* was challenging but fun. I was trying to share things that were familiar to me that I thought might be useful to others.

Writing this book, however, required me to write about things I have *not* experienced and about a man I had not met till a few weeks before I started the project. I feel a responsibility not only to the readers to weave together a compelling story but also to Mr. John I. Unger to accurately and vividly depict his extraordinary life.

Brian Unger, one of John's two sons, has been a friend and colleague of mine for three decades. He and his wife, Jacki, have been valued friends to my wife, Randi, and me. Brian and Jacki had been helping his dad to clean out his house after he and his wife, Alice, had moved into an assisted-living facility. In the course of cleaning John's house, while working on the attic, Brian and Jacki discovered letters John had written to Alice before and after World War II, during the time he served as a Navy Hospital Corpsman. Among the many interesting aspects of the letters was that no one knew they existed.

Brian eventually shared his discovery of the letters with me and suggested that it would be a great idea if someone wrote a book about it. As the conversation continued, he asked if I'd be interested in writing the book. At the time, I was retired and just finishing my first book, which had taken a great deal of time. Also, I had never met John, so I did not have a connection with him other than the references Brian had made about him being a great guy and a special father. Shortly after, I came out of retirement and returned to work for thirty months in a very demanding job. Accordingly, the notion of writing another book was out of the question.

I retired again in March of 2018, and, after a re-retirement celebratory cruise with my family out of Cape Canaveral, Florida, Randi and I went to visit Brian and Jacki at their home in Palm Coast. We had seen them only once in the thirty months since I'd returned to work, so we were looking forward to the visit. Suffice it to say that it resulted in an unexpected opportunity.

Our visit with Brian and Jacki was over Easter weekend. On Sunday, Brian was planning to take his dad to church and asked Randi and me if we'd like to join them. We accepted and went to pick John up. It was the first time I'd met him. John was ninety-seven at the time, and, from our very first greeting, I was struck by his thoughtfulness and alacrity. My initial thought was, *I'd love to be like this guy if I make it to ninety-seven.*

John was wearing a World War II Veterans hat, and, as we walked into church, several parishioners thanked him for his service. One gentleman in particular went on and on expressing his gratitude, to a degree that was almost uncomfortable. John listened to him attentively and graciously, and then humbly thanked him.

John was fighting some intestinal problems, so, after church, we dropped him off at his place, and we went off to Easter dinner at Brian and Jacki's house. John warmly bid his goodbyes to us and thanked us for joining him for church. I vividly recall that, as I shook his hand, he grasped both of mine and warmly wished me the best. It was one of those small gestures that convey a lot more than a mere formality. To me, it conveyed a great deal about the man.

Later that day, Jacki decided to take some Easter pie to John, and the four of us went to deliver it. I was glad to be able to see him again. Brian started asking John about his war experience as a Prisoner of War. Once again, I was struck by John's humility and thoughtfulness as he answered Brian's questions. Brian asked if there was anything I wanted to know, and, at first, I declined. I did not want to intrude. But as I listened to John talk about his horrific experiences in a matter-of-fact manner, I couldn't help myself. I jumped in with some questions of my own. One response in particular that got us all laughing was what John wanted to eat first after being released from captivity as a Prisoner of War. He pondered the question for a minute and then laughingly said, "I can't remember what I wanted to eat, but I knew for sure I never wanted to eat uncooked rice anymore; that's about all they fed us."

We said our goodbyes to John again, and, later that evening, Jacki shared a couple of the letters John had written to Alice. Not surprisingly, they were thoughtful, loving, and engaging—exactly like the man I'd met earlier that day. Suffice it to say that, the more I heard, the more my admiration grew. Brian then posed the question again that he had asked four years earlier: Would I consider writing a book about John? I told him I'd think about it and get back to him.

After talking to Randi and reflecting on the opportunity to write about an exemplary and humble man who has lived an extraordinary life, I decided to give it a try. It has been an honor and privilege to write this book. As you read it, you may realize that my intent was to portray a man who has positively touched countless lives and has overcome incredible obstacles during his remarkable life. If, after reading the book, that is not your conclusion, the failure is all mine and not a reflection on John I. Unger.

★ ★ ★

CHAPTER 1

"THOSE ARE BOMBS!"

December 8, 1941

The bombs started falling on the Wake Atoll shortly before noon. The shock for most of the men on the atoll, military and civilian alike, was terrifying. Almost immediately, casualties started mounting, especially at the airstrip. The Pan American Hotel was one of the first structures to go up in flames, and the Pan American Clipper (amphibious plane) was hit with machine gun fire but would survive. Some civilians helped where they could, but most of them ran for their lives. At the gun batteries, the Marines took shelter inside the bunkers and fired their 3-inch and 5-inch guns (antiaircraft and armor-piercing rounds). These, however, were ineffective because the bombers were flying too low. The fierce surprise attack had taken mere minutes, but it had been accurate and deadly. While John was trying to figure out what was happening, the inescapable reality for everyone at Wake Island was that America was at war.

Arguably, if one were to pinpoint the "Middle of Nowhere," the coordinates are latitude **19.308552** and longitude **166.631012**,[1] otherwise known as Wake Island or, more accurately, the Wake Atoll, which consists of three islets: Wake, Peale, and Wilkes. It is 4,656 miles from Los Angeles, 2,303 from Honolulu, and 1,992 from Tokyo[2] in the Pacific Ocean.

On Monday, December 8, 1941 (Sunday, December 7 in the U.S., on the other side of the international dateline), at seven in the morning, twenty-one-year-old John Ignacious Unger, Navy Corpsman (medic) 3rd Class, was having breakfast, as usual, at the mess hall in Camp 2 on Wake Island, before reporting for duty at Peale Island. There, he provided medical support to the Marines of the 1st Defense Battalion at Toki point, who manned the machine guns and the 3- and 5-inch antiaircraft guns. The 5-inch battery consisted of two guns under the command of First Lieutenant Woodrow M. Kessler. The 3-inch battery consisted of four guns commanded by Captain Bryghte D. Godbold. Both officers were supported by First Sergeant Johnalson E. Wright. Wright was a mountain of a man, big in both stature and girth, and a veteran of previous campaigns. Wright was the senior enlisted Marine in charge of all the enlisted men in B and D Batteries. John liked Wright as a person but also thought the veteran Sergeant was someone who could teach him a lot about what to do and how to do it the right way.

At approximately the same time, Army Captain Henry Wilson's radio truck had intercepted a message from Hawaii that Hickam Air Force Base, adjacent to Pearl Harbor on the Island of Oahu, had been attacked by Japanese dive bombers. Wilson ran into the command post of Major James P. Devereux, Commanding Officer of the 1st Defense Battalion, U.S. Marine Corps deployed at Wake, and shared the news about Pearl.[3] In a matter of hours, the men at Wake would join their brothers at Pearl Harbor in fighting the earliest American battles of World War II.

John was one of seven Corpsmen at Wake. There was no Chief Hospital Corpsmen on the atoll, so the highest ranking among them was Corpsman First Class Jessee R. Chambliss, who coordinated the Corpsmen's efforts. Chambliss made sure that the Corpsmen had the necessary supplies on hand to support the Marines, Navy, and Army personnel. Accordingly, he traveled throughout the entire atoll. Four Corpsmen, including John, were assigned to support gun batteries on each of the islands, and two were assigned to the military aid station on Wake. John's best friend, Navy Corpsman Second Class Artie T. Brewer, was supporting the Marines at Peacock Point, near the airfield. Artie was from Arkansas and shared a tent with John. They had met during their time together at Pearl Harbor before traveling together to Wake. Because he was Second Class, Artie rated a bunk, as opposed to John, who was Third Class and had only a cot. Artie felt bad about that, but John said, "That was fine. It didn't bother me at all."

In addition to the seven Corpsmen, there were 517 military personnel at Wake, including 449 Marines, 6 Army and another 62 Navy. Also on the atoll were 1,145 civilians who worked for Morrison-Knudsen Civil Engineering Company, who had been contracted to build a military base, and 72 Pan American employees.[4] Pan American had used Wake as a refueling station for trans-Pacific PBY Clippers since 1935.[5] The PBYs were amphibious aircraft that would transport passengers to and from the west coast of the U.S. to Japan and the Philippines.

Shortly after Devereux got word of the attack on Hickam, he tried contacting Navy Commander Winfield S. Cunningham (who was the senior Naval Officer in charge of the Naval Base) but failed to reach him. Devereux then contacted the Navy radio shack and asked if there had been any priority messages from Pearl Harbor. He was told "Yes" and that it was being decoded. Devereux did not wait for any further clarity and ordered the bugler to "sound a call to arms." He also told those near the command center that "this is not a drill and to pass the word along to all the men."[6] At that time, few of them on the atoll, including John, knew that Pearl Harbor had been attacked.

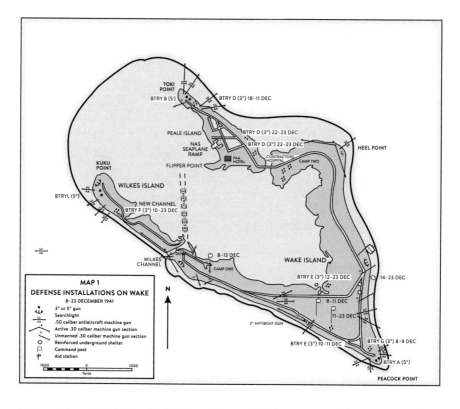

Military Map of the Wake Atoll (Colonel James P. S. Devereux U.S.M.C. from *The Story of Wake Island*)

At the airfield, Major Paul A. Putnam was the Commanding Officer in charge of the twelve F4F fighters from VMF-211 that had been positioned to help defend the atoll. Major Putnam did get word of the attack on Pearl as the two-plane morning patrol was about to take off. Putnam increased the patrol to four planes and ordered that there be planes in the air at all times.[7]

As soon as he'd arrived at Wake, in early November, John was issued a station wagon to enable him to move quickly between batteries B and

D. The batteries were about six minutes apart by vehicle. On occasion, he would also drive to the military aid station near Camp 1 to see if he could help in any way. On December 8, as John was leaving the mess hall to support the Marines at B and D batteries on Toki Point, Jessee Chambliss came over to him with an extra supply of bandages and morphine. John asked, "What is all this for?" and Chambliss replied, "There has been a call to arms, and this is no drill. So just take these—you might need them." With that scant information, John headed off to Battery B.

As he approached Battery B, John could see that the Marines had already received the word by field radio about the call to arms because they were all hunkered down in or near the bunkers. He went back and forth between batteries during the morning, to ensure everyone was all right. Shortly before noon, he saw a large group of planes approaching from the south of the atoll toward Peacock Point. This was not unusual, as both military and civilian planes stopped at Wake on a regular basis to refuel on their way to or from the Philippines. He and the Marines at B Battery thought the planes were ours. Somebody made a comment that "the wheels on the planes are falling off." Then, in the blink of an eye, the realization hit them: "Those aren't wheels—those are bombs!" Some of the men were actually waving at the planes till the bombs started falling.

Everything went crazy for John in an instant. His first thoughts were: *What do I do? Where do I go?* "I was scared stiff for a few moments, but then I said to myself, "*This is your job; this is what you are paid to do. Go do your job.*" Specifically, John told himself, "Hold your ground and support the Marines in any way you can."

Marine Private Ewing E. Laporte, stationed at Toki Point with John, would later say, "I looked, and, about one-and-a-half miles away, the planes were dropping bombs on the airport. We threw our coffee and stew away—I'd regret that later—and got our butts into a hole and watched them come over. They hit the Pan Am Hotel. They flew right over us, but they weren't after our positions."[8]

John vividly remembers that every bomb that hit—regardless of where it landed—was felt by everyone. "The whole atoll shook. Regardless of where they hit, it felt like they were right on top of you." The tremors caused by the ones that hit near his position felt monstrous. Luckily, some of the bombs fell in the lagoon and out of harm's way. There was nothing in his Navy boot camp training or his subsequent Marine boot camp training that could have prepared him for the sensation of a bomb exploding, let alone those that fell within spitting distance of where he was working or taking cover. "We had daily training at Wake with the Marines on the range. They would shoot at a target being towed by one of our planes, and that got really noisy; but there is no noise and no feeling like bombs falling on you. It was an awful, deafening noise."

Though there were no serious injuries at B and D Batteries from the first attack, John attended to the cuts and bruises of the men as he shuttled back and forth in his vehicle. He also administered morphine to those that needed it. Almost all the injuries he treated that day were caused by shrapnel, flying coral breaking up as the bombs hit, or the concussions caused by the bombs. John remembers, "Everyone was thinking, *This is crazy! Our lives have just completely changed.* We were also wondering, *What's next?*"

"We could see fires everywhere. They were especially strong where the gasoline tanks and the ammunition dump had been hit." John recalls looking across the lagoon toward the smoldering and damaged airfield on Wake Island, where the four scout planes were trying to land. Three landed safely, but one did not, causing significant propeller damage to the aircraft. John thought the pilot might be injured or dead, but he saw him later at the Officers Club, and he was fine. Since arriving on the Island, John had worked as a bartender at the Officers Club in his off-duty time, to earn extra money. The pilot, Captain Henry T. Elrod, felt bad about losing the aircraft, but he had literally lived to fight another day. Elrod would be the sole Congressional Medal of Honor recipient from the Battle of Wake Island, for his actions in the air and on the ground.[9]

John is a "glass half-full" person. After the attack, he thought, regardless of the shock factor, "We were lucky that first day. In my area, no one got hurt too bad." The Japs' first attack had taken only ten minutes, but it had felt much longer. As John recalls, "The Jap bombers had taken only one pass over the gun batteries at Toki Point, and, though the attack was short, it made you think, for sure."

The rest of the atoll had not been as lucky. A confluence of circumstances had dealt the Marines and civilians on the atoll a severe blow on that first day of the battle. Only four days prior, on December 4, the *USS Enterprise*, a carrier, had sailed within flying range of Wake to deliver twelve planes to the defense of the atoll.[10] The four scout planes that Major Putnam had put in the air to look for enemy planes had been flying at twelve thousand[11] feet and well above the Japs, who approached the atoll below a cloud cover, at less than two thousand feet.[12] The scout planes never saw the Jap planes approaching. In addition, the base had not received their radar equipment, which, as far as Devereux knew, was sitting on a dock at Pearl Harbor, waiting to be delivered to Wake.[13] Finally, the constant surf around the atoll drowned out other sounds, including those of approaching aircraft. As John shared, "We simply got used to the sound of the surf and didn't pay attention to it, but the constant pounding of waves made it difficult, if not impossible, to hear incoming planes till they were almost on top of us." The twenty-seven Jap Mitsubishi Attack Bombers which had flown from Roi, an island in the north part of the Kwajalein Atoll in the Marshall Islands, had been precise, destructive, and deadly.[14] Nine of the planes had focused on Peale Island, but most of the attack on that first day was concentrated on Wake.

Regardless of the almost five-hour warning after the attack on Pearl and the subsequent call to arms, the Wake defenders had been taken by surprise. The guns that were fired at the Japs were ineffective. The Japs were flying too low for the 3-inch and 5-inch guns to be effective, and, by the time the machine guns started firing from Wilkes and Wake Islands, the Jap planes were too far away and could not be reached. Neither of the antiaircraft guns at Batteries B and D got a chance to fire at the Japs. Seven of the eight planes at the airfield were destroyed. The eighth was damaged beyond repair but would later be used for spare parts. At the airfield, there were thirty-four military casualties, many of the refueling gas tanks were burning, and most of the Pan Am facilities on Peale Island were destroyed. The Pan Am Hotel, which had taken a direct hit, suffered the loss of ten Chamorro (see page 9) employees who had transferred there from Guam.[15] John recalls that, "Miraculously, the Pan Am Clipper, which had been hit by machine gun fire while docked on Peale Island, was not seriously damaged and could still fly."

The pilots on the ground had tried desperately to reach their planes to try to get them in the air and join the fight. They were running through strafing fire from the Jap bombers. Second Lieutenant Frank J. Holden was cut to pieces by bullets. Second Lieutenant Harry G. Webb was shot in the stomach and feet and could not move but would survive. All over the airfield there were dazed, wounded, or dead men.[16] Earlier in the day, First Lieutenant George A. Graves and Second Lieutenant Robert Conderman had been assigned to escort the Clipper partway to Midway Island.[17] The two pilots had been furiously running to their planes. Graves reached his plane but never had a chance to get off the ground, as he took a direct hit from a Jap bomb. Conderman was hit by machine-gun fire before reaching his plane. Some of the men tried to help him, but he ordered them away. He knew he was dying and told the men to help the other wounded he could see all around him.[18] John knew all of them from his work at the Officers Club and would mourn the three pilots who perished.

Captain of the Pan Am Clipper, J. H. Hamilton, inspected the damage to the Clipper and decided that it could fly. He hurriedly found Commander Cunningham and requested permission to evacuate the handful of passengers who had come from the Philippines plus his crew of eight and the twenty-seven remaining Pan Am "white" personnel. This resulted in a total passenger load much heavier than normal. The dark-complexioned Chamorros were indigenous people from the Mariana Islands and employees of Pan Am. Cunningham would later write that he was taken aback that the plans had not included taking the Chamorros. According to Cunningham, Hamilton had explained that there was no room for them. Cunningham would say, "It seemed to me an unfortunate time to draw the color line."[19] The Clipper would take off at 1:30 PM, needing three tries to take off because of the extra weight. It would fly to Midway for refueling before going on to Pearl Harbor, where the Captain and passengers were questioned about the conditions at Wake.[20]

At the time of the first attack on December 8, there were two health-care facilities on the atoll. One was the civilian hospital located near Camp 2 on the north part of Wake Island. The second was a military aid station, or sick bay, located near Camp 1 on the south side of the island in a bunker. Navy Lieutenant Gustav Mason Kahn, who had been a dermatologist prior to joining the service, supported the military personnel, and the civilians relied on Dr. Lawton Ely Shark for their medical care. Sometime that afternoon, John drove to the civilian hospital to see if he could be of help. Both doctors were performing surgeries on the wounded, and he was told that things were under control. He also checked on his close friend Artie Brewer at the gun batteries on Peacock Point. Artie told John, "All is good." Both were happy to see each other and that they had survived the first awful bombing.

Late in the day, bone-tired from the action and the tension, John reflected on what had happened. Most notably, he was happy to be alive. He thought about the turmoil all over the island and wondered what tomorrow would bring. That night, unable to retire to his tent, he found a piece of tarp near Battery B and lay down to rest under the stars. All military personnel had been told to stay at their stations, as no one knew when the next attack would come. Someone from the mess hall brought water and sandwiches out to the gun batteries. John can't remember what time that was, but he recalls it was welcome nourishment. He was grateful. Sometime that night, he must have fallen asleep because he recalls someone tripping over him and then not being able to get back to sleep.

In one of countless ironies at Wake, one of John's buddies at Peale Island, Private First Class Verne L. Wallace, knew he had a letter from his girlfriend in Pennsylvania. He was intending to read it, but the order came to man the guns. It was not till the early morning hours of the next day that he finally read the letter, which said, in part:

> *As long as you have to be away, darling, I'm so very, very happy you are in the Pacific, where you won't be in danger if war comes.*[21]

Meanwhile, in Washington DC, Admiral Kichisaburō Nomura, Japanese Ambassador to the United States, there to broker a peace agreement with President Franklin D. Roosevelt, steadfastly claimed that he was not aware that his country was about to attack Allied forces all over the Pacific while he was conducting diplomatic negotiations.[22]

In Japan, Prime Minister Hideki Tojo addressed the Japanese people and told them, "I hereby promise you that Japan will win final victory" and reminded them that, in 2,600 years, Japan had never been defeated in a war.[23]

In England, Winston Churchill, Prime Minister of the United Kingdom, after hearing from Roosevelt about the attack on Pearl Harbor, wrote, "I slept the sleep of the saved and thankful, convinced now that we had won the war. England would live."[24] Though certainly logical for Churchill to welcome the U.S. might and power to the war, it was tragically ironic for John, his fellow defenders at Wake, and hundreds of thousands of Allied soldiers all over the Pacific. All of them felt anything but safe or saved.

The next day, President Roosevelt delivered his famous "Infamy" speech to the Senate and House of Representatives in Washington, DC. Below is an excerpt from the speech:

Yesterday, December 7, 1941—a date which will live in infamy—the United States of America was suddenly and deliberately attacked by naval and air forces of the Empire of Japan.

The United States was at peace with that Nation and, at the solicitation of Japan, was still in conversation with its Government and its Emperor looking toward the maintenance of peace in the Pacific. Indeed, one hour after Japanese air squadrons had commenced bombing in the American Island of Oahu, the Japanese Ambassador to the United States and his colleague delivered to our Secretary of State a formal reply to a recent

American message. And while this reply stated that it seemed use-
less to continue the existing diplomatic negotiations, it contained
no threat or hint of war or of armed attack.

It will be recorded that the distance of Hawaii from Japan
makes it obvious that the attack was deliberately planned
many days or even weeks ago. During the intervening time,
the Japanese Government has deliberately sought to deceive the
United States by false statements and expressions of hope for con-
tinued peace.

The attack yesterday on the Hawaiian Islands has caused
severe damage to American naval and military forces. I regret to
tell you that very many American lives have been lost.

Yesterday the Japanese Government also launched an attack
against Malaya. Last night Japanese forces attacked Hong Kong.

Last night Japanese forces attacked Guam. Last night
Japanese forces attacked the Philippine Islands. Last night the
Japanese attacked Wake Island. And this morning, the Japanese
attacked Midway Island.

As Commander in Chief of the Army and Navy I have
directed that all measures be taken for our defense.

No matter how long it may take us to overcome this premedi-
tated invasion, the American people in their righteous might will
win through to absolute victory.

With confidence in our armed forces—with the unbounding
determination of our people—we will gain the inevitable tri-
umph, so help us God.

I ask that the Congress declare that since the unprovoked and
dastardly attack by Japan on Sunday, December 7, 1941, a state of
war has existed between the United States and the Japanese Empire.[25]

On December 8, Montanan Jeanette Rankin, the first woman elected to Congress and a dedicated, lifelong pacifist, cast the sole Congressional vote against the U.S. declaration of war on Japan. Rankin cared little about the damage her beliefs caused her political career.[26]

It was now December 9 on Wake, and John and his fellow defenders waited—for what, they did not know.

★　　★　　★

CHAPTER 2

"JOHN, YOU SHOULD NOT DO THAT EVER AGAIN."

June 23, 1920 to January 1932

Johan I. Unger Jr. was born near Deutsch-Schützen, Austria, on June 23, 1920, and was baptized on June 28, 1920, in a Roman Catholic church in the state of Burgenland in the region of Oberwart. He was raised as a devout Catholic. To this day, he still attends church on Sundays and takes communion every chance he gets. If he misses mass on Sunday, he attends service on Monday at the assisted-living facility where he lives. Johann was named after his father and would change his name to John when he moved to America. For simplicity, I'll refer to Johan Jr. as John from this point forward.

Deutsch-Schützen is a small farming town in Southeastern Austria, near the Pinka River, close to the Hungarian border. John was born during uncertain and dangerous times, between World Wars. World War I, ironically dubbed "The War to End All Wars," had ended two years before John was born and would pale in comparison to the death and destruction wreaked by World War II. Austria played a central role at the beginning of both wars.

World War I was sparked by the assassination of Austrian Archduke Franz Ferdinand and lasted from 1914 to 1918. It culminated with the signing of the treaty of Versailles, which, some argued, placed overly harsh conditions on Germany and led to its nationalistic resurgence, Adolph Hitler's rise to power, and, eventually, World War II. The treaty was primarily negotiated by the Allied powers, with little involvement by Germany. Among its many provisions, the country's boundaries were reassigned. Germany was assigned liability for severe monetary reparations and also held to stringent military restrictions.[1]

Hitler came to power as Chancellor in 1933, and, in 1938, he annexed Austria. With the annexation, his quest for territories in Europe had begun. In 1935, Benito Mussolini, Prime Minister of Italy since 1922, was the first of the Fascist leaders. He began his own territorial quests the winter of 1935-36 by conquering Ethiopia, in Northeastern Africa.[2] Finally, Japan had taken its first steps toward the military domination of East Asia with the occupation of Manchuria in 1931 and subsequently Nanking in December of 1937. Japan's move into China would lead to the massacre of more than 350,000 civilians and come to be known as "The Rape of Nanking."[3] Some have argued that World War II really began in 1931 in Manchuria. The unholy and destructive Axis alliance (Germany, Japan, and Italy) would eventually come together in 1940 with the signing of the Tripartite Pact.[4] Together, the three countries would wreak havoc on the world.

John and his family, younger brother Wilhelm (or "Bill," as he would be called after moving to the U.S.), grandma Anna Standor, mother Anna Unger, and father Unger Sr., lived in a log cabin on a small farm outside of Deutsch-Schützen. They had no electricity or indoor plumbing, and the cabin had dirt floors. In short, it was a meager home. John described it as being "just like where Abe Lincoln grew up." John described Grandma Anna as "a tall, stern, and statuesque lady."

John with his parents Anna and John Sr. and brother Wilhelm in Austria (From the personal collection of John I. Unger)

Tragically, John's first recollection of life was being at his mother's bedside when she died. There were lots of trees on the property, and John was playing and running through them one day, when his grandmother called him inside. John, along with his grandmother and brother, were by Anna's bedside when she passed from complications with pneumonia. He was four years old at the time, and his mother was in her early twenties. As best as John knows, Anna had walked from their home to catch a train in town and missed it. Both the trip to and from the train station occurred in a driving rainstorm, which caused her illness and her subsequent demise. A fair-complexioned, long-haired, beautiful lady, she would not see her two sons grow up.

John's father had worked in a bakery, dabbled in making his own liquor, and did odd jobs to make money. Johan Sr. had left Austria in August of 1922, before John had any recollections of him. He was not present when his wife passed away. As the story goes, Johan Sr. had a friend who had been accused of murder, stealing, or both. Johan Sr. put his friend up for a night, and the police suspected him of being an accomplice to the crimes. John's father had a history of other relatively minor brushes with the law, which, as he later learned from his father, "were usually resolved by giving the judge or policeman a bottle of whiskey to settle the matter." Based on his past history with the law and this current and more potentially damaging situation, Johan Sr. figured out a way to flee to St. Louis, Missouri. Johan Sr.'s father Michael lived among a large German and Austrian community. John and Wilhelm would not see or know their father from 1922 till 1932. For ten years, grandma Anna was their surrogate mother and caregiver. Grandma Anna had visited St. Louis prior to John's birth but did not like it and returned to Austria to live at her modest farm.

The official language of Austria is German and John's first language. Speaking German would serve him well during his war years. Though he doesn't recollect being hungry as a child, he did not grow up with an abundance of food. That would also serve him well during his years as a Prisoner of War (POW). John's family had some fruit trees on their small farm, a goat that provided milk, and some chickens that produced eggs; the family also planted potatoes. According to John, Grandma Anna used to say, "When you plant one potato, you get a dozen in return." As such there were always potatoes on the menu, especially when nothing else was available. He remembers having a couple of pigs at one time that lived in a pen that was almost attached to the cabin. The pigs eventually grew too old, and grandma butchered them. The pigs provided the three of them with some meat for a short time. There was no money to buy new pigs.

Deutsch-Schützen and agricultural fields, 2018 (From the personal collection of Brian L. Unger)

Though John didn't know any different as a young child growing up, he retrospectively recognizes that "I was raised without food practically. It was a special treat at Christmas time to get an orange." Eight decades later, his grandson Tim Unger would say of his grandfather: "I really believe the way grandpa grew up had a lot to do with him surviving the war, especially the Prisoner of War camps experience. I'm convinced that his meager diet as a child and his faith in God got him through it. He grew up as an old school Austrian Catholic, and that helped him."

Besides getting an orange during the holidays, John has fond memories of his first Christmas tree. He was six at the time. The primary decorations on the tree were small candles that grandma would light in the evening. "She had to be careful to ensure the tree didn't go up in smoke." They had no electricity, so evening lights from a tree were a real treat. According to John, "the rich people in town had electricity, but they could have only one light bulb on at a time. "If you wanted light in one room, you had to turn the light off in the other room. Electricity and lights had not been around that long in that part of the country, and only a few families could afford it." He and his brother Wilhelm's sleeping arrangements were interesting in that they both slept on top of a hearth that was used for both cooking and heating the cabin. There was no mattress, but the heat from the hearth kept them warm in the winter.

Clothing was also a luxury for them. The two boys could not wear shoes year-round for fear of wearing them out. Shoes would be worn only when the weather was too cold to go barefoot. As such, for several months every year, they would go around barefoot, even at school. The school they attended was also modest. It consisted of one room that housed all the children in their rural area, regardless of age. The teacher would constantly switch subjects and the level of difficulty to accommodate the age spectrum of the children attending the school.

As the two of them grew up, they developed a reputation as some of the toughest kids in the area. As John described it, "We were rough, some of the roughest." Rough-and-tough kids will get in trouble, but Grandma was tough herself and not shy about administering discipline. When a bit of corporal punishment was in order, she would make John and or his brother "kneel on a rough block of wood" for specified periods of time. John and Wilhelm would revel in standing up or pushing off the block when grandma wasn't looking. It was the only way to get some relief from the pain that would inevitably soar through their knees, legs, and backs. "We got off that block of wood every time we thought we could get away with it and then got back on it as quickly and gracefully as we could without her noticing. It didn't always work out."

One aspect of "rough and tough," especially without a mom or dad to look after them, was learning some things the hard way. One distinctly personal memory still fresh in John's mind was a day he and some other boys were horsing around in an old church that had been condemned. The fact it was condemned made it more enticing for them to break in and play. A feature of the church was a high steeple that could be reached only via a rickety ladder. One day (he cannot remember what possessed him to do so), John brought an umbrella with him and climbed up to the steeple, planning to jump down. He thought the umbrella would act as a sort of parachute and all would be well. He jumped, and though the umbrella did not break the fall, on his way down he was fortunate to hit a couple of bushy trees and escaped without a scratch. A couple of days later, the boys were back at the church, and John was contemplating jumping from the steeple again. To this day, he swears he heard a woman's voice saying to him, "John, you should not do that ever again. You are going to hurt yourself." John explained, "To me, that voice felt like it was my mother. None of the other boys heard it, but I know I did. I didn't jump off the steeple that day, and I never did go back to that church after that." As John told that story, I couldn't help but think that Anna took over as his guardian angel that day and devoted herself to protecting him to this day. That incident would be the first but not the last time in his life that John would cheat death.

John loved to swim as a youngster. Starting at seven, he would swim every day, as long as the weather allowed it. He swam on the Pinka River, which, at some points, acts as a border between Austria and Hungary, not far from their cabin. His first swimming experience was involuntary. One day, he was on a horse-drawn buggy going across the river. He could not recall who he was with, but he does recall getting to midriver and the current sending the horse one way, the buggy the other, and John into the water. Never having had lessons, instinct took over, and he simply started kicking and moving his arms in a sweeping motion till he got back on solid ground. That would be his first swim and, though somewhat traumatic, marked the beginning of a pastime that he would enjoy the rest of his life.

Some of the men in the area would occasionally seek him out and ask him to swim across the river to Hungary to buy cigarettes. Cigarettes were cheaper in Hungary, and, by asking John to swim across the river, the men would avoid the hassles of having to present passports to border guards or having to declare goods on their return to Austria. John would swim across and then walk into the village of Pornoapati to purchase them. When he was on a cigarette-purchase mission, John learned to cross the river, current and all, by kicking his legs. He would take his clothes off and hold them over his head while using only his legs to navigate the river. On the return swim, he'd do the same but now also carrying the cigarettes. Every once in a while, the current was too strong, and he'd go underwater. Clothes and cigarettes would get soaked, but that only served as a catalyst for him to refine his swimming stroke and do better the next time.

When the weather got too cold to swim John would ice skate at a pond near the cabin. Since they had no money for skates, he improvised by attaching wires to the bottom of his shoes. Whether swimming, skating, or jumping off church steeples, John was nothing if not ingenious.

Around the age of nine, a tree fell on the cabin and made it uninhabitable. Luckily, no one was in the cabin at the time. John believes that either his dad or grandfather sent Grandma Anna money for the three of them to move into town. Deutsch-Schützen was a small town with few houses, but life there was very different from living at the cabin. A big change was that living off the land was now going to be much more challenging.

One indelible memory John has of his childhood was a trip to Hungary with some friends of the family. John does not recall the town they went to but remembers his relatives paying to see a black man manacled in a cage. The man was billed as a "Man Eater." It was an unfortunate and scary experience for him and the first and only black person John would see or know till he arrived in America. That depiction of blacks as cannibals would not be dispelled in John's mind till he had a much different experience on his arrival in America.

Another indelible experience that would change his life forever occurred in early January of 1932. John and his brother were in school, and, as he described it, "Soldiers came in and told us to get our belongings, that we were going to America." Why soldiers were involved, John does not know, nor did he ever discuss it with his father. The soldiers took the boys to their house and Grandma Anna gathered what little belongings they had and gave them some food, and money their father had sent from America. Johan Sr. had also arranged for three different people to shepherd the boys on different legs of their trip. The soldiers took the boys to Eisenberg An Der Pinka, a town about three kilometers northwest of Deutsch-Schützen. At Eisenberg An Der Pinka, they were turned over to the first stranger, a friend of their father's who the next day would put them on train to Hamburg, where a second man unknown to the boys was waiting for them. Though exciting on one level, there was also apprehension for both boys. They were leaving their grandmother, who for all intents and purposes was the only family they had ever known; they had no idea what the journey would bring. They would never see Grandma Anna again. Just like that, John, who was eleven-and-a-half years old, and Wilhelm, who was ten, began their journey to America.

Meanwhile, a few months earlier, in 1931, before John began his travels to the U.S., Japan had seized Manchuria in the Northeast of China, bordering Mongolia, Russia, and what was then unified Korea (now known as North Korea). Their aim, beyond their wanton imperialism, was to secure the region's raw materials and to control the area's rail resources.[5] Japan's relentless quest for the domination of East Asia had begun.

★ ★ ★

CHAPTER 3

"I WAS NINETEEN AND INVINCIBLE."

January 14, 1932 to May 1940

John and Wilhelm's (soon to be John and Bill) first night in Eisenberg An Der Pinka after leaving their grandmother was spent with the family of his father's friend. John does not recall their names, but he does remember that they were treated to a good meal and then taken to see a movie. Though in 1932 there were "Talkies," they had not yet made it to that part of Austria. After the silent movie and a good night's sleep, they were put on a train to Hamburg, Germany. They had no chaperone on the train. It was just the two boys headed on a seven-hundred-mile trip, to meet another person they did not know.

John remembers the overnight trip and he and his brother exploring the train from top to bottom. "It was not scary," John said. "It was an adventure for us." In Hamburg, a second stranger met them and took them to the Port of Hamburg. Visas in hand, they were ready to sail to New York on the *S.S. Roosevelt*. Johan Sr. had arranged for the boys' visas in Austria. They had been issued in Vienna on December 29, 1931, according to the Alien Passengers to the United States Manifest from the Port of New York.

UNITED STATES LINES   S. S. PRESIDENT ROOSEVELT   U. S. GOVERNMENT SHIP

The ship that took John and Wilhelm to America (Pinterest.com)

It was January 19, 1932. It would take the *S.S. Roosevelt* eleven days to make the transatlantic voyage. The boys had third-class tickets that, at the time, were also referred to as "steerage" accommodations. Steerage tickets were the cheapest way to travel on the cross-oceanic ships, and the accommodations were located on the lower decks of the ship. Once again, the boys had practically no chaperone for this longer portion of the trip. There was an unknown woman who spoke German who looked after the boys—a decision she would soon regret.

Two rambunctious preteen boys, on a big ship for the first time in their lives for eleven days: a perfect recipe for mischief. The boys played, ran, jumped, and explored. Mostly, they were everywhere they weren't supposed to be. Each of the different classes of passengers (first, second, and steerage) had specific areas of the ship dedicated to their status.

For example, each had a different dining room and sun deck. John and Wilhelm decided early on that those restrictions did not apply to them. They explored and played throughout the ship, often culminating in one of the crew hauling them back down to the steerage, which is where they were supposed to be. The lady who looked after them would admonish them, but in no time at all, they were back at it again. More than once, they were locked up in their sleeping quarters so that she and the staff could control them and know where they were for the moment— that, and to take a breather from the boys' hell-raising. One day, to the dismay of the captain and crew, they managed to get into the bridge area, which resulted in a longer lockdown than usual.

After eleven days, most of the crew and staff on the *S.S. Roosevelt* were happy to be rid of the Unger boys. Some, however, had enjoyed the antics of the two spirited Austrian boys. Though their trip on the ship was done, the mischief was not. As the ship was coming into New York, the boys were awed by the size and grandeur of the skyscrapers. After the ship docked, in the hustle and bustle of disembarking, somehow the boys managed to walk down a gangplank and started a stroll through the city. They lost all track of time as the hours passed, mesmerized by the big city and crowds. They did not speak a word of English and had no idea where they were going.

It was not clear to John whether the authorities on the ship or customs knew they were missing. An alert New York policeman thought it strange that two young boys would be wandering the streets lugging their bags. He could not communicate with them but surmised that they had just disembarked from a ship. The cop herded them back to the port and figured out that they had not cleared customs. Somehow, he also connected with the lady who'd been semi-in-charge of the boys, to learn that they should be taken to the railroad station. After clearing customs and becoming officially "John" and "Bill," they would begin the last leg of their almost five-thousand-mile trip between Deutsch-Schützen and St. Louis to reunite with their father.

It was January 30, 1932, and, in three days, the Unger boys would see their father for the first time in ten years—for John, since the age of two. Shortly after the train departed New York, John had his second life encounter with a black man. As the boys were settling in, a black porter came by selling bananas. The boys had never seen a banana before and didn't know what it was. After getting over the shock of seeing the potential "man eater," John used some of the money their father had sent them and bought a banana. The porter, having determined that John did not speak English, made an eating gesture, and John proceeded to stuff the banana into his mouth without peeling it. The porter went from the eating gesture to shock and quickly pulled the banana out of John's mouth. He also showed him how to peel it. John proceeded to eat it, and all was good. Better yet was the fact that John's second encounter with a black man was that of an attentive and kind person showing him how to eat a banana, rather than eating him. In 2014 and again in 2018, John would become the proud great-grandfather of two biracial, half African American children. Rachel, Jacki and Brian (John's younger son) Unger's daughter, would marry Jamil Branch, an African American, and together they would bring Hayden and Hayes into the world and into the loving arms of great-grandpa John.

Arrival in St. Louis was on February 2, 1932, where the boys met their new family. Johan Sr. had remarried in 1925 to Theresa, their new stepmother, and together they had two children, Frank and Theresa. Ergo, the younger Theresa (their stepsister) was referred to by her nickname, "Babe." The family lived in the North St. Louis area on 21st Street and worshipped at the Most Holy Trinity (MHT) Catholic Church, established in 1848,[1] a short distance from their home on 14th Street.

From left to right, Bill, Frank, Johan Sr., Theresa (Babe), John, and Theresa (From the personal collection of John I. Unger)

Life in America was much different than in Deutsch-Schützen. Though they lived in a large German community, where most of the people spoke their language, there was the challenge of learning English and dealing with American-born children who knew little and cared less about where the Unger boys had come from. Some, thinking the boys were Hungarian, soon referred to them by the slur "Hunkie." Soon after that, the wrestling matches and fistfights started, particularly with John, who was the bigger of the two boys. The challenges did not faze John, as he had been one of the rougher boys in Deutsch-Schützen. As far as he was concerned, this was just another rite of passage that he welcomed. Also, because he did not speak English, he was originally placed in the first grade with kids three to four years younger. As John described it, with a big smile on his face, "It was easy to whip any of the kids in first grade."

Soon after they arrived, the boys ended up going to different schools. Bill chose to attend a Catholic school. John chose a public school because there was a teacher at the school who spoke German. He surmised, at the wise old age of eleven, that being in a school with a bilingual teacher would accelerate the process of learning a new language. In fact, learning English became his primary pursuit. While other boys enjoyed sports and other interests, John focused on learning English. He remembers talking regularly to the bilingual teacher, often after school. The discussions made translation and picking up the language easier and faster for him. She would have him read books every night and write book reports to accelerate his learning.

At home, it was a different matter, as the children were expected to speak German. Failure to do so would occasionally result in a slap on the mouth. Though both his father and stepmother had been in the U.S. for years, they spoke broken English. John's English-speaking ability soon surpassed theirs, but it occasionally got him in trouble.

Though his focus was learning the new language, John still enjoyed swimming every chance he got. In his new home, swimming was at a large outdoor public pool near his home. It was large enough, according to John, to "have a hundred kids line up, dive into the pool, and race to the other end." John took great pride in sharing that he won those races more often than not and that the pool monitor would always praise him by saying, "John, you did it again."

John's educational history took a circuitous but interesting path. Though initially assigned to first grade because of his language deficiencies, John quickly progressed from one grade to the next and, in less than a year, was in a class with children his own age. The bottom line is that he had a gift as a quick learner, not just in language but across a spectrum of subjects. Ironically, he started high school but did not finish before enlisting in the Navy. He would not complete his high school education till after returning from the war in 1947. That did not mean he would stop his education.

October of 1929 marked the beginning of "The Great Depression," with the collapse of the stock market. It would last till 1939 and would become the worst economic period America had ever known. In 1930, the unemployment rate was 9 percent, but, by 1932, it had jumped to 24 percent.[2] It would mark the ascendency of Franklin Delano Roosevelt to the presidency when he defeated incumbent Herbert Hoover and ushered in the "New Deal," whose aim was to bring prosperity back to Americans, through the creation of government jobs and projects.[3]

Johan Sr.'s primary work was as a baker, but work during the Depression years was hard to get, so he did other odd jobs to earn extra money. He also fashioned a distillery to make alcohol for himself and to sell and generate additional income. Having access to yeast at the bakeries was convenient for the creation of his beloved whiskeys and beers. As John put it, "My dad liked to drink . . . a lot." With six mouths to feed and not a whole lot of money coming in, it was clear to

John that going to work would help things at home. Being the oldest of the children, he decided shortly after finishing grade school that it was time to go to work.

At first, John did any odd job to earn money but eventually worked for a combination travel agency and bookkeeping business. The owner of that business paid for John to go to a business school to learn bookkeeping, shorthand, and typing, skills he would use in his military service. However, that job did not provide steady income, so he went to work in a factory that manufactured cardboard boxes. That job provided full-time work but only modest wages. At one point, John went to a trade school and was certified as a car-engine mechanic. In short, he would do anything necessary to make money but was bouncing from job to job without a clear vision of the future.

That is, till some friends from the neighborhood suggested they go to a Navy Recruitment Office to learn about what opportunities that might present. It was 1939, and though the New Deal projects and increased defense spending had reduced unemployment, it was still hovering at 14 to 15 percent.[4] The bottom line was that meaningful employment would continue to be a challenge for millions of young guys like John, or so they thought.

John listened to the recruiter talk about the Navy and became interested in the idea of serving on a ship and traveling the world. Specifically, the recruiter talked to him about a six-year commitment, at least half of which would be served at sea. It sounded intriguing and adventuresome, and when asked if he would be willing to take a test, John enthusiastically agreed. He doesn't recall all the specifics of the test but clearly remembers the recruiter telling him that he was the only person who had scored 100 percent on the exam. John then proceeded to take a physical, and, as he laughingly told me, "I was rejected because I had a cavity in one of my teeth. Some of my friends were rejected because they had flat feet, but I was okay in that regard. I went and got my cavity fixed, and the next thing I know, I'm on my way to the Naval Training Center in San Diego."

John remembers telling his father that he had joined the Navy, and he sensed a bit of relief from Johan Sr. that he would now have one fewer person to provide for in the house. Shortly after John enlisted on August 11, 1939, Bill also left home and eventually ended up working in a farm in Wisconsin. It was the first time the Unger boys, now young men, would not be sleeping under the same roof. Though John did not know it at the time, years later, he was grateful that he and Bill had moved to America when they did because, as John put it, "we would have most assuredly been conscripted into Hitler's Nazi Army."

The war in Europe and Asia was now in full force. On the Asian front, Japan was now in the throes of the destruction and slaughter in Nanking, China. In Europe, Hitler had invaded Czechoslovakia in March and would invade Poland in September of 1939. The invasion of Poland led to France and England declaring war on Germany. In 1938, Neville Chamberlain, then Prime Minister of Britain, had written to a relative about Hitler: "In spite of the harshness and ruthlessness I thought I saw in Hitler's face, I got the impression that he was a man who could be relied upon when he had given his word."[5] Finally, Hitler had planted the seeds for what would become the "Holocaust"—the barbaric extermination of millions of innocent Jews.[6]

In Washington, President Roosevelt had long recognized the inevitability of war. However, the "Isolationists," led by, among others, Charles Lindbergh, the great aviator, were predicting mass riots in the streets if the U.S. were to enter the war.[7] Among the primary issues of the Isolationist were that the costs both in casualties and dollars of World War I had been too high to jump into war again—that and the fact that the war was being fought in Asia and Europe, not on our turf. The president recognized that some Isolationists were earnest in their beliefs, while others were in denial about what was happening in Europe and Asia. These "cheerful idiots," as he would later call them in public, naively bought into the fantasy that the United States could always pursue its peaceful and unique course in the world.[8] Despite all of that, many in America, including John, did not think about the possibility of America entering the war. John was not at all concerned that he could soon be in the middle of it. "I was nineteen and invincible. America being drawn into war was the furthest thing from my mind. My focus was on the next chapter of my life and what was ahead of me at Navy boot camp."

John's entry into the Navy started with eight weeks of boot camp involving fitness activities, learning the rules and disciplines of life in the Navy, and overall being prepared for duty, wherever and whatever that might be. A key part of the training was the Blue Jacket's Manual, which covered all subjects enlisted men needed to learn, for example, Deck Seamanship, Boat Seamanship (literally learning how to row a boat), Navigation and Piloting, Communications and Signals, and on and on. Physical-fitness drills were also a daily routine, especially learning how to carry and row what John referred to as "the big whale boats." There were basic things that could get you in trouble if you did not do them correctly—things like how to fold your uniforms and pack them in a sea bag or make a bed. One day, John did not make his bed to the specifications required by the Petty Officer, and he was ordered to march, carrying his bed, till he was told to stop. John, being the driven guy that he is, decided to run rather than merely march. The Petty Officer let him go for a while and then ordered him, "Stop before you kill yourself, Unger."

His stated duty preference was to serve on a submarine or a "Tin Can," which was the slang word for a destroyer. "I just wanted to be at sea." Instead, after boot camp he was told, not asked, that he was being sent for training to become a Hospital Corpsman. In retrospect, that was his first hint that America was preparing for war. John would say, "As I look back, you sort of felt that we were preparing for trouble." There were plenty of guys who could serve on ships, but not many that were asking for or had the smarts to be trained as Corpsmen. He didn't know for certain if the test he took at the Naval Recruiting Center had anything to do with the assignment to Corpsman, but he suspected that it did. John was not thrilled with the assignment, but he would soon appreciate the opportunity.

After boot camp, he was assigned to duty at the Hospital Corpsman School in San Diego. John remembers his training lasting almost nine months. The nine-month training included first aid, minor surgery, nursing care, hygiene and sanitation, pharmacy, chemistry, anatomy, and physiology. To this day, John was positively amazed at the extent of the training and appreciative of all the things he learned. Once the war started, Corpsman training was shortened to ten to twelve weeks, focusing on the Corpsman's specialty. Though all the Corpsmen received the same basic training, some would go on to study for additional certifications like dentistry. The Navy Hospital Corpsman specializing in dentistry assigned to Wake Island, and one of John's buddies, was Ernest Christian Vaale, one of the seven Corpsmen at Wake. As he said, "I would not have had the opportunity to learn so much had I been assigned to serve on a ship as a seaman."

His Navy Hospital Corpsman training concluded in early 1940, and he was assigned to the U.S. Marine Corps. The Marines are part of the Department of the Navy, from whom they receive medical support.

Accordingly, the Navy provides all medical support, including Corpsmen assigned within front-line units. As a result of this assignment, John was ordered to complete the Marine Corps boot camp in San Diego. Also, by being assigned to the Marines, it meant his initial duty would not be on a ship. Rather, he would be assigned to a specific battalion and provide medical support wherever the unit was sent.

Marine boot camp, as John recalled, was significantly more physically demanding than the Navy boot camp had been. It had been several months since the first boot camp, but John had maintained his fitness, making it easier to survive the more-demanding Marine boot camp. In addition to physical fitness, the Marines emphasized coordination and stamina. More important, at Marine boot camp, John learned how to shoot a rifle. As John said, "I learned how to row in the Navy and shoot in the Marines." After boot camp, John and his fellow Corpsmen were taught how to use Marine field equipment, ground combat tactics, and advanced combat medical skills such as: bandaging, splinting, treatment of shock, casualty evacuation, and field sanitation. By virtue of being assigned to support the Marines, John now wore two uniforms: Marine and Navy. While stationed with the Marines at Wake, he wore both uniforms.

John's education and his affinity for the service kept increasing by the day. After Marine boot camp, John was sent to Mare Island Naval Hospital in Vallejo, California, near San Francisco. There, he would meet the girl who would change his life forever—the girl who would become the love of his life.

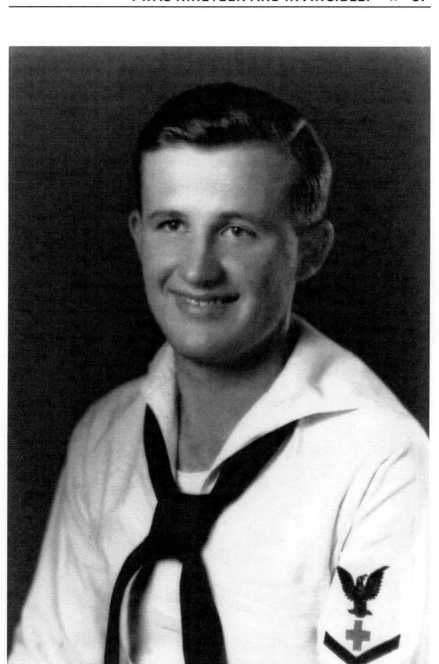

John in his Navy whites at age nineteen (From the personal collection of John I. Unger)

★　★　★

CHAPTER 4

"I JUST HAD THIS FEELING, YOU KNOW, SHE WAS SO PRETTY."

May 1940 to December 10, 1940

Mare Island was first discovered in 1775 by European settlers. Explorer Don Felix Ayala named it "Isla Plana" or Flat Island. In 1835 General Mariano Vallejo, a Mexican Commander renamed it "Isla de la Yegua," or Mare Island. As the story goes, the general's white mare fell overboard from a barge only to reappear later on the island, ergo, the name "Mare." In 1854, the U.S. Navy built a Naval yard, and in 1859, the first of more than 500 ships would be built there. In 1869, the first Naval Hospital was built, and during World War II, it would gain acclaim for its work in prosthetics for injured veterans. Between 1939 and 1944, the island reached its peak productivity, employing 41,000 workers, including 9,000 women, many living in Quonset huts on the island.[1]

In Europe, Hitler invaded Belgium and France in May. Between May 26 and June 4, Britain had turned disaster into a miracle at Dunkirk,

France, on the coast of Flanders. Of the approximately 400,000 Allied troops who had retreated to Dunkirk under the onslaught of the German Army and Luftwaffe, 342,000 had been saved by a flotilla of almost 1,000 vessels, including 700 civilian boats.[2] Almost all had been taken to England, 4,000 had been ferried to Cherbourg and other French ports still in Allied hands.[3] The Allied troops who were saved were primarily British and French, but Belgians and Dutch soldiers were also included. At the beginning of what would be called "Operation Dynamo," Vice-Admiral Bertram Ramsay, in charge of the operation, did not expect to rescue more than 45,000 men, before the evacuation would probably be halted by enemy actions.[4] Afterward, Winston Churchill would call it a "miracle of deliverance."[5] Despite the war in Europe and Churchill's pleas for help, America was still more than a year away from being drawn into the conflict.

John's duty on Mare Island was primarily to continue his training. He and his fellow Corpsmen were rotating from one unit to another every couple of months, augmenting their earlier training in San Diego, only now, on an active basis. After an orientation to each unit, they would jump in and assist doctors in various procedures or perform the medical tasks they had been trained to execute. The hospital served active and veteran service personnel.

In his spare time, John went to the bars with his buddies to enjoy a beer or whiskey or spent time at hamburger joints. He enjoyed seeing the pretty girls, but none interested him enough to ask them on a date. In July of 1940, that would change. One day early into his assignment at the hospital, John was on his way to lunch and walked past an area where patients went for physicals and minor procedures. John described who he saw on the other side of a window as he looked into the room: "Oh, yeah. She was sixteen or so, with a nice hat on and long hair. I looked in, but she never looked up. I kept walking, but, after finishing my lunch, I went back to see if she was still there." I asked John what was it that so captivating about her. He replied, "I don't know. I just had this feeling, you know, she was so pretty."

Unfortunately, she wasn't there when he returned from lunch, but that didn't stop him from trying to find her. John knew the Corpsman who had been treating her and asked him to pull her records so he could get her address. The Corpsman did so and shared the information with John. Her name was Alice Faleogo Hurtado. John did not know it at that moment, but Alice was of Samoan descent. She was born on September 13, 1923, in Aua Village, Tutuila, American Samoa. Her dark eyes, complexion, and long hair were like no one this blond, light-complexioned boy from Austria had ever seen. He was smitten.

With address in hand, John went to Benicia, about ten miles from Mare Island. Alice was babysitting when John knocked on the door and introduced himself. She politely told John she could not meet with him as she was busy but invited him to return the next day. John returned the next day and the next day after that and the one after that. He lovingly said, "We got acquainted quickly." Alice would later tell him, "I knew right away that you were the guy I was going to marry."

With Cupid's arrows embedded deeply in their respective hearts, their chance meeting would mark the beginning of a loving relationship that would last more than seventy-five years—seventy-four of them as husband and wife. And though Alice would pass away in 2014, the love and affection John feels for her still burns bright.

I vividly recall the first time I sat with John to start interviewing him for this book. We started by getting to know each other a little bit and then our discussion turned to the war and what it was like on Wake. About an hour into the interview, I asked him about Alice for the first time. Without saying a word, his eyes open wide, and he looked at me with a smile that lit up the room. The expression on his face was so blissful that it left me speechless for a moment. It was, to me, the epitome of a picture telling a thousand words. That brief moment told me volumes about both John and Alice. Afterward, I, too, started smiling. At that moment, I started regretting that I had not had the pleasure of meeting Alice.

Alice came from a family of four, including sister Julia and brothers Richard and Leon. Their father Leon Hurtado Sr., was a Navy Petty Officer, which is why the family was living in Benicia near the Naval Base at Mare Island. Alice's mom was also named Julia. Leon Sr. had been reassigned to a base in Florida for duty, and, sometime after, he and Julia had divorced.

Alice's mom, Julia, worked as a supervisor in a cannery in Benicia. Alice, at 16, was a junior at Benicia High School and the oldest of the four siblings; she babysat to bring some extra money to the now-fatherless household.

Julia was not at all pleased about her daughter spending more and more time with a sailor. According to John, Mom told Alice in no uncertain terms to "stay away from that sailor."

John and Alice's respective ages of nineteen and sixteen and Julia's recent breakup with Naval Chief Hurtado after bearing four children with him most likely contributed to her concerns. But John would not be deterred. When he could not see Alice because of his responsibilities at the hospital, he would write to her to express his love and to keep her up to date on what was going on in his life. Alice would also write, and their respective letters became a significant aspect of their bond to each other. An amazing sign of Alice's early commitment and devotion to John is that she kept all of his letters from their early romance and right through and after the war.

Alice in her teens (From the personal collection of Julie Ikeya)

Below is one of John's first letters to Alice undated, but likely late July of 1940:

Dearest Alice,

Right now, I'm contemplating on when it would be a good time to see you. If I do not hear from you, I will be over on Sunday afternoon or please state a different time you wish and I will speedily come so that we can again spent time together.

Till then, with lots of Love.
John

P.S. The fellow that has the watch next weekend has just now asked me to stand his watch Sunday evening as he is a married man, saying that he will do the same for me as soon as I get married. So please expect me Saturday morning.

John wasn't wasting any time insinuating about marriage in his early letters. On August 2, 1940, he wrote:

Dearest Alice,

It is now getting to be Monday evening and almost ten hours since I have seen you. Leaving you this morning, I waited for the bus for quite a while then a fellow came by and said it was 7:20 AM so I thought your watch was wrong. I was very much surprised when I remembered I was in Benicia. I then thumbed my way and it was exactly 8:00 AM when I arrived in Vallejo. Knowing that a jitney (an unlicensed taxicab) *would not get me there on time, I took a cab and was in the yard at 8:20. Still in civilian clothes, I turned in my liberty reporting myself 20 minutes over time and without waiting for an answer, about faced and ran to my quarters. Upon entering the quarters, I was stopped and asked the purpose of my speed. Having answered him, he gave me a response that really made me swear. His reply was, "today is a Holiday and special details are off duty."* (John's diligence and haste to return to base was for naught as he had the day off). *For a minute, I wanted to go right back to you again but I finally shaved, took a shower and went back to sleep.*

I feel very fine right now, except of course, the loony time in my head which will no doubt remain. Here is hoping you are in the best of condition and I shall try my best to be over Wednesday evening.

So, till Wednesday, when I shall see you again I'm hoping that I will find you as interesting and lovely as I did the last time.

Lots of love,
John

On some of his visits, John had stayed overnight in her family's house so they could spend more time together. With each letter, it was clear that there was little on John's mind besides Alice. Meanwhile, because of his typing and filing skills, he was transferred from hospital duties to work the veteran's office responding to various requests. That gave him access to a typewriter, and his letters were now typed and being composed while on duty. On a letter dated August 4, 1940, he ended it with the following:

Till I see you again Wednesday night, I shall think of you
always and remain,

Your ever-loving husband,
John

P.S. A husband that wouldn't flirt with another girl while he
was with you nor would date other girls except on Wednesday
and Saturdays (Wednesdays and Saturdays were the usual days
John and Alice saw each other).

In less than a month of seeing each other, John was beyond insinuating marriage, but formally he had not yet asked the question. John
would continue to see Alice through mid-September of 1940, before
receiving his orders to return to San Diego, where he was again assigned
to hospital duty. There he would wait for further orders to be deployed
for duty somewhere in the Pacific.

In a letter August 14, 1940, John expressed his frustrations with his
commander's indecisiveness regarding his days off.

I probably would have written before but there is a change
in watches here in this department giving me the watch yes-
terday, and then I don't know when I will have it again. If I
don't have it this weekend I will be sure to have it Wednesday.
Therefor my dear the only dates I can see open will be Tuesday
or Thursday. So please upon your answer to this letter state
what date you wish me to come and see you. I wish someone
would make up their mind for me. When I try to think around
here I get reminded that a person here in the Navy is getting a

lot of money to do the thinking for me. But he sure can't think for a person in love, rather he stumbles along in the darkness.

John then used a series of asterisks to denote a profanity. In the same letter, he asked Alice what she preferred for her upcoming birthday. John's mood switched from frustration to head-scratching.

Your birthday is drawing near and if there is anything worse than buying a present for a girl, well you tell me. Now if it was a man I could get him a box of cigars or do you smoke? Considering that I don't know what to buy you I have three means of letting you know it's your birthday and celebrate it accordingly.

1. Buy you a present of anything starting from candy to cigars or things like that

2. Give you at least $25 for a present wrapped up

3. Having, after I pay all my debts and sending a few dollars home about $50 for spending purposes, we could take the $50 and go over to the fair the week end of your birthday

Please let me know as this is quite a burden on my mind.

So, my darling, till I see you again here is hoping that you stay as beautiful as you are.

Will remain forever and always ever and ever as long as I shall see you, your most fervent lover,

John

It is noteworthy to point out that $25 in 1940 adjusted for inflation to the present amounts to about $437; $50 would, of course, be double that. John was not messing around. Though he was confused about what gift was most appropriate, he was not at all confused about his love and devotion to a girl he'd known for only a few weeks.

John's last letter before he'd have to return to San Diego, dated August 18, 1940, clearly expressed his frustration over not being able to spend more time with Alice, including having to fulfill other family commitments that would further reduce their time together.

> *It has been a rather long time since I've seen you and am getting mighty lonesome. Right now, I'm contemplating as to the time when I could come over without inconvenience to anyone. I have concluded that I will be over Tuesday on the 6 o'clock bus. I guess this letter will arrive in time. You said that you could have come over here on Saturday. I wish I could have gotten in touch with you, so that I could have told you that I stood my watch in the O.O.D.'s* (meaning Officer of the Day), *and you could have easily come up here and we could have spent some time together in the recreation room.*
>
> *I have just gotten a letter from home through the Captain and my father was saying that I don't write often enough and wants me to come home. Being away from home now for over a year. And the Captain called my attention to the fact. As yet, I do not know when I will comply with his request but it might be in the near future, so as to get it over with.*
>
> *So, I will be sure to be over Tuesday and here is hoping you pester me not too much as pestering might lead to excessive measures. You follow me sweetheart? But it really does tickle.*
>
> *Hoping you get your heart's desire, no matter what your wish might be. Am signing off.*

Vieles gluck and kusse (German for "much luck and kisses")
John

The trip to visit the family in St. Louis would not happen. He received his orders to report to San Diego the first week in September and arrived there September 14. His second time in San Diego was more challenging. First and foremost, he was now away from Alice. After meeting the one and only woman he would ever have a love affair with and their short-but-torrid romance, John was in a bit of a spiral. Second, he was now working with Marines on a daily basis, and the first few days had not gone well.

His first letter to Alice after returning to San Diego, dated September 21, expressed John's frustrations.

Dearest Alice,

Received your most interesting letter on Friday and I'm sorry to hear that you miss me so much. Having been here for a week now, I find myself rather lonely and really would have liked to spent the week end with you.

The service here with the Marines is not as pleasant as it was on Mare Island, which only contributes to my loneliness. I feel rather moody today, so there isn't much I can write that you don't already know. With love to you and the rest of the family, I'll close and hope to hear and also see you soon.

Lovingly Yours,
John

P.S. Will send you a picture as soon as possible.

Nine days later, John's mood was improving, though his concerns about not seeing Alice were not abating.

September 23, 1940:

Dearest Alice,

I have just received your letter, which I was very glad to get. I guess the Marines here aren't so bad after all. Today about six of them came to me for advice on illnesses and various sores. They even address me as "Doc" as I just treat them the best I can. One fellow came by and wanted to know what he could do with his toes as they were bleeding. I painted his toes with an athlete's foot mixture as that was what he had. They really seem to appreciate it as they are more or less afraid of the doctors who are usually handy with a knife. I myself have just received my first aid jacket containing various bandages, forceps, tape and scissors and with a knife which I hope to get soon will hold a regular sick call among those dumb crazy Marines.

I have skated quite a few times since being here. I have not skated with a girl and have not been out with Curry or his girl-friends. I find that I can really behave myself if I want to. The climate here is very nice. I'll try to make it to the beach for a weekend swim.

So, lots of love and kisses from yours always,
John

John continued writing to Alice every few days, and each kept a diary that they agreed to share when they were together again. He would write more than four hundred pages of letters to her between the time they met and the attack on Wake. Unfortunately, all of Alice's letters to him would be lost at Wake. In his letters from San Diego, he continued to tell her about what he was doing and how much he wanted to be with her again. He shared a story of helping a Marine who was having an appendicitis attack and the ambulance going eighty miles an hour between the sick ward and the hospital. He promised Alice he would send pictures soon of him in both his Navy and Marine uniforms. In one story, he chided the Marines.

> *They have changed my detail and am now working in the one and only medical ward they have here dedicated solely to the active Marines. And what a bunch of babies they are.*

In their letters back and forth, they would ask each other lots of questions, including subtle ones to get at whether either of them was seeing other people. Then, in late September, Alice stopped writing. On a letter to Alice on the 27th, John frustratingly wrote the following:

> *I believe this is the second letter now since I have received yours and for a girl who said she wanted to write every day, you are certainly not doing it. But if you do write I find your letters very interesting and it even makes me think twice about the service.*

On October 1, his letter to Alice referred to the last couple of letters he had received from her. Something was going on with Alice that was baffling him.

I received your letter saying you wanted to come to San Diego and that short letter which sounded really mysterious. Please rewrite that letter again and please don't leave out any details.

I'm not even writing anymore after this time till I receive your letter and which must sound right without any beating around the bush.

So please answer soon and not so stern and hard as your last letter. Closing and hope to hear from you soon.

Love John
P.S. Love to all

John held out for nine days but did not hold true to his commitment not to write again till he had received a detailed letter from Alice. Love will do that to a guy. In any event, he wrote to Alice again on the 10th:

Dearest Alice,

I expected a letter from you a few days ago, but since none arrived and me having duty today, with nothing to do but let my mind wonder, which would picture you clearly with many memories, well, I just had to write.

For some important reason you have surely neglected your own promise and have not written, which is quite surprising to me. However, if I have offended you in any way you could surely inform me of my error and thereby at least write.

In that same letter, John told Alice that he was considering taking flying lessons, trying to evoke some response about him taking up such a dangerous hobby. He also shared that word was going around that he, along with a contingent of Marines, would be deployed to Alaska in the coming weeks. He still had not been assigned to a specific battalion, so nothing was certain. That said, the possibility of going to Alaska became more real, when he was told to get measurements for heavy clothing. As he explained to Alice, *"that means that any day, unknown to me, I shall be Alaska bound; snow shoes, skis etc."*

John did not know where in Alaska he might be stationed. At the time, the Navy had a small seaplane base at Sitka and two direction finder stations in Soapstone Point on Cross Sound and at Cape Hinchinbrook on Prince William Sound. The only radio station and Coast Guard operations were located at Dutch Harbor on Unalaska Island. With the potential of war, Congress had appropriated $19 million to enlarge the base at Sitka and to establish seaplane and submarine bases at Kodiak and at Dutch Harbor.[6] In short, John could be sent to any one of those bases in Alaska.

Still getting no response from Alice, John wrote to her again on October 16, raising the volume on the issue of marriage. He was trying to be practical about finances, which caused him to vacillate on the question. That said, he had raised the marital issue yet again, which spoke volumes about where his heart lie.

> *Marriage has really occurred to me. Being in the service it had been out of my mind but with the various changes in the Navy program, a sailor can almost get married if he makes second class. That rating is however, uncertain, as you can't never tell about getting rated if this war keeps up. I myself might make it in one to two years from now. But in peace time it usually takes about four years.*

Should I make second class, and if marriage appeals to me, I certainly would ask you to make a fool of yourself, but by that time you will probably be happily married with everything you want.

I would like to hear your side of this, also please in your next letter explain your letter of a while back (this was in reference to the letter John had written on October 1).

So, till I hear from you, lots of love and kisses always
John

It would be three more weeks before John would write another letter, and there was still no word from Alice. He had been temporarily transferred from San Diego to Camp Elliott. The camp was still under construction, so John and the Marines slept two to a tent. Prior to and during the war, the Camp would serve as a training ground for fifty thousand Marines bound for the war in the Pacific. The camp would also serve as the training site for the famous Navajo Code Talkers, who were deployed in the Pacific to use their native language to transmit secret military messages and confuse the Japs trying to decode the communications.[7] John described it as "a dusty place in the sticks about twelve miles from the Marine Base in San Diego. It is cold at night so we got small stoves to keep warm. There is no hot water, making the showers ice cold."

On a letter on November 8, he described Camp Elliott and included the following love-sick passages:

Dearest Alice,

It certainly has been a long time since I've heard from you and I really do miss your letters. I thought surely that you would answer the last letter I sent you. But you have probably fallen in love with some other handsome fellow and have forgotten all about me. Or could it be that you are ill and could not write.

I really wish that I would have stayed in Vallejo, so I would not have to write to you but just see you every day. I guess I must have liked you more than I thought at the beginning because there is never a day that goes by without you coming into my mind.

In your last letter you said that you were enclosing a letter from Julie (Alice's sister) *but I could not find it. Or did you leave it out on purpose, as she was always trying to cut in before.*

I'll close by really hoping to hear from you again and to please explain you not writing me anymore. Well toots, lots of love and kisses.

Always,
John

P.S. Love to your mother, brothers and Julie. Auf Wiedersehen (Goodbye)

In the same letter, John shared that he had bought a car and was spending lots of time on maintenance (it was a 1933 model) and driving his buddies around. He'd bought the car with another guy. He couldn't remember his name, but he does remember the guy almost wrecking the car and causing damage to one wheel that had to be replaced. He told the guy, "Go to hell—and keep the car." John rationalized that he was spending too much time and money with the car and said, "I didn't care for that car any more as it only kept me broke all the time."

Around Thanksgiving, Alice finally broke the silence and sent John a very short letter, most likely closer to a note, with a new picture of her and the letter from Julia that she had failed to send earlier. John was ecstatic. When he and I talked about Alice making contact again, he laughed and said to me, "Yeah—I was getting a little worried there for a while. I thought she was done with me." Though happy to have heard from Alice, he was still concerned about what else might be going on with her that she wasn't sharing.

On November 20, John's letter included the following:

Dearest Alice,

This is indeed a Happy day, at noon I received your most wonderful picture and at 4PM your letter together with Julia's. You asked me up for Thanksgiving but your letter was late in coming and Thanksgiving is tomorrow.

Alice had written the letter the first week in November but it was sent at first to San Diego and then to Camp Elliott. John had just left the camp and missed the letter. Eventually it made it back to San Diego but too late for John to decide to visit Alice. After finally hearing from her, circumstances were working against him. Beyond the invitation to visit her, he had a strong sense from the letter that there was something she wanted to tell him directly.

In the same letter, John updated Alice that he was now back in school. He wrote:

I'm now back in Field Medical School that keeps me very busy, as a matter of fact, all of my spare time. And will I be glad when it's over. Perhaps after the course is over, I can get enough time to come and see you soon. I do hope it's soon or sooner.

I think I'm really getting terrible; do you know that since I saw you I haven't even so much as taken a girl to a movie.

He was terrible, all right—terrible at telling Alice that she was the only one for him. John continued:

I'm really glad to see by your picture that you are still as beautiful as when I left you. I guess it's my turn to send you my picture but if I can see you soon, I would rather wait and have one taken together.

Well, if you will excuse me now darling, I have some studying to do yet. Please give all my love and thanks to Julie for her letter and am so sorry not to have time to write her personally.

So, lots of love and kisses.
Love,
John

In early December John wrote to Alice that he could arrange to get seven days' leave to go visit her for Christmas, but he thought if he waited a few more days, he might be able to get a one-month leave. That would be great, as he wanted to see her so badly. However, in the same letter, he also expressed concern that the redeployment to Alaska may happen as soon as January 3, 1941. If he went to Alaska, he'd been told, it would be for at least six months. He felt if he was gone that long, she would surely meet someone else and get married. As always, he updated her on what he was up to now: yet another series of courses, including: Organization of the Marine Corps, Military First Aid, Chemical Warfare, Medical Field Tactics, and what he referred to as, "the driest of them all," Topography. He ended that letter by asking Alice some direct questions, including:

> *By the way, how is your health these fine days? Are you still as beautiful as ever and slowly forgetting me? Could you let me know of what your future plans are? Like how long you are going to go to school, get married and to whom?*
> *This ought to keep you writing now and perhaps you'll write a long letter on those subjects. So, with love to all, with hopes of a real letter from you soon.*
>
> *Love and kisses,*
> *Always*
> *John*

On December 9, as he was leaving school, he received word to call a certain number and on doing so found out it was a telegram from Alice asking him to take his leave as soon as possible and to please come visit her. Doing so would limit him to five days, so he responded to her as follows:

> *All I could possibly take is five days. But if you definitely want me to come, that could give us about 3 days in which to see each other* (it would take two days to travel to and from San Diego

to Vallejo by train). *Couldn't you please confirm your telegram by letter and thereby not make my heart do a Rhumba. But then again, it not only takes a telegram to get that effect, as I quite often experience something of that sort whenever you looked at me.*

On receiving that response to her telegram, Alice finally wrote a more detailed letter to John to inform him that she was pregnant.

★　★　★

CHAPTER 5

"THERE WAS A TIME I LOVED THE SEA."

December 11, 1940 to February 27, 1941

As 1940 was coming to an end, America's relationship with Japan was in rapid decline. In the spring, Washington allowed its fifty-year-old trade agreement with Japan to expire. Months later, Roosevelt declared an embargo on all shipments of steel and aviation gas to the Japanese. In September, Japan signed the Tripartite Pact with Germany and Italy, and Washington responded by barring the export of all scrap metal to Japan. Oil was the only, but most vital, export to Japan that was left untouched. More than 80 percent of Japan's fuel supplies came from the U.S.[1] In addition, the ever-growing love for cars had propelled the United States to the largest rubber goods industry in the world. However, 98 percent of its rubber and 90 percent of its tin were imported from Southeast Asia. In all, the area provided more than half of America's need for fifteen vital commodities. Policymakers in Washington were prepared to go to war to ensure America's freedom to continue to trade for these resources. In his congressional confirmation hearings, Secretary of the Navy Frank Knox had clearly stated America's interest in the region: "We should not allow Japan to take the Dutch East Indies, a vital source of oil, rubber, and tin. . . . We must face frankly the fact that to deny the Dutch Indies to Japan may mean war."[2]

Meanwhile, in mid-December of 1940, John Ignacious Unger's head was spinning. He had been preparing himself to believe that Alice did not love him and or that she'd found another beau. He was not prepared, however, to learn that he was about to be a father. Alice had been pregnant since September. Their torrid love affair had produced much more than two love-sick people who were crazy for each other. Alice's silence for so many weeks now made sense. She had, most likely, been struggling with how to accept the fact she was pregnant, and then with how she would tell John. She had honorably tried to get him to visit her to break the news to him in person, but when that didn't work, he gave her no choice but to break it to him by mail. I asked John when Julia found out about her daughter's pregnancy and he said, "I have no idea, but I'm sure she figured it out long before I learned of it."

After the shock of learning of his pending fatherhood, John's thoughts went immediately to figuring out a way to see Alice as soon as possible. He could not risk getting reassigned to Alaska—or any other place—without seeing her. In fact, the same week he had heard that now Honolulu was also a possibility but that it may not occur till March of 1941. His preference was to have her come to San Diego as soon as possible. In an undated letter, most likely sent around December 13, John asked Alice to come to San Diego. He also offered to send her money so she could take the train. An excerpt from the letter lays out his plan:

Should you decide against coming down here, which you will
please inform me in your next letter, then I would try my best to
get leave immediately and which I'm sure I can get even if I have
to tell them that my mother is dying.

Clearly, John was desperate to see Alice, if he was willing to go as
far as putting his stepmother in a deathbed to get his commanders to
approve a leave. It was a much more convenient excuse than telling them
his girlfriend was pregnant. He ended the letter with the following:

This rather sounds like a business letter so please do not think
too harsh of it. So, I'll sign off now as I have to prepare for my
hike and it even looks like rain.
Please write soon and till then my little sweetie-pie.

Lots of love, hugs and kisses.

P.S. Supposing you discuss it with your mother, perhaps she could
give us some motherly advice. And also give her my love.

John would tell me, "Julia was not at all supportive of Alice going
to San Diego." Presumably without her mother's consent, Alice went
anyway. John does not recall the exact date Alice arrived in San Diego
but he knows it was a few days before Christmas. "Everything was such
a whirlwind that it is difficult to remember it all." I asked him if he ever
formally proposed marriage to Alice, and he laughed and said, "No, I
think she proposed to me." My wife, Randi, who was involved in all
the interviews, and I laughed with John, and then we told him, "That
was a hard one to believe."

Their reunion went from exhilaration to the decision to get married. Believing that Alice was not at the age of consent to marry and that they would need Julia's blessing and signature (which they probably wouldn't get), they decided to head to Tijuana, Mexico, where such a formality would not be an issue. John claims it was Alice who talked him into heading to Tijuana. One thing is a certainty: Alice did not hesitate at all to make decisions, especially when it came to matters of the heart.

They married on Christmas Eve 1940. John hailed a cab and asked to be taken to a Justice of the Peace on the Mexico side of the border. Interestingly, the cabbie knew exactly where to go. It leads one to believe that cross-border weddings were not uncommon. As a testament to the whirlwind nature of the days leading up to their wedding, they had no rings and had not thought about who would act as a witness. They had no Maid of Honor or Best Man, and there were no friends or family present. The cabbie dutifully acted as a witness before ferrying them back to San Diego. John thinks it cost him about five dollars for the ceremony and the wedding certificate; that was less than what they paid the cabbie for the round trip. They celebrated their honeymoon by spending a few days at the New Plaza Hotel in San Diego.

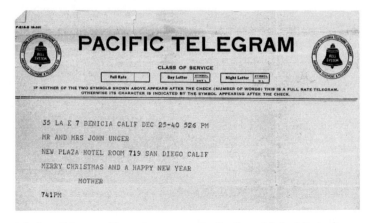

Congratulations Telegram (From the personal collection of John I. Unger)

Julia had been informed by Alice of the planned nuptial but John does not recall how. Julia, being a loving mother and, I surmise, wanting the best for her daughter, must have had a change of heart about the sailor. On the evening of Christmas Day, she sent the newly married couple the following telegram:

Mr. and Mrs. John Unger
New Plaza Hotel Room 719 San Diego California
Merry Christmas and a Happy New Year

Mother

What was done was done. Julia now had to figure out how to best support her pregnant daughter and her new son-in-law.

Their honeymoon at the New Plaza Hotel was short, as Alice returned to Benicia a couple of days later. John was still unsure of where his next duty was going to be. Though Alaska was still a possibility, there was now more talk about being shipped to Pearl Harbor in Hawaii. Excerpts from his first letter to Alice after they were married had a different, much happier tone than the letters he had written her leading up to her announcement about her pregnancy.

The New Plaza Hotel in San Diego (From the personal collection of John I. Unger)

December 31, 1940,

Dearest Alice,

I have just received your letter and am very glad to hear that you arrived safely at home. But I'm sorry to hear of a severe cold suffered by your mother and here's hoping for a speedy recovery.

No one missed me Christmas Day so all is well. It certainly rains down here something awful, and I believe I read every magazine in camp to keep me occupied. Still in all, I'm all smiles. As a matter of fact, all of my friends are contemplating marrying, as they say I'm such a happy fellow now. But then it's too bad that they all can't get as lovely a wife as I have.

You know dear, I really do miss you terribly. I wish I was still up in Mare Island. But you don't have to worry about my behavior as I can really keep myself occupied in Camp. Pleasant memories of you really keep me happy.

I had my leave papers fixed so that I could come up to see you at Christmas but that you came down here made me neglect those papers so yesterday they raised "hell" because I didn't take the leave. Now that is just like the Marine Corps for you to always do the opposite of the expected.

In his haste to spend time with Alice when she decided to come visit him, John had forgotten to get formal approval for the days he had been away from the base. He had asked for the leave, but it had not been approved. Technically, he had been AWOL (away without leave).

It appears that the nature of his absence and that he had no intentions to desert helped him avoid any discipline. His letter went on:

> *The Marines still don't know that they can't make a Marine out of a sailor, so the laugh is still on them—the sea-going bell-hops.*
>
> *Well toots, how is your condition as to your health? Do you still love me like you used to before we met and the way you love me now? You know some times I show a sign of being a practical joker but this time I don't think I'll burden you with any. . . . I wonder did you ever hear the one about the traveling salesman? Did you say which one? Oh, I'm sorry I'm forgetting myself.*
>
> *So sweetest, I'm signing off and till death do us part, promise to love you always.*
>
> *Love and kisses,*
> *John*
>
> *P.S. My love to all: especially Julie. Kindly give her my love and tell her that I would still marry her if I could have two wives.*

In early January, John was finally assigned to a specific unit: the 1st Defense Battalion, U.S. Marine Corps. That battalion, he was told, would be deployed to Honolulu, but it was not a certainty. At the time, a Marine defense battalion consisted of eight-hundred and fifty men.[3] John would be one of several Corpsmen assigned to the 1st Defense Battalion. In the meantime, he wondered when he'd see Alice again. He not only wanted to spend time with her, he also wanted to give her the wedding ring he had purchased since their wedding. On a letter on January 7, 1941, he wrote the following:

Dearest Alice,

    For some reason I haven't received a letter from you in answer to my last one but before I get a wrong impression it might be because I have been transferred to a different company (the 1ˢᵗ Defense Battalion).

    Now that I'm transferred I hope I don't have to go to Alaska. My new company is scheduled to go to Honolulu. This is very indefinite so it shouldn't worry us any.

    I'm planning on coming to Benicia within a month. I might only have enough time to say hello and be off again but I shall be there and I shall inform you of the right date as soon as I know. And I will also deliver your ring in person.

    By reading a book on astrology yesterday I found a paragraph in which it stated that a man born in 1920, would find his loved born between September 5ᵗʰ through September 29 (that is the period of time that their intimacy and passion had resulted in her pregnancy). *So here is hoping or rather, here is when I start believing in Astrology.*

    Now I'm at my new place of work, in the dressing room (bandaging wounds), *where hundreds of people come in with all kinds of messes and sometime when I start day dreaming about you, well you should see the result on the patient I'm working on in that particular moment.*

Saying John was crazy in love would be a gross understatement. In an attempt to express his love in different ways, his next letter, on January 13, 1941 included this:

At the beginning, I only dreamt of you, but now I can't keep my mind off you for a minute. It must be love, huh! And while you are haunting me again, here is a poem (author unknown) *which I just ran across:*

There was a time I loved the sea,
And torpid blood would tingle,
When tall waves crashed defiantly,
Or crooned across white shingle.

There was a time I loved a hill,
All autumn-drenched or vernal,
With lofty pinnacles so still,
So close to the eternal.

There was a time when I loved towers,
And crowded, hurried places,
The human pageant, smiles and frowns,
That filled a million faces.

But nowadays those thrills are through,
And fled their fascination;
Strange, that a little elf like you,
Can blot out all creation.

Dearest, I can usually keep myself busy by working in the dressing room where all sorts of patients come in while listening to their troubles and keep from being too lonesome, but it must be awful tiresome for you. Is it?

Here's closing and hoping to hear from you very, very soon,
Viele Grüße und Küsse von mir (Many greetings and kisses
from me)
John

A week later, John asked the doctor he reported to for leave but was denied. The superior believed that the departure of the battalion was imminent and a leave would not be appropriate. He wrote Alice that he was doing what he could to get some time to visit her the first week in February. It was rumored that the battalion would be shipping off to Honolulu on March 1. The dates had switched before, so he wrote:

> *"This has me in a tailspin as I don't trust the Marine Corps.*
> *If it wasn't for me in this Marine Corps, all would be well. But I*
> *guess love always finds a way."*

John was desperately trying to find a way to see her before he had to ship off. Given the uncertainty of when, or if, the battalion would go to Hawaii, John turned his thoughts to finding an apartment for them to live in, off the base. He spent days looking for a suitable arrangement but got nowhere. By this time, Alice, as she had done in December, suggested that it would be easier if she travel to San Diego to ensure they could see each other before he was deployed.

As January turned to February, John still had not found a place for them to live near the base, and there was no further clarity as to when his outfit would be redeployed. A concern for both of them was that, if Alice moved to San Diego and his orders came for duty somewhere else, she may have to face delivering the baby and caring for it without her mother. One group of Marines was said to be going to Samoa by the end of the month, but, as far as he knew, that did not include him. In a letter to Alice on February 2, he wrote in part:

Mein Liebchen (My Sweetheart),

I know other girls have babies without their mother being present but it's just impossible for a girl to be alone after having a baby. But I guess I just don't understand girls. Someday I'll just take a certain one apart and see what makes her tick.

The latest news about the chances of us moving out of San Diego is thus: Notices have been given to all married men in the 1ˢᵗ Defense Battalion to adjust themselves for leaving at any day.

I was just sitting here absorbed in my letter writing and a fellow came up and said that he knows of a place that will be vacated in a month. So, I'll look into this, and see what can be done. That would perhaps be alright, if it wasn't for this outfit trying to move out all the time.

So dearest, I'll close and when I hear from you I hope that you request my presence with you.

So, till then, love and kisses forever,
John

P.S. Please give my love to all.

By February 8, John's deployment orders arrived, and his thoughts immediately turned to financial matters. He wanted to ensure that Alice and the baby would have the resources they needed in his absence. Excerpts from one of his longest letters to Alice follow:

Mein Liebchen,

All of my worries about me leaving, well—it's finally come home. We are all packed, that is the 1ˢᵗ Defense Battalion and are ready to move. We are to leave San Diego the latter part of next week to a destination that is still a secret but to be some place near Honolulu. We are to fortify the area as we are taking all our ammunition.

I'm really sick today, a sickness to which there isn't even a cure. And it's taken all the energy I have to write this letter. I hate to think ahead of the months we are going to be separated not seeing each other and enjoying each other's company. I never was home sick but this time, I'm sure it will be unavoidable. And after all you are really my life and my happiness.

Now please do not raise too much heck with me in your next letter as I really could not take it, but now that you do know that I'm leaving, I guess I can expect the worst letter from you. But whatever you say, I'll just love you more for it, so I'm sure you will be very easy with me.

So, I believe as when a married fellow gets transferred, the usual procedure is to make out an allotment to his wife. So, I guess I will have to explain my financial position and you will have to decide on your share. You are familiar with Navy ratings and the pay for each rating. When enlisting in the Navy $21 a month is paid to recruit for four months after which he gets rated (in my particular branch) to Hospital Apprentice 2ⁿᵈ class (HA2c.). Six months thereafter, if he successfully passes an examination, he gets to Hospital Apprentice 1ˢᵗ Class (HA1c.) paying $54 a month. And which is my rating at present. But the

16th *of this month, having passed my examination, I get rated to*
Pharmacists Mate 3rd Class (PhM3c.), paying $60 a month and
if the fellow is married and living ashore, his wife gets $15 extra
for rations. Too bad we can't get it now.

So now I'm making $60 a month minus a few cents less than
$6 for insurance amounting to $3,000, payable to you, in case of
my death. It was formerly made out to my father, but it will soon be
changed to you. Now that leaves $54.00 a month. So, in your next
letter please give me the amount which is required for you to get by on.

I should make PhM2c. in about nine months which will pay
a base of $72 a month. So, that is something to look forward to.

I guess I had better close this letter so it still gets out this
morning so that I might receive a quick reply. So, till I hear from
you, with lots of love, hugs and kisses.

Always,
John

P.S. Please inform your mother of my departure and give her my
love, also to your sister and brothers.

Upon receiving the letter, Alice immediately arranged for a bus to
take her to San Diego. She could not bear John leaving without seeing
him again. They also had important financial and family matters to
discuss that she would not do by mail. John does not recall the exact
dates Alice was in San Diego, most likely between the 11th and 14th
(St. Valentine's Day). He does recall that the couple of days they were
together, were, once again "a whirlwind." Besides enjoying each other,
they had agreed on finances and reaffirmed their love and commitment

to each other. Unbeknown to them at the time, it would be 1,700 days or almost 56 months, before they'd see each other again.

Many other marriages or close relationships had to endure similar circumstances to what John and Alice would face, and some of those did not survive. Theirs would, because from the very beginning they knew their love for each other was special. As John had written in a letter on January 19 expressing his frustrations about the uncertainty of his leave and deployment dates,

"I guess love always does find a way."

On February 16, a couple of days after seeing each other, John wrote to Alice:

Mein Liebchen,

I hope you arrived safely at home and all is well. I tried my best to sleep last night but I just couldn't. I awoke every hour and tried to think whereabouts you would be. And today I find myself very sick, but I couldn't tell you where the pain is.

I know one thing for certain and that is, if I can stand to be away from you for a year, I know I'd never leave you again. I surely hope this year will pass very quickly.

I can't understand what the matter is with me. I just seem to be floating through air and I'm having the worst time with this let-ter as I can't concentrate and I seem to drop off after each sentence.

Dearest I could just keep writing and say "I love you" and write a thousand pages of it. But should I do that, you would probably think I'm crazy, but consider it written anyhow.

Precious, you must excuse me for closing so soon but I would rather retire and just dream of you. I promise to write you a book in the near future. So, I hope you are in a better condition than I am and wish to hear from you real soon.

Love and lots of hugs and kisses,
Always,

John

John continued writing his lovesick letters throughout February. Several times he thought they would be shipping out the next day, only to be delayed. He tried to reassure Alice that, despite the distance and the time away from each other, *"everything is going to be just fine with us."*

The ship that would ferry him and the Marines to Hawaii was packed and ready to go on February 18 but would not leave San Diego till the 28th. On the 18th, John had worked with the Marines till midnight to ensure all the necessary supplies were on board. The ship was the *USS William P. Biddle*, named after a Commandant of the Marine Corps who retired in 1914 after almost forty years of service. Biddle saw action as an officer in several campaigns including the Spanish-American War in the Philippines and the Boxer Rebellion in China. The ship had been built in California in 1919 for the British and sold several times before it was purchased by the U. S. Navy and converted to a transport. It had the capacity to transport more than a thousand troops.[4]

In addition to his heavy heart, John asked Alice if she hated him for not being with her when the baby was born. He kiddingly wrote: *"I would gladly bear the child for us (or would I?).* He expressed his concern over her condition, as she had written that she was very uncomfortable as the pregnancy progressed. He wrote back: *"I'm scared. I believe I'll have a worse time than you till our baby arrives and after that, twice as bad till I see you and the baby."* He asked for the names of boys or girls that she liked so they could agree on one. He ended one letter with the following postscript.

P.S. My love to all and please keep me informed as to your condition so my imagination does not run away with me. And please do not worry about me.

On February 22, John wrote his last letter to Alice before embarking on the *USS Biddle*. They were being told that their departure was imminent, but days passed, and they were still in San Diego. He speculated: *"I guess there must be a German submarine outside the harbor causing the delays."* He concluded that letter with the following:

Princess, I have just this moment received your letter in which you were considering the name of Anna Theresa for our baby. If you remember, I told you that when trying to think of a name, you naturally judge the name by a person who you've known by that name. Anna would remind me of my mother, now dead and it would probably be a very appropriate name. Theresa, reminds me of my stepmother. My stepmother was a good woman but not a very good mother, and besides our child will never have a stepmother, so that is out. So, coming back again to judge from a person you once knew by that name, the name would have to be Alice. And that sweetheart, is final, unless you can give me 101 reasons why Alice would not be the name. By the way, how do you know it's going to be a girl? And if a girl, and you do not like the name of Alice, we will just call her "Toots" because you like that so much.

Darling, have you been to the hospital yet, and what is your present condition?

So, "my one and only," I'll close now hoping to hear from you very soon.

With lots of Love and Kisses
Forever yours,
John

P.S. Alice my darling, I love you. I thought I would remind you of it so you wouldn't forget. Ain't you surprised?

In six days, John was on the *USS Biddle,* headed for Hawaii. In San Diego, he and Alice had been five hundred miles apart, which, to both of them, seemed like a world away from each other. When he arrived in Hawaii, they were more than 2,400 miles from each other and the looming war would continue to pull them farther and farther apart.

★　　★　　★

CHAPTER 6

"ALWAYS FAITHFUL"

February 28, 1941 to July 2, 1941

John and the 1ˢᵗ Defense Marine Battalion left San Diego at 3:00 PM the afternoon of February 28, 1941, under heavy wind and rough seas. They arrived at Pearl Harbor on the following Thursday, March 6, 1941. As John explained, "By 6:00 PM on the first day, half the crew and most of the Marines were seasick."

Since his letter on February 22, John would not write to Alice again till March 8 from Pearl Harbor. That marked the longest stretch of time between John's letters to Alice since they'd met. The crowded ship, tight accommodations, and the weather all contributed to the letter-writing drought. In that first letter after arriving in Hawaii, John went into greater detail about the conditions onboard.

The sick Marines were a pitiful sight. But concerning myself, watching all those people "heave," I finally took my turn, and did it turn my stomach over. And then those flat-footed Marines, they having a little worse than me, asked me what to do for seasickness.

*And did I tell them the treatment, why I even showed them by
hanging over the rail and groaned, spit etc. but nothing came up.*

*At bedtime the first night, I felt pretty good but when the
Chief woke me up the next day I never got my second shoe on I
was moving so fast to empty my stomach. You should have seen
me take off. Though I didn't feel so bad after that, I sure didn't
eat a thing for the next two days.*

*But the third day till the end of the voyage, I was very gay.
The entire trip was rainy and a very strong wind blowing all the
way, making the ship roll and toss a great deal. After the second
day, the more furious the storm, the better I liked it. Anyhow I
showed those Marines I had a little salt in me.*

After arriving at Pearl Harbor, John, being one of the few guys
who felt okay, was put to work unloading and checking goods till after
midnight. He started working again the next day at 6:00 AM. He had
been too busy and too tired to do much thinking; then thoughts of
Alice colored his view of Hawaii. He would write:

I don't like it here at all. I guess the reason is that I miss you too much.

*We are expected to remain here at Pearl Harbor for about
a month or two to get in shape again before continuing to our
lonely Island which will probably be "Johnson Island"—I guess
you can find it on a map.*

John was referring to Johnston Atoll, which consisted of four small
islets about 825 miles southwest of Honolulu. The atoll was placed under
the U.S. Navy in 1934, and with the advent of war. they had been building an air station in 1941.[1] He continued his first letter from Hawaii:

Here in Pearl Harbor, we are in new barracks, much more suitable than in San Diego, so our living conditions are very good. Looking out of the window from here, I see a very beautiful view, mountains all around, sloping in various ways with various colors. It really looks peaceful. I don't know how much you know about this burg but I'll give you full details as soon as I have time to get around. I went to Honolulu with the ambulance last night and we rode around town quite a bit to get an idea of the town. And though it looks better than San Diego, I still didn't get much of an impression of the town.

So, my darling, I'll close and consider this letter only to tell you that I love you, that I arrived and I'm still very, very much in love with you and I'll write another letter later, by which time I hope to feel a little better.

Till tomorrow, lots of love, kisses and hugs. Yours always.
John

John was hoping to get into a routine in Hawaii so he could concentrate on his studies, swimming, and going to Mass on Sundays. It was not to be. Due in large part to his good work and his willingness to help wherever he could, his superiors kept assigning him to different jobs. On arriving at Pearl, he had been assigned to messenger duties for the Battalion. In that role, he would deliver messages between officers stationed at different locations. Some messages were verbal, while others were typed, which made his typing and shorthand skills come in handy. He was basically at the beck and call of the Officer of the Day while on duty. Speed and accuracy were paramount, and some messages took him to different places on Oahu, which gave him the opportunity to see the island. In his spare time, he wrote to Alice and asked about a myriad of issues but mostly about the baby. He wrote her the following on March 9:

The last letter I got from you, you stated that you measure 40 inches. Keep it up, you are doing fine. Say, I'm getting curious, what have you got, a boy or a girl, how big and how much does she eat for breakfast. Or is it twins. And if it is twins, I think Johnny will just keep on going, instead of rushing back.

You know sweetheart, now that I have a year to myself, you could give me your idea of a model husband and I'll see if I can fill the bill. So, let's have some details and don't say you'll take me the way I am.

The weather down here is certainly wonderful at present. Fair and not too hot at all. I would like to go swimming at Waikaki Beach (or however you spell it), (Waikiki) this afternoon and if only you were here, it would just be too perfect.

So, hoping this letter reaches you in best of health and humor, with loads of Kisses and hugs,

Always yours,
John

John was now writing all his letters on Marine Corps letterhead, which includes the Marine emblem. The emblem depicts an eagle, a globe, an anchor, and the phrase *"Semper Fidelis"* meaning "Always Faithful."

As I was reading John's letters, it struck me that a common theme was to make sure Alice knew she was his one and only love. Though John often kidded Alice about other girls, he wanted her to know that his love for her was "Always Faithful."

John and Alice were still undecided about the baby's name but in a letter on March 16, he tried to bring the matter to a close.

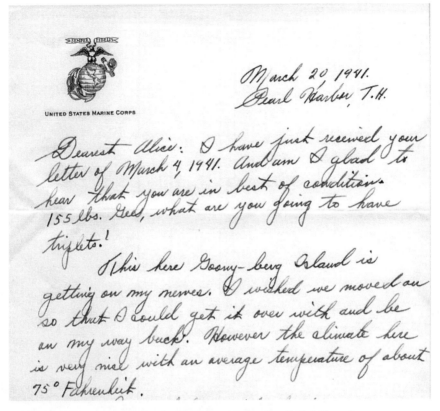

Letter on Marine Corps letterhead (Personal Collection John I. Unger)

Well "Toots," as to the name of our child, I'm finally con-
vinced and with your approval that the following name will be
accepted. In case of a girl, the name will be Alice. And in case of
a boy, if you are going to call him "John," you can if you want to
but the "Ignacious" is out. And as I don't like John very well, and
if you know a better name please use it.

John thought about Alice night and day. When he wasn't on duty,
he tried to keep busy to avoid, as he said, "becoming melancholy." One
day on a trip to deliver a message he was so wrapped up thinking of

Alice that he ended up on the opposite side of Oahu from where he was supposed to be. Driving around aimlessly was soon remedied when the Captain, *"got me a motorcycle; one with a side car and including a driver."* That solved the issue of getting lost while delivering messages but gave him more time to think about Alice. In the end, he'd chance lapsing into melancholy over getting less time to revel in his memories of his sweetheart.

Since going out with the other guys looking for girls was not an option, John looked for other activities to occupy his time. He started spending time with a group of Marines that went swimming on a regular basis and liked having "Doc" around. Not having swam in the ocean before, the only downside was the occasional mouthful of salt water. There was always coconut tree climbing and occasionally, he'd go on excursions around the island with the same group of Marines. In the evenings, "since I was pretty good at it, I'd iron shirts for some of the guys, including the Chief."

Back in Benicia, Alice was watching her health and continuing to gain weight. By mid-March she was up to 155 pounds. John wrote:

> *Gees, what are you going to have triplets!*

In the same letter, dated March 20th, John again turned to poetry but this time with a different twist.

> *Before I forget, following is a small poem* (author unknown) *that fits me to a "T."*

> *There is a man who never drinks,*
> *Nor smokes, nor chews, nor swears,*

Who never gambles, never flirts,
And shuns all sinful snare;
He's paralyzed.

There is a man who never does
Anything that is not right,
His wife can tell just where he is
At morning, noon and night;
He's dead.

And just think, I'm neither dead nor paralyzed. It also
reminds me that I have not drunk anything since the first of this
year; that wine—remember?
I hope not.

He concluded that letter by raising a topic that had not discussed before.

Say sugar does your father know about your marriage
already? I bet you never told him, or have you? I wonder when I
will be able to meet him and under what circumstances.

Loads of love, kisses and hugs.
Forever Yours,
John

P.S. My love to the baby.

John would never meet Alice's father. As best as he recalls, there simply was no contact with him or by him.

Due to the irregularity of mail delivery to the island, John would sometimes receive multiple letters from Alice. Those days were special and made him, *"a very happy man"*, at least for a few hours. He would write her, *"I seem to enjoy each and every letter more than the previous one."* It did not help to know that Alice also missed him terribly. On March 25th, he shared with Alice what got him through some of the days without her.

> *Sorry to hear that you miss me so much. Being more or less of a religious kind, I usually trust in God and hope for him to guide or decide my way. And perhaps this is the way it is meant to be—only, I can't see that way at all. Now it has to be this way, and for all our pains now, we will get our reward for a happy life thereafter. I'm sure that we will both be thankful for it.*

John's prescience and his faith in God would get him through the most difficult times. He and Alice would indeed be rewarded with many happy years together, but not before they tackled much more challenging obstacles than simply being apart from each other. On the same letter, John enclosed twenty dollars that he called, *"excess money on my side and will be handy till the allotment arrives."* It would be a practice that he'd maintain throughout his life: to put his family first and ensure that they were taken care of.

A challenge that both of them faced after being apart for a couple of months and knowing they'd be apart for at least ten more months was convincingly expressing their love for each other through mere words. You could argue that both were learning a hard lesson, captured by Shakespeare's proverb in the play *A Midsummer Night's Dream*, that: *"The course of love never did run smooth."* John expressed his frustration in a letter dated March 31.

There is a certain line dear, in which you stated in your last letter and also previously about me finding it very hard to get rid of you—probably referring to future years. I guess my letter writing must be a failure, since you are saying that you are not assured of my love for you.

I guess no matter whatever I tell you, you just won't ever know how much I do love you. So, you must just realize, that I absolutely adore you! And you must understand that, I get much more satisfaction in planning an ever-happy future for us, than in trying to get rid of you. You have my solemn promise that never such an idea will occur in my mind. Darling, how can we fail if we mutually cooperate. If you are not yet convinced (of my love for you), the only thing left for me to do is to prove it. I don't think I've ever felt more serious in all my life and with the help of God, will be sure that everything is going to turn out all right with us.

As John often does, he couldn't help himself but to add a playful twist.

There is however, just one catch—should you get four babies, the above statement is void.

Time was dragging for John regarding final orders. He surmised that he would not be staying in Hawaii and wanted very much to get on with getting to his final destination. He was not aware of it at the time, but in addition to Johnston Atoll, Midway Island and the Wake Atoll were distinct possibilities for the deployment of the 1st Defense Marine Battalion.

Midway Atoll consisted of two islands, Eastern and Sand. It is located more than 1,300 miles Northwest of Honolulu and, in 1941, was already on Japan's strategic radar screen. It had been annexed by the U.S. in 1867, and President Theodore Roosevelt had placed it under the control of the U.S. Navy in 1903. In 1940, the Navy had begun work on an air and submarine base.[2]

The Wake Atoll is located almost 2,300 miles west of Honolulu. It was first sighted by the Spanish in 1567, but they considered it too desolate, so they sailed away. In 1796, British Captain Samuel Wake gave the atoll and islets their names when he anchored offshore. In 1841, Lieutenant Charles Wilkes of the United States Navy anchored at Wake as part of his mission to explore Pacific Islands. He named one island after himself and another after a naturalist who was on the expedition, Titian Peale. In 1898, the United States claimed the atoll.[3] It was used as a temporary stopping point for ships traveling between the U.S. and the Philippines and remained uninhabited till 1935, when Pan American established its station for refueling its trans-Pacific Clippers.[4] It was clear that Wake was of strategic importance to any future conflict with the Japanese, and by 1941, there was work underway to build a naval base. As Major Devereux would later write, "The only question in 1941 was whether the construction could be completed before the start of the war we expected sooner or later."[5]

John continued to keep Alice updated on what he was doing and where his next stop might be. He shared a story about his second attempt to climb a coconut tree *"native style,"* wearing only his swimming trunks. The long and short of it is that he slipped, fell, and ended up with scrapes from head to toe. He was relieved to have heard from Alice in April that she had received her monthly spouse allotment that he had arranged in February. Alice had also shared that the hospital bill for the delivery of the baby would be $35, to which John responded, *"Why, at that rate we can have one every month. How many did you say you wanted?"* He shared that he had heard that a detachment of Marines from the 1ˢᵗ Defense Battalion was headed for Johnston Atoll and added, *"I don't know whether or not I'll go this time, but I'll get there soon enough."* On Easter, he sent Alice a postcard with a Hula Girl and told her his holiday would not be a happy one, as he would spend it without her.

By mid-April John began to inquire in his letters about when the baby would be born. On April 11, he wrote about swimming now being a daily occurrence with a group of Marines who left at 12:30 PM and returned around 5:00 PM. They would go to a Navy beach where, as he wrote, *"There are no girls present—what a pity, huh?"* He then related a story to highlight his fidelity.

> *Two days ago, I had an encounter which was more or less fun. It started this way: I worked in my white Navy uniform all morning and then headed out with some Marines but did not change my uniform. As usual, we all got on top of a large Marine truck and you can imagine me sticking out in my whites against all those Marines. After a great swim and on the way back, a 1941 convertible sedan Buick pulled up behind us containing three young girls. As usual my thoughts were of you. After the usual cheering between Marines and girls they suddenly focused on me. If I hadn't seen the proofs of the pictures of me, I would have attributed it to my good looks, but I know better. I guess the credit goes to my Navy uniform. They soon made it plain that they wanted to make my acquaintance. Probably because I like to be different than the rest of the fellows, they never succeeded. When questioned as to whether I wanted to ride in their car or if I wanted a date, I just shook my head no, without saying a word. They kept asking questions and I kept shaking my head no. When they taunted me*

by saying I was going to break their hearts smiling and winking, I
somehow started to blush, much to the Marines enjoyment.

I gathered from this experience that I'm more in love with
you than I can imagine if not even 3 girls and a car can get my
thoughts and attention from one as lovely as you. I always hoped
to have such an experience to prove that I not only think that
I love you but now that I'm certain of my true love, I feel very
happy and pray to God, that no one will ever come between us.

Perhaps I'm wrong to break down and tell you of my love for
you. When I asked you not to fall in love with me, you said you
did. So now that I want you to love me I wonder if you'll do the
opposite. Will you?

In the same eight-page letter, he talked about swimming, and a
Mr. Bennett, at the Mare Island hospital. Alice had met Bennett, and
John told her that he was *"one of the finest people there."* The subject then
changed to answering an important question she had asked him that
allowed John to play a role in helping with the baby.

My darling, hemorrhage means bleeding. You didn't tell me
the name of the pill but I think it's called "ergot." This pill is a
vasoconstrictor, used as a stimulant to the uterus and is also good
for congestion. But its main function is to keep you from bleeding
internally. It comes in quite handy while having the baby. Please
take as much as you are supposed to and when you're supposed to.
That dear, is an order. You will get more pills at the hospital that
must be taken without the slightest hesitation.

If there would be something wrong with your blood pressure,
you should report it right away to someone at the hospital and

they will do what is necessary to correct it. So, you have nothing to worry about that.

He ended that letter with a reference to a letter he had received from his father, whom Alice had not met. He had twisted the truth about the day they were married, to avoid questions about the timing of Alice's pregnancy.

> *I received a letter today from my father and all he said was the best of luck to you (John). I don't think he was referring to my marriage. I told him we were married on July 4, 1940. Maybe he still won't believe me, as he never expected me to get married. So, if you send him a birth announcement he might be convinced*
>
> *So, my ever-thoughtful wife, I'll close now and hope that all this was not very boring.*

Many, many kisses, love and hugs.
Forever your ever-loving husband,
John

P.S. 160 lbs. Gee whiz! I like a stout girl but not that stout. Between the baby and me, we will keep you so busy that you'll look like a shadow of yourself before we get through with you.

As the days passed, John thought more and more about Alice and the baby's health. It was clear in his letters he wished he could be with her to help. He continued to write about his daily swimming and that he was getting darker and looking more like a native Hawaiian every day. He shared stories about his work, including a ghastly one about a guy whose crushed finger would not stop bleeding. After that story he wrote: *"Now there I go trying to make you feel bad again. So sorry."* Their letters to each other filled the void of not being together and trying as much as possible to have regular conversations, though they were more than two thousand miles away from each other. To make matters worse, there was now only one ship carrying mail back and forth from the mainland each week instead of the customary two. In a letter he wrote on April 5, 1941, he was anxious to hear about the baby and once again tried to reassure her that all would go well.

> *Probably by the time you get this letter, you will be on your way to the hospital to have our baby. Since I worked in that ward for a time, it would be a good idea for me to tell you a few things about it, so you won't worry yourself unnecessarily.*
>
> *While working in the obstetrical ward, seeing women before and after delivery and one during the labor, I used to think that if I ever should have a wife in the same condition, I wouldn't worry myself in the least. That might still be true, but now that I'm so far away, I find myself quite the opposite and truly worried.*
>
> *To get back to what I was trying to say: When you arrive at the hospital (and please get there in plenty of time), you will feel yourself more or less excited and the nurses will try to make you feel comfortable. As soon as the nurse knows your baby is arriving, she gets you on a stretcher and immediately wheels you into the delivery room that you'll find contains the most modern equipment. Usually, there are two doctors and two nurses present.*

From here, your mother has probably already told you the procedure.

It appears that John chose discretion as the better part of valor by leaving it up to Mom Julia to instruct Alice on the physical part of the childbirth. While trying to be helpful to Alice, he recognized his limitations. His letter continued:

Your ten days in the hospital will begin and darling I promise to be with you every minute of the day and night. Just close your eyes and I'm sure you will feel the nearness of me. During those ten days, the nurses take care of you in every way and the Corpsmen will bring you your meals and nourishment. They usually have cheerful Corpsmen on this ward and I'm sure if you want anything they will do it for you. Perhaps they will be anxious as they haven't ever seen a more beautiful girl in this ward.

So darling, please hurry and have the baby so you can tell me all about it. I must surely be more anxious than you are. I guess you will forget all about me, being too interested in the baby: will you?

Hoping to see you and the baby real soon, I'm closing with Loads of love, kisses and hugs.

Forever and ever yours,
John

On the sixth of May, the baby had not been born but John sent Alice a card that would hopefully get there in time for Mother's Day on the 11th. The Hallmark card included a prayer: *"This brings a prayer on Mother's Day, that God will always bless your life in his most tender way with special happiness."*

Since his role as a messenger, John had returned to the hospital to continue his training and work wherever he was needed. In early May, he was learning how to perform various blood and urine tests. As part of his lab responsibilities, he would draw blood from patients. He was fascinated with the lab work, and it kept him busy. Keeping busy kept his mind off the rumors that they would soon be moving on again. In a letter on May 10, he shared his new experiences with Alice.

> *Well, darling, there is a rumor going around that we will move again shortly but it is not official yet. I'm certainly staying busy now that I got interested in laboratory work. From morning till night, you can see me looking at bugs through the microscope.*
>
> *I've extracted so much blood and stuck so many people already, that they are now afraid to get near me. A good friend of mine went ashore yesterday and asked if he could bring me anything. I asked him to bring back a dose of "clap" so that I can look at it on the telescope.*
>
> *Oh, my darling sometimes I just start wishing that I might be with you and be able to tell you directly how much I love you. I feel so low at times that the fellows can't understand me and wonder what the trouble is.*

The baby finally arrived on May 16th. It was a boy, and Alice had decided to name him John Wayne after his father and the movie actor. John had been clear that his middle name, Ignacious, was not an option. So, "Wayne" it was. She did not send a telegram, rather a birth notice that John had not received as of May 19 when he wrote to her.

Again, I have the happy task of writing you a letter, but I must remind you, that I still have not received the long-awaited news. So please do not keep me waiting too long.

Saturday, I had the duty and a young Marine came in complaining of losing twenty pounds within the last two weeks. He also complained of headaches and a sore spinal column. All the doctors were ashore so I took it upon myself to take him in our ward.

The senior man aboard said to give him a dose of castor oil and let him go as he thought he was only pretending. Another fellow said he might have TB but he couldn't prove it. I had my own suspicion so I did a urinalysis test. I guess it was more luck than anything but I found some abnormalities including high sugar which pointed to diabetes. He is at the hospital right now and the diabetes has been confirmed and he is in bad shape. I was certainly treated with respect Monday morning when the doctors came in and were told about it.

Sweetheart, please remember that I love you, love you every second of every day and so greatly that I couldn't put it in writing. Perhaps when I get back I might be able to tell you in person.

Will close now darling and hope to hear some wonderful news soon. Tomorrow I hope and till then and forever afterwards, your ever-loving husband.

John

Alice had been asking John to have someone take a picture of him climbing a palm tree. On May 22, still not knowing he was a father, he sent her a postcard of a native climbing a tree. He wrote:

> *"Dearest since you wanted a picture of me climbing a coconut tree. How do you like this one? Love John."*

Postcard of local climbing a tree in Oahu
(Personal collection of John I. Unger)

A couple of days later John finally received John Wayne's birth notice, but ironically, he would not be able to write Alice for a week as his workload had increased dramatically. On June 1, he wrote:

My Darling wife,

On account of heightened activities around here, I was unable to write before this. I hope you will forgive me for neglecting you for such a very long time.

It has been quite a while since I received your birth announcement and I was happy and gay when I did. But I did not go out and get myself plastered as I will take your advice and wait till I get back and the three of us shall paint the town red. That's a date huh?

So, my darling was wrong, we got a boy instead of a girl. I'm sure the boy arrived because you wished it. I guess it must have been a boy I wished for, but if it had been a girl as beautiful as the mother is, I'm sure I would likewise have enjoyed her. You are sure now sweetheart it wasn't twins?

Darling, Wayne is a very beautiful name. But where did you get that name of John at? Must have been that you once loved a fellow by that name before you met me, huh? And tell me how did such a young girl like you ever get such a heavy baby? Why he must be fatter than me and probably stronger. According to you, the baby must be very cute. I guess that is the reason I'm getting so cranky lately, because I can't see him in person.

Sweetheart, it feels great to be a daddy but I wonder how my father feels about being a grandpa and him being only 39 years old. I'm awful glad you like the baby so much dear and you wrote so little about your labor pain, that I guess you did not have too much trouble.

Will close now darling with loads of love, kisses and hugs to you and Johnny. Always your loving husband.

John

A contingent of Marines, including Corpsmen, had been shipped to Johnston Island by mid-June. With fewer Corpsmen at Pearl, John's workload continued to increase. Before, he had been writing to Alice two to three times a week, but now three weeks had almost passed before he wrote again. He would continue to keep her abreast of his activities, including that he was on his best behavior. "Best behavior" included staying on the base and not going into town, going to church every Sunday and concentrating on his studies. He had turned twenty-one on June 23 and asked Alice in one of his letters if she *still loved an old guy like him and that perhaps a young chicken like her had better find a younger man."*

Alice's letter writing had also slowed since she was now caring for John Wayne. She had sent John's parents a birth announcement, but neither of them heard from them. On a letter on June 25, John wrote to Alice:

> *I don't write many letters home but I expected to hear from them in answer to your birth announcement but I certainly didn't. They used to say that there wasn't a girl good-looking enough to attract me so maybe they still don't believe it.*

On June 28, John received orders that he was shipping out to Midway Island the following week. He wrote:

> *By the time you get this letter I will probably have a good case of sea sickness. It will be only about once a month that a ship gets there so I guess our letters will be very scarce. Maybe it will be worth it. A couple of months there and then back to the States I hope.*
>
> *At least when I write you from there and tell you I don't pay any attention to the girls, you might believe me as I hear there are only two married women on the island.*

The idea of going further away from you really doesn't appeal to me. I hope my imagination and ability to visualize you every day will not be affected by this distance.

I hope you haven't forgotten the picture of the baby you are going to send me as I'm still anxiously awaiting it. By now he must be big enough to talk back to his mother. And did he ask for me, what does he say?

I guess I better start packing. There are 5 Corpsmen going and 10 are staying here. I will again have the dressing room duty at Midway.

Lots and lots of love, kisses and hugs sweetheart and a great big kiss for the baby. Forever your loving husband.

John

P.S. Are you calling the baby Johnny or just baby?

After much internal debate, Japan's government and military agreed on July 2, 1941, to occupy all of Indochina. American cryptologists had broken the Japanese diplomatic code, and Roosevelt knew that this move was the first step toward the invasion of British Malaya and the Netherlands East Indies. Moreover, it meant that the Japanese were ready to go to war with Great Britain and the U.S. In response, Roosevelt ordered a freeze on Japanese assets in the United States. He had not intended to cut off oil, assuming that would be an excessive provocation, but the freezing of assets became a de facto embargo when the State Department persuaded the Treasury Department to refuse to release the frozen funds to Japan to purchase oil. The severing of trade would irreparably damage Japanese-American relations, for Japan saw it as a threat to its survival.[6]

As America was heading for war, John and his brothers-in-arms still did not worry much about getting drawn into it. In one of my interviews with John, we spoke about this time period and what was going on in Europe and the Pacific. I asked him if that was creating any angst for him and his friends, and his response was, "We were all just having a good time and also thinking that no one would have the nerve to attack America."

★   ★   ★

CHAPTER 7

"I MISS YOUR KISSES SOMETHING AWFUL."

July 3, 1941 to December 7, 1941

In the first few days of July of 1941, John, along with a group of Marines from the 1st Defense Battalion, were finishing their preparations to embark to Midway on July 5th on the *USS Portland*. The *USS Portland*, a Cruiser, had been commissioned in 1933 and would be one of the most decorated ships in World War II, receiving sixteen battle stars. She would serve throughout the Pacific during the war fighting at Midway, the Coral Sea, Guadalcanal, the Aleutians, the Gilbert and Marshall Islands, New Guinea, at Peleliu, and taking part in the battle of Leyte Gulf and the invasion of Okinawa. She would suffer a torpedo hit in 1942 but survived to finish the war.[1]

On the 4th of July in Washington, DC, President Roosevelt delivered what the *New York Times* described as a "somber" speech. In the radio address, Roosevelt said: "In our generation—in the past few years—a new resistance, in the form of several new practices of tyranny, has been making such headway that the fundamentals of 1776 are being struck down abroad and, definitely, they are threatened here. It is, indeed, a fallacy, based on no logic at all, for any American to suggest that the rule of force can defeat human freedom in all the other parts of the world and permit it to survive in the United States alone."[2] As America celebrated its 165th birthday, the president was telling the country that we could not stand by while the world was ravaged by tyrants. He ended his speech by pledging "our work, our will and, if it be necessary, our very lives" to the cause of freedom.[3]

The *USS Portland* left Pearl Harbor at 2:00 PM on Saturday, July 5 and arrived at Midway the following Tuesday. When he arrived at Midway, John and Alice were now 3,217 miles apart. John met many friends aboard the *USS Portland* with whom he had trained two years earlier. On arriving at Midway, the troops that had been there a while seemed to like the atoll, which consisted of two islands. That said, John wasn't so sure he was going to like this place. As he described it, "There was plenty of water to go swimming, but there are lots of fish that bite. And if I swam out farther, I'd probably run into a shark, and I'm afraid the shark wouldn't like that very much."

He could walk from one end of the bigger island to the other in about ninety minutes but had to be cautious of the thousands of birds everywhere. He described some that were as big as geese and so heavy that they'd "take off like an airplane, running for a stretch and then take off. The entire island was covered in white sand and the sun shone fiercely all day." He wrote his first letter to Alice from Midway on July 11.

I'm still anxiously waiting for those pictures of the baby sweetheart. Almost two months old, he must certainly be big already, and must be more trouble as he is no doubt getting more active every day. I try not to let it get me down not seeing you both but I believe it's working on me. I used to treat patients with a smile and now all I do is yell at them.

Ships coming to Midway are very irregular but I believe a Clipper comes and goes almost once a week. So, I think you'll able to get a letter every week.

I'd like very much to hear about the baby and how you are after the delivery. How much do you weigh and are there other changes?

Will close now darling and hope this letter reaches you and the baby in the best of health. Forever your loving husband,

John

Back home in Benicia, Alice had been suffering from complications that eventually required surgery for the removal of one of her kidneys. She had told John she was suffering from kidney problems but not that it had led to surgery. She did not share that till after she'd had the operation to avoid him worrying about it. She did not want him feeling helpless, not being with her to offer his support. On the 25th of July, John wrote to her after learning of her operation.

My dearest beloved,

I received your letter on the last Clipper. I was very surprised to hear about your operation. I thought a few pills would surely fix your kidney trouble. It's a lucky thing that I received your letter after the operation, otherwise I would have been a very worried young man. You will no doubt already be at home by the time this letter reaches you. I wish you a speedy recovery. I guess I just like to make myself feel good by hoping that you are in the best of health and happiness. In your next letter I wish you would tell me more about your operation.

Darling I'm still waiting for those pictures of the baby and hope it will also contain a snapshot of you. I've been on this isolated island for two weeks and turning black from the sun. I went spear fishing the other day and actually caught one. I also speared an octopus. There are supposed to be quite a few sharks here but so far, I haven't met any. They are probably afraid, when they see me coming with glasses and a wicked looking spear in my hand.

Sweetheart, how is Johnny doing? Is he still getting fatter and getting to be more trouble now as he increases in age?

A Marine Gunny Sergeant has just died from a heart attack that was very sudden. It's keeping some of the Corpsmen busy getting him ready for his trip home. Working in the dressing room is certainly keeping me busy. The other day in about 30 minutes, I gave a hypodermic needle to 230 Marines. I'm really good at it now.

Darling I'm getting very lonesome. I wish so much to be with you and Johnny that I get very moody and cranky. And so far, there is not a word about us going back. With your imagination and intuition, when do you expect me? I try my best to imagine myself with you but I just can't make it feel real.

My darling I'll close now and hope with all my heart that you are now in the best of health and remain so forever.

Lots of love, kisses and hugs to the baby and you. Forever your darling husband,

John

P.S. I love you very, very much.

After three weeks on Midway, John could not understand why most of the other guys liked it. He was not at all enamored with the island, though most everyone else seemed to enjoy it. He shared a story about two Marines who took a small sailboat out beyond the reef and discovered that the waves were really high on the other side. Their boat capsized and for several hours, they were hanging on for dear life. They had gone out at midday but no one missed them till after dark. A search party luckily found them and brought them to sick bay at about three in the morning, where John was on duty. They were scraped and bruised but otherwise okay. According to John, "They were pretty lucky to get out of it easy and were sent back to duty right away."

A different incident involving John was when he and three of his fellow Corpsmen took a boat out and were rowing for twenty minutes before discovering that their anchor was still down. After correcting the problem, they rowed further, and one of the Corpsmen, named Sommers, got seasick. The story got around the island and, eventually, it was published in the local newspaper, called the *Gooney Gazette*. According to John, all four of them were razzed for days, but Sommers got the worst of it. It seems like the crazier the story, the better the chances it had of making the *Gooney*. John said, "Thinking back on it, maybe it was lucky the anchor was down or perhaps they would have found us at the bottom of the reef."

In a letter on August 7, John wrote:

I still love you more and more and more and wish I was still with you and the baby but it just seems impossible. Instead of me going back, there is talk of going out further and it's likely true.

Two days later, John got orders to return to Pearl Harbor. On August 14, he wrote a short letter to Alice from Pearl.

Darling,

I didn't mail this letter because the Clipper was delayed due to bad storms we've been having. Instead of the Clipper it went to Pearl Harbor and me with it. It happened so sudden that I was unable to tell you of the change before. I left Midway Sunday and arrived at Pearl Thursday evening. I had a very nice trip and didn't even get seasick.

I'm expected to be in Pearl Harbor for only a short time and will soon take off for another island. The only thing I'm worried about is the picture of the baby. It's probably at Midway now and by the time it gets back here I'll probably be away again.

I'll write soon again sweetheart.

John

P.S. Still love me darling?

In one of Alice's letters, she told John that a picture of the baby was on its way to him, but as John feared, it had been sent to Midway. He'd have to continue to wait to see the image of his son. Alice's weight had gone above 160 pounds during the pregnancy, but she wrote that she was now back to 128 and still working on getting back into prepregnancy shape. She shared with John that Johnny always wanted to play with her long hair and that he did not like to be kissed. John responded he *did* like her kisses and *"I miss your kisses something awful."*

On August 28, he wrote her a letter anticipating his promotion to Hospital Corpsman Second Class:

My Dearest Darling,

I study so much that I'm practically as smart as a doctor. When I make Second Class, I'll double my money to about $125 a month. That is a nice sum and worth studying for. I'm eligible to be rated Second Class on December 16 – 41. I have hopes of being Second Class by the time I see you and everything will be OK then. And darling, when I make Second Class, I won't try to send you home like I did before in San Diego. I was kind of worried living together and me being only Third Class.

Johnny saying phooey to kissing means he is taking after me. I don't know how many times my mother kissed me but my step mother kissed me at my graduation and she got mad at me because I wiped it off. So, sweetheart that makes you the first girl I really kissed. And if you teach me really good, I should learn to kiss you very nicely; right?

Darling, so far, I have found it very easy to keep women out of my mind and I feel very proud. But should I break that vow, I'm sure I would never see you again because I know I could never face you afterwards.

I'll close now darling, with all my love to you and Johnny. Forever, your loving husband.

John

The next day (August 29) John sent Alice a birthday card. Alice was turning eighteen.

Most likely in anticipation of Christmas, Alice had asked John for details regarding his clothing sizes. He wrote her the following on September 6.

My Dearest Darling,

I don't know why you are interested in the size clothes I wear. But I'll try to give you a description. I'm 21 and in love. I only love brunettes. I will never smoke and so far, don't drink (much).

I'm 5 feet 9 inches tall and my average weight is 154 lbs. Waist is 30 but seems to be increasing. Length of trousers is about 31 inches. Chest 38 inches. Hat size 7 and shoe size is 8½ E.

I guess that is about the best I can do and hope that meets your requirements. And about pajamas darling, I'd rather see you in a night gown, even if it's up to your neck. I would like pajamas if I were at home but since hardly any one wears them in the service, it would cause too much talk and I would rather do without it.

I spent too much time at church this morning so I missed the Clipper and if I don't close now I'll miss the mail ship also.

On the same day, the Japanese attempted one last time to forge a peace agreement and made a critical decision that would plunge America into war. At a cabinet meeting that included Emperor Hirohito, Japanese leaders agreed to continue the talks in Washington and sent Saburo Kurusu as a special envoy to help Admiral Nomura restore relations with the Americans. However, Japan would not give up its newly acquired colonies nor disengage from its invasion of China. If no suitable agreement was reached with the U.S. by the beginning of October, the cabinet agreed to prepare for war with the Americans.[4]

John wrote again on the twelfth expressing his disappointment that he would not be with Alice the next day to help her celebrate her eighteenth birthday. In the same letter, he bared his soul regarding some deeply personal issues that had literally been causing him nightmares. In her last letter to him she had asked what was troubling him. Two poignant things he shared were that he never liked his father or stepmother because he had learned that, *"they had been keeping company with each other before his mother died."* Also, that he could never forgive his father for that. He then wrote her about several of his married buddies cheating on their wives some, with prostitutes. When he questioned them about their infidelity, they told him that, *"after six months, you, too, will be doing it."* It was an ironic twist and a testament to John's faith in God and himself, along with his devotion to Alice, that doing right was causing him to have frightful dreams. He ended the letter by writing the following:

That worried me quite a bit and had me quite upset. But now that we have been apart for more than 6 months, I find that I love you more and more and now definitely know, that I will never go with other women. I'm so sure that I would swear it on a bible.

Sweetheart I hope this satisfies your question and if you say you never get nightmares, well then, no doubt you trust and believe me and you are not worried about such thoughts: Are you? After all this, I had better close darling before I tire you too much.

Lots of love, kisses and hugs to the baby and you. Forever your darling husband,

John

After John's soul-baring letter and subsequent letters by Alice, John was desperate for a leave. On October 3, he wrote to her to say he wished his promotion to Second Class would happen soon and if it did, he was sure he could request and be granted leave. In the same letter he wrote:

> *I would like to ask you what your imagination and dreams are but I guess they are the same as mine. Specifically, a very happy future among us, enough to fill a book.*
>
> *Darling, your description of your days with the baby seem very busy and it's good that you are keeping a good diet. Wait till I get back, Johnny and I won't take a shower but once a week. Then we'll take one whether we need it or not. Our diet will consist of a hamburger with a scotch and soda and a beer for a chaser. Just wait you'll see.*
>
> *Darling, what sailors are you talking to that give you those misleading facts about service men. I don't know whether they talk more than girls about those things (sex) but sailors are not very particular about their speech and can be really filthy. As for me, I wouldn't have anything to talk about, for which I have you to thank for. If I hadn't met you, no matter how good a boy I was before, I would have probably been influenced by that bad element and gone to the dogs.*
>
> *I thought I knew everything about the Catholic religion but now I'm stuck, so maybe you can help me out. If a boy and a girl both Catholic get married outside the church they would have to be married again by a priest in order to stay in good graces with the church. In the mean time you cannot go to confession but it's OK to continue to go to mass.*

During their breakneck speed romance and subsequent marriage, John and Alice had failed to cross the t's and dot the i's regarding things like religion. Though Alice was a Christian, she had not been baptized in the Catholic church, a matter that they would resolve years later. In many ways, they knew much more about each other through their letters than from the time they had spent together. In their almost fifteen months, they had spent the majority of the time away from each other.

In Japan, the early October deadline had passed, and there was still no agreement with the United States. In late October, the Emperor would replace Prime Minister Fumimaro Kanoe with the much more aggressive and former War Minister, Hideki Tojo. Now in control of the cabinet, Tojo admitted to "some uneasiness about a protracted war" with the powerful Americans. He emphasized that due to our limited oil reserves, "I fear we would become a third-class nation after two or three years if we just sat tight." Accordingly, the government blessed a war plan designed by Admiral Isoroku Yamamoto that entailed a secret and preemptive strike on the U.S. fleet at Pearl Harbor and a simultaneous attack on the Philippines and other strategic targets in the Pacific,[5] including Wake.

Yamamoto erroneously believed that, by crippling the U.S. Navy in a decisive battle, it would encourage the Americans into a negotiated peace and avoid a "protracted and dirty war." He believed that was Japan's only hope for success in a war that he loyally supported but believed his country should have avoided.[6]

Meanwhile, it appeared as if John would be staying at Pearl Harbor for an extended period, but that would change by his own doing by the end of the month. On the fifteenth of October, he sent Alice an eight-page letter covering a variety of topics. Of highest importance were his studies and pending promotion to Second Class.

My Dearest Sweetheart,

I got a tip that we were going to have a 2nd Class examination. So, I really hit the books and did I study. The situation was this. There are no vacancies for Second Class but because of the increase in personnel in the Navy, the bureau sometimes overlooks that and still rates some fellows. There were four fellows, including me, that went up for it last Friday. I waited to send this letter till I could get my grades. And darling, I got the highest mark out of the four. You didn't know I was smart, did you? My mark was 86. There were 9 different subjects on the exam.

But as I had the least time in the service, one fellow got a ½ point more than I did. And I'm mad. If he would have gotten a higher mark because he was smarter than me, everything would be OK but just because he had a few more months in the service he got ahead of me. I even helped him with the examination. That's what you get for being so kind. So, the situation is this: Our exam papers are being forwarded to the bureau and if they don't rate all four of us, one or two might get rated. So darling, you better keep your fingers crossed.

If I get rated on the first chance, it would be on or after November 1st. If I don't make it, I'm sure I will, shortly thereafter. And darling you know what Second Class means to us. $34.50 a month more for housing allowance, plus $15 if I'm living ashore with you. Plus, travel allowance for my wife and child. So, here's hoping and I'll let you know if I hear any more on the subject.

Though madly in love with each other, they simply did not know each other well. To bridge that gap, John wrote: *"Darling, I still expect a life history of yourself and you no doubt need one of me."* He went on to share that there was no chance he'd be home for Christmas but he was hopeful that he could arrange time after the holidays. Alice had written that she was worried about him and what the future would bring for him, but he assured her that there was nothing to worry about. He went on to tell her that the only thing that worried him was when he'd be able to see her and the baby.

The next week John made a decision that would change their lives forever. Not enjoying the worldly pleasures of Oahu and because doing anything there was too expensive, he decided to switch duty with a Corpsman who had been ordered to Wake Island. John surmised that by going to Wake he would save money, still enjoy his love of swimming, and possibly get his Second Class rating sooner than by staying at Pearl. He does not recall the name of the Corpsman but does recall both of them going to Chief Hospital Corpsman Hall and asking for a switch in assignments. Their request was readily approved. The other Corpsman was happy to stay in Hawaii, and John was feeling good about being able to save more money for his family.

John was not alone in his decision to choose to go to Wake for financial reasons. Many of the men at Wake, especially the civilians, had volunteered for duty there. William Taylor, one of the few men to escape from a Japanese POW camp in China, wrote a book, *"Rescued by Mao: World War II, Wake Island, and My Remarkable Escape to Freedom Across Mainland China,"* in which he wrote:

> *So, what did we have to worry about? For a guy wanting to*
> *get paid three times what he could make on the mainland, it was*
> *just great. However, I must note that a majority of the men were*
> *married with families on the mainland, so even though they were*
> *paid great wages and bonuses to entice them to stay after their*

contracts expired, most of them could hardly wait to get on the
boat or the clipper and return to the "good old USA."[7]

When John arrived at Wake, there were about 200 Marines on the island from the 1st Defense Battalion, along with some Navy personnel, including other Corpsmen and the 1,200 civilians who worked for Morrison-Knudsen and Pan American Airlines. According to John, the Marines were spending most of their time setting up the gun positions to fortify the atoll. They also ran regular drills, including antiaircraft target practice. The civilians were busy building barracks, docks, and other structures that would be part of the naval base. John and the six other Corpsmen were assigned to different responsibilities. His responsibility was to support the Marines at Toki Point on Peale Island, at the northernmost point on the atoll.

John was taken to Wake on the *USS Castor*, known as a General Stores Issue Ship used for ferrying men and supplies. It was commissioned the *USS Castor* on March 12, 1941. The ship was at Pearl Harbor on the day of the attack but escaped damage. It would serve out of Pearl and then at Tarawa and Okinawa during WW II and then in the Korean War and Vietnam.[8]

Within a couple of days of being on the island, John became the bartender at the Officers Club where, among others, he'd meet Devereux, Cunningham, and the twelve pilots who had arrived at Wake on December 4th. He enjoyed spending time with the officers, and the extra money came in handy. On Halloween of 1941, he wrote his first letter to Alice from Wake Island:

My Dearest Sweetheart,

Here I am way out on Wake Island; 2,004 miles from
Pearl Harbor and about 4,000 miles away from you. I left

Pearl Harbor Saturday at 6:00 PM and arrived here Thursday October 30. The reason it took so long was that we stopped at Johnston Island for 2 days. Wake Island is much nicer and bigger than Midway. And so far, I seem to like this place. The only thing wrong is that it's a little too close to the Japs for comfort. But if the worst comes, I'm a very good swimmer and with you waiting for me, I could cut a wicked path through this ocean to you. And if they don't give me leave pretty soon, I'll swim for it anyhow.

Wake Island is densely wooded and is composed of three Islands that are more or less connected together and make a horseshoe shape with a lagoon in the center. On one side is the Pacific Ocean and on close inspection, I find that on the other side is also the Pacific Ocean. They even have malted milk out here, movies every night, and beer, but usually they are out of it.

The trip out here was very rugged, storming all the way. And the vessel that was a supply ship rocked all the way. But darling I'm so salty that I didn't even get sick. It was so stormy that for two days we could not get close to the island. Anything you want to know about this island I'll be glad to tell you, except of course, its defenses.

I try to keep myself busy out here so I don't feel so bad, for sweetheart how I miss you and if I don't get to see you and the kid pretty soon, I'll go over the "hill." I'll sit around and my mind starts wondering, and soon I imagine us three together being happy and I feel so good. But when I come around, what a feeling! I guess there is no need telling you about it, as you must have the same feelings.

Alice had asked John about a watch he had sold, and wanted to know if he wanted a new one for Christmas. The answer was a resounding "No," as *"watches don't last long in the heat and humidity."* If she could, he'd like an electric shaver, as he was expected to shave every day, and razors rusted easily, making a mess of his face. He shared that the two Clippers and two steamers alternated stopping there every two weeks so that they could continue to write to each other every week. He lamented about the price of a stamp that was three-and-a-half cents. and the number of sharks around the island. So many, that they had to fence an area for the swimmers that was right outside his tent. He finished that letter with the following:

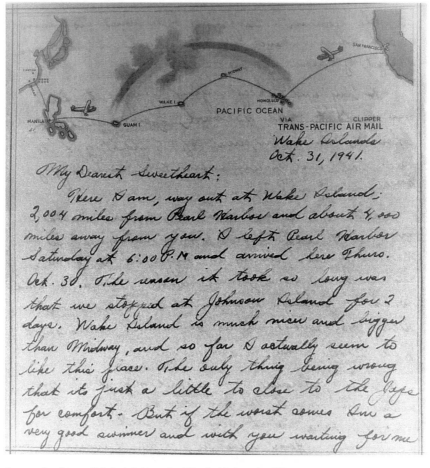

A sample of one of John's letters to Alice in his handwriting

*I'm just so anxious to gaze into your eyes that seem to haunt
me so much as I can always see them. And that wonderful hair,
how I'd like to get my hand in it. Most of all, I miss your kisses
from those lips that are so sweet and tender.*

*I never knew it was possible to love anyone as much as I
love you. Words, I know, can't describe it but I'll surely try to
tell you when I see you in person. Darling, I will have plenty
of time to read your complete life history so please do not disappoint me.*

*I'll close now darling with lots of love, kisses and hugs, for-
ever your ever-loving husband,*

John

Though John had made the conscious decision to go to Wake, it
was clear to him that the prospect of war with Japan was now very real.
So, too, was the case with Major Devereux, who had arrived at Wake
to take over command of the 1st Defense Battalion on October 15th.
He would write in his book that *"Initially, the 6th Defense Battalion had
been scheduled for Wake, but it was decided that they needed more training
before being sent to a Sea Frontier. A small detachment of the 1st would be
assigned to Wake till the 6th was ready to take over."*[9] For John, that meant
that, barring a leave being granted, he would stay on Wake till the 1st
Defense Battalion was deployed elsewhere.

From the time he arrived on the island, Devereux had concerns about
defending an all-out attack on Wake. The bare training allowance of a
defense battalion at that time was about 850 men. Devereux had only
180 Marines when he arrived, and that number would not increase till
10 days before the war broke out. At that time, he would have a total of

378 men to do a job requiring 850.[10] The balance of the Marines from the 1st Defense Battalion remained at Pearl Harbor and the Johnston Atoll. Before leaving Pearl Harbor, Devereux had discussed the deficiencies of the military power at Wake with Colonel Harry Pickett, who reported to Rear Admiral Husband E. Kimmel, Commander of the Pacific Fleet. Pickett and Devereux agreed that the mission of the Marines on Wake was only to withstand a "minor raid."[11]

On November 15, 1941, John would write the last letter that Alice would receive from him till July of 1943. She would not know whether he was dead or alive till January 14, 1943. Below is the letter of November 15, in its entirety.

My dearest Darling,

It certainly took a long time to hear from you, but when the ship came in I got four of your letters, including the pictures. And after receiving those lovely pictures of you and Johnny, I was really full of joy. I just can't keep away from them. I spent all day looking at them and still, I feel as if I haven't seen them enough.

I see where you have your hair fixed a different way which looks very nice but I really don't know which way I like it the most. Just give me time; I'll find out. Also, the dress you have on really makes you look appealing. How a wonderful girl like you can love a person like me, is far beyond me. And if those pictures do Johnny any justice at all, why no wonder you say he is adorable. He really looks cute and quite the man.

Darling, a lucky thing all your letters came together so I don't have to look very far for the snapshot of Mary Jane (Alice's friend) *and Johnny together. With his fists closed, he really looks tough but his face spoils it. He took too much after you, he's just too lovely.*

Honey, I'm not trying to answer all of your questions in this letter, I'm just making a general round up to answer your most important questions. Regarding your inquiry as to whether or not you should buy Savings Bonds, that sweetheart not only sounds patriotic but is also most undoubtedly, the best way to invest money. If you still think greatly of an immediate purchase, please do so but I have two reasons why a later purchase of Bonds might be more convenient. One is that I'm trying to get some leave, but I'm not making much headway. If the unexpected happens, it might be in a month or two and if I haven't got it three months from now, I'm going to be hard to get along with. If they think they are getting bothered now, they won't know the meaning of being bothered, as I'll really go after them. And besides darling, you know I usually get what I want, and this, I want more than anything else.

Second, I expect to make my rate by the first of the year if not before which would give me all the money you need for Johnny's investment. So, the only thing wrong, is that everything is so uncertain. As soon as I make my next rate, I'll just pull rank. A 2nd Class rate is pretty good in the Marine Corps, as there are only two more rates till I make Chief.

We are getting a new doctor by the name of Kelley with whom I worked with at Mare Island and he should still remember me. I'll have him get me my rate and my leave. His rate is Commander and he should get what he wants.

I'll close now darling with loads of love, kisses and hugs to Johnny and you. Always your loving husband,

John

P. S. I love you very, very, very much darling

On December 5, in Washington, Roosevelt learned that two large convoys of Japanese ships had been sighted off the coast of China, but no one knew where they were headed. Siam, Malaya, Singapore, or the Dutch Indies were all possibilities. No one in the administration believed that Hawaii might be a target. Some speculated the Philippines might be a target, but it was ridiculous to think Pearl Harbor might be in danger. Hawaii was just too far from Japan. These beliefs persisted, despite warnings from Navy intelligence that the Japs might precipitate a war by conducting a sneak attack on Pearl Harbor.[12]

★ ★ ★

CHAPTER 8

"IT WAS MY JOB."

December 9, 1941 to December 11, 1941

There is an allure to many tropical islands that brings smiles to those who have the opportunity to enjoy them. From the amalgam of blues where the sea meets the sky to the warm breezes that flow throughout the day, they are a gift of nature, meant to be enjoyed. But on December 9, 1941, no one, including John, on the tropical Islands of Peale, Wilkes, or Wake, was enjoying anything. Many were thanking God that they had survived the swift attack by the Japanese the previous day, yet most of the inhabitants at Wake on that Tuesday morning were tense and apprehensive about what the enemy had in store for them. The more seriously wounded were being cared for at the civilian hospital. The less critically wounded had been patched up by John and his fellow Corpsmen at their gun stations or at the sick bay near the airfield. Unfortunately, there had been no time to bury the dead. The previous night had been spent reinforcing battery positions and bunkers and digging in, in anticipation of the next attack.

After a couple of hours of sleep, John had been up most of the night. At daybreak, he met Chambliss, and, after ensuring that he had an ample supply of bandages and morphine, he started his usual shuttling between B and D Batteries. As he did so, he was vigilant of any planes that might be approaching the islands. When he met with Chambliss that morning, it was the first time he had heard about the apparent damage that had been wrought on Pearl Harbor. The news did not spark confidence, as John was well aware of the incredible might the U. S. military had at Pearl. At the time, Chambliss did not have specific details, but 2,330 military personnel had perished, and another 1,143 had been wounded. Additionally, 68 civilians had been killed and 35 wounded.[1] More than 1,000 men died on the battleship *USS Arizona* when the missile credited to the veteran Bombardier and Petty Officer Noboru Kanai hit beside the No. 2 turret and detonated the forward magazine.[2] Eventually 1,177 would die on the *Arizona,* including 23 sets of brothers.[3] Among the ships lost at Pearl were the *Arizona, Utah, Cassin, Shaw,* and *Ogala.* Several others were damaged including the battleship *Oklahoma.*[4] The U. S. Pacific fleet had three carriers, the *Enterprise,* the *Saratoga,* and the *Lexington;* fortuitously, none of them were at Pearl at the time of the attack. That fortunate timing would come back to haunt the Japs at Midway.

Though tired, John was as ready as he was going to be for whatever havoc the Japs had in store for them on what was a beautiful morning with clear skies. As was customary, he checked with Sergeant Wright to see if he needed anything but especially now that the war had started. He wanted to learn as much from the sergeant as he could, especially about staying alive. Wright was more than three hundred pounds and stood six feet, six inches tall. The veteran, who had fought in Nicaragua, was plain spoken and to the point. When the situation called for him to be loud and even more direct, Wright would not hesitate. His vocabulary was colorful at times, including a full array of well-placed cuss words. He was hard on his men and harder on civilians that couldn't or wouldn't carry their weight. When he disagreed with an opinion or perspective from one of his men that didn't suit him, he was known to respond-ing with, "You're not paid to think, you are paid to fight." He was also known for always carrying a lucky silver dollar with him that he believed would safeguard him through the toughest situations. Above all, he was a respected leader, which is what had drawn John to the big man.

At about eleven forty-five in the morning, twenty-seven Jap bombers again approached the Islands from the south. John recalls getting some warning this time, "but not much." The warnings were shots fired in the air that alerted all to take cover or for the Marines at the batteries to man the guns. Before the bombers reached the island, Lieutenant David D. Kliewer and Sergeant William J. Hamilton, who had been flying patrol, spotted the bombers and immediately engaged; two against twenty-seven. The nimbler American fighter planes downed one bomber, making it the first kill for the defenders at Wake. The bombers were coming in above eight thousand feet, which meant that the 3-inch guns had a chance of fighting back.[5]

John had been trained by Sergeant Wright to use the pathfinder scope. The scope is a range finder that controls the direction of the 3-inch guns. The pathfinder is wired to the guns and directs them where to fire. Whoever is on the pathfinders tracks the planes and tells the Marines when to open fire. When the attack started, Wright who usu-ally manned the pathfinder, was not in the control center. Accordingly, John immediately took over the pathfinder and directed the 3-inch guns at Peale till Wright made it back. As usual, John had been happy to do what he could above and beyond his duties as a Corpsman.

The Japs focused most of their attack on day two on Camp 2 and what was left of any structures on Peale. The 3-inch guns on Peale, where John was stationed, and at Peacock Point fired a barrage of rounds at the bombers. From his vantage point, John could see three of the Jap planes smoking as they headed back to their base. A fourth plane exploded in midair. John and everyone around him jumped for joy at the sight. In his usual understated way, John smiled and said to me, "Yeah, we were happy about that." The guns at Peale and Peacock had hit their mark. What John didn't know at the time, was that the civilian hospital had been hit, and almost everyone inside had been killed. The red cross on the building, marking it as a hospital, did not matter to the Japs; they dropped their bombs anyway. They not only didn't care—they had *targeted* it for destruction.

In all, twenty-one patients had been killed, including ten civilians and eleven Marines.[6] After the bombing, the men near the hospital and those inside who were still mobile rushed to help anyone still alive. Drs. Kahn and Shank repeatedly ran in and out of the flaming building to try to save the wounded and to retrieve as many of the medical supplies and equipment as possible.[7] Devereux wrote in his book that fifty civilian casualties had been reported to him, mostly wounded, but he believed there had been duplications in the report.[8] A different estimate had thirty civilians dying near Camp 2 and seven Marines killed at different places around the atoll.[9]

John had more wounded to tend to on day two, including five civilians who had been helping fill sandbags when the Japs hit. He did what he could for the wounded and, not knowing the condition of the hospital, sent them there for further care if they needed it. He would not learn about the carnage at the hospital till much later that day. In one of his status checks, Chambliss would tell him about the men killed at the hospital.

Once again, the noise and impact of the bombs had been horrific, but John would tell me, "At some point I got used to it—it became a routine for us." He kept telling himself, "This is what you trained for, so do what you are supposed to do, and don't worry about things you can't control. This is the way things are going to go, so do your job." I asked John if there was any talk about reinforcements coming to Wake, and his simple answer was, "No—that wasn't my job, so I didn't think about it."

An aerial view of the Wake Atoll. The V-shaped island on the bottom is Wake, at top center is Wilkes, and on the right side is Peale (Warfare History Network).

Devereux made two critical decisions on the 9th. First, he began to move gun positions to confuse the Japanese. Second, since the civilian hospital was now gone, he ordered two sick bays be set up by the airfield in the magazines (reinforced concrete shelters about forty by twenty feet in size and fifteen-foot ceilings). The shelters offered more protection for the wounded than the hospital building had.[10] John recalled that, as the planes were headed back to their base, one of them left the formation and took another pass over the atoll but did not fire or drop bombs. It was, most likely, taking pictures for the next bombing raid. Ergo Devereux's decision to move the 3-inch guns.

That night, the Marines worked feverishly moving guns. John offered to help the guys at Peale, but they told him, "No, Doc—keep your hands clean, in case you have to treat someone." As John described it, "Conditions were not too sanitary, and the Marines wanted to make sure I was always ready to help anyone wounded." As he had done the previous day, he drove to Peacock Point to check on his friend Brewer and then headed back to Peale, to sleep under the stars by the gun positions. He said, "It was no big deal; the weather was nice, and my orders were to stay near B and D batteries."

As December 9th turned into the 10th all concerns were again on what the Japs would throw at them today. The shortage of Marines literally prevented Devereux from manning all the gun batteries. Throughout the island, while most civilians were taking shelter, some were doing anything and everything they could to support the Marines. One group of six civilians manned a new gun position that Devereux had ordered Marine Corporal John S. Johnson to set up on Wilkes Island. According to Johnson, one civilian in particular, Leo Nonn, was invaluable.[11] Another fourteen civilians showed up at Toki Point and Sergeant Wallace A. Bowsher placed them on his unmanned 3-inch gun and instructed them on the fundamentals of using the weapon.[12] For John, it meant he had more men to look after, but getting more antiaircraft guns in the fight was a welcome development.

John went through his usual routines, ensuring he had plenty of medical supplies and continuing to shuttle between the batteries on Peale. What island you were on, on any given day, literally made the difference between life and death. The Japanese had focused on Wake the first day and Peale on the second. Today was Wilkes' turn to take the brunt of the attack that started at 10:45 AM and included eighteen bombers that were coming in much higher, at around eighteen thousand feet. Though all three islands were hit, the heavier concentration was on Wilkes. At Wilkes, the 3- and 5-inch guns were damaged as well as a storage facility with more than one hundred tons of dynamite, causing a horrendous explosion.[13] John recalls the sight and sound of the dynamite blowing up. He is sure anyone watching could see it from any place on the atoll. On Peale, at the 3-inch gun battery, the power failed, knocking out the pathfinder. Accordingly, the antiaircraft gunners were firing on instinct without the aid of the tracking mechanism. After the attack, the power would be restored to the pathfinder.

John also recalls that, due to the high altitude of the bombers, most of the bombs aimed at Peale mercifully dropped into the lagoon. "There were a lot of dead fish, but the guys had been spared." In the air, our remaining four planes were taking on the Japs, and Captain Elrod, who by now had been christened with the nickname "Hammering Hank," would be credited with downing two of the Jap planes. Around the atoll casualties had been amazingly light.[14]

On December 11, activities would start before dawn, and it would become a historic day for the Wake defenders and for America. Japanese Admiral Sadamichi Kajioka had sailed from the Marshall Islands on December 8 on his flagship, the light cruiser *Yubari*, along with a taskforce of fifteen other ships: two other light cruisers—the *Tenryu* and the *Tatsuta*—along with six destroyers, three submarines, and four troop transports that carried 450 Special Naval landing forces. Kajioka was confident that the three previous days of bombings, along with the firepower about to be delivered by his ships, would have significantly weakened, if not totally destroyed, the American defenses.[15]

Shortly before 3:00 AM, Devereux had been roused from his sleep with a report of movement at sea, south of the island. He was aware that there was no American task force nearby, so it had to be the Japs. Shortly before daybreak, he confirmed that it was a taskforce of Japanese ships, and he gave the order to prepare for battle but to "hold your fire till I give the order." This would be the time to bring the 5-inch guns into the defense of the atoll. He then called Major Putnam to get the four planes ready to take off but not till our guns began firing. He wanted to draw the Japanese in as close as possible before opening fire and did not want planes taking off, giving away the element of surprise.[16]

The Japs sent a cruiser ahead of the task force that opened fire on the atoll at about seven thousand feet off shore, by Wilkes. The cruiser was followed by three destroyers that also opened up. They were firing to kill but also to draw fire from the Americans to gauge what they had left. The Marines at all gun positions were getting antsy if not downright mad that Devereux had not given the order to fire. Devereux waited till the ships were within 4,500 yards and then gave the order to "commence firing!"[17]

Almost in unison, the 5-inch guns opened fire from all three islands. The guns on Battery A registered a hit on Kajioka's flagship, the *Yubari*, which immediately tried to reverse course. Two more shells hit the ship, and then one of the destroyers put down a smoke screen to try to shield the stricken vessel. It, too, was hit by another salvo from Battery A.[18]

On Wilkes at Battery L, Lieutenant John A. McAllister, firing without the benefit of a rangefinder (it had been destroyed in an earlier bombing raid) zeroed in on the destroyer *Hayate*, one of several ships within range of his guns. On his third attempt, a shell hit the destroyer and detonated its magazine, causing a ferocious explosion, splitting the ship, which sank in less than two minutes, taking all 168 sailors to their death. It was the first ship to be sunk by the Americans in World War II.[19]

At Peale, on Battery D, Kessler and his men were under heavy fire and narrowly avoided disaster when a shell landed between two rows of ammunition handlers. Had the shell landed on either side, it would have killed a good number of the men at Battery B. Kessler's team eventually hit two destroyers that were trying to maneuver around the north end of Wilkes Island.[20]

During the battle Kessler climbed to the top of the lookout tower and, in the process, caught some shrapnel on the bridge of his nose that was bleeding profusely. John was called to help and had to travel between D and B batteries with shells falling all over the area. When he got there, he raced to the top of the tower. From that vantage point, he would say, "I could see the ships in the distance all around. They were firing and just going around and around." John patched Kessler up and then headed back down to Battery B.

More than five decades later, in June of 1995, Kessler would write a letter to Jim Kelly, John's nephew and also a Navy Chief Petty Officer, in which he said, in part:

Dear Mr. Kelly,

I was the first Lt. in command of "B" battery at Toki Point, Peale Island. On the first day of WW II, 8 December on Wake, some men were wounded by the bombing. John was attending to them very quickly, although he had to come over from "D" battery. He was very efficient in treating their wounds and administering morphine.

Again, on December 11, my position was heavily shelled by Japanese ships, and I received a cut on the bridge of my nose from flying shell fragments. John Unger showed up soon after. The cut bled profusely, and John applied a double band aid and I was back to work. "Efficient" is how I would describe John Unger's handiwork. He was everywhere, wherever he was needed.

Sincerely,
Woodrow M. Kessler

Jim Kelly had contacted the Editor of the *Wake Island Wig-Wag* newsletter, asking anyone who had served with John to contact him with stories about John. The *Wig-Wag* was originally published at Wake to keep the military personnel up to date on activities on the island and news from back home. After the war, Corporal Franklin D. Gross, one of the Marines on Wake, revived the newsletter sometime in the seventies. Kessler had come across Kelly's request and subsequently wrote him the letter. Kessler had retired from the Marine Corps as a Brigadier General.

When I talked to John about Kessler's letter, he laughed and said, "That was good of Kessler to say, but we didn't have any band aids. I had to improvise with what I had because he was bleeding pretty bad. I think it was some gauze and tape, fashioned into a sort of a butterfly shape, to stop the bleeding." Regarding going from one battery to the other, while shells were falling everywhere, his response was simply, "It was my job." During the many interviews we conducted with John, some of his most horrifying experiences were usually explained by him saying, "It was my job."

Meanwhile, the battle continued, and our four planes were running sortie after sortie against the Jap ships. Major Putnam and Captains Elrod, Frank C. Tharin, and Herbert C. Freuler scouted at fifteen thousand feet to intercept enemy aircraft or spot a potential carrier. When none were sighted, they joined the fight. Each plane could carry only two one-hundred-pound bombs in addition to their machine guns. After dropping their bombs, they would strafe the ships with machine-gun fire, return to the airstrip to reload, and take off again. The four pilots were relieved by Lieutenant John F. Kinney and Sergeant Hamilton. Japanese Submarine Lieutenant Shigeyosi Ozeki would later write about our pilots. "We were hounded out to sea by fanatical American fighters who strafed us relentlessly and dropped bombs with impunity."[21]

Captain Elrod would be credited with the sinking of a cruiser and once again would have to apply all his skill to land his plane, which eventually crash-landed on the beach. All of our planes had been hit with flak from the enemy ships, and, after the battle, only two would be able to fly again.[22] John remembers seeing Elrod's plane coming in for the landing from across the lagoon. "It was coming in all wobbly; you could tell he was in trouble." John eventually lost sight of it as Elrod landed on the beach. Later in the day, Captain Kliewer, out scouting, spotted an enemy sub about twenty-five miles from Wake and dropped two bombs close enough to cause damage; it supposedly sunk.[23]

One of our submarines, the *Triton*, had been in the area, but the men at Wake did not know if the sub was still around or if it had engaged in the battle. It was indeed in the area, had fired at one of the destroyers, and hit it, but it is uncertain if the sub or our planes sank the ship.

The estimates of Japanese casualties on the 11th vary, but a conservative estimate is that at least seven hundred of the enemy perished that day. The Japs also suffered the loss of two destroyers, and two transports were heavily shelled although not technically sunk. Five other ships, including two light cruisers were disabled or damaged.[24] The Marines, Navy, and Army had four casualties, none of them fatal.[25] Just as important was that the Japanese landing force never got close enough to invade the island.

The Japanese destroyer *Hayate*, one of the ships sunk by the Marines on Dec. 11 (National Archives)

In all, it was a resounding victory for the defenders of Wake and a deflating defeat for the Japanese. On the cover of every volume of the *Wake Island Wig-Wag*, there is a quote from Masatake Okumiya, Commander, Japanese Imperial Navy, referring to the attempted landing. "Considering the power accumulated for the invasion of Wake Island and the meager forces of the defenders, it was one of the most humiliating defeats the Japanese Navy had ever suffered."

December 11 had been America's first victory of World War II. Every military man and many civilians had played a part. Whether at the batteries, in the air, or supporting those who were delivering destruction to the enemy, every man contributed. It was interesting to me, in talking to John, how little had been shared among the troops about their success that day. This was due, in part, to the fact that they did not know the extent of the damage they had inflicted but also because all of them knew that this fight was not over.

The day ended in somewhat of a bizarre way for John. As was his custom, he checked in on both B and D Batteries and then on his friend Brewer at Peacock Point. He was then flagged down by Devereux to go around the island, to check for any dead Japs who might be floating about. John executed his duty and reported back that he had not seen any floating Japs. He told me, "I have no idea what I would have done if I had seen one."

John thought often about Alice and Johnny but kept grounding himself in the reality that there was nothing he could do to get back to them. At this point, he couldn't even write to them. I asked John what else was going through his mind, and he responded with his usual, "I had to focus on doing my job." He added, "I was making thirty bucks a month, and I had to earn it." I told him, "John, you were getting bombed for thirty bucks a month." He said, "Heck, before I made Third Class, I was being paid twenty-one bucks a month and had to pay for my own haircut." At that point I gave up. Clearly, this man was cut from a very special piece of cloth. Back in the States, Alice, like most Americans, knew that Wake had been attacked and that the men were defending the island. But neither she nor any other relative, sweetheart, or friend of the men at Wake had any idea whether their loved ones were alive.

★　　★　　★

CHAPTER 9

"KEEP RUNNING, DOC!"

December 12, 1941 to December 21, 1941

Once again, John's day started by meeting with Chambliss, who asked John if he was okay and if he needed anything. The previous day's casualties had been light, so John said, "All is good, and I'm ready to go." He had all the supplies he needed, and he was focused on "doing his job." Chambliss made no mention of the incredible victory the previous day. This was a new day, and no one would be resting on their laurels.

On the mainland, newspapers reported on the heroic defense of the atoll. When asked by a reporter to express his thoughts about Wake on December 12, President Roosevelt responded, "So far as we know, Wake Island is holding out—has done a perfectly magnificent job. We are all very proud of that very small group of Marines who are holding the island." All the major newspapers and magazines were covering the activities at Wake. *Newsweek* stated that "Out in the middle of the Pacific, on the tiny Wake Island, a Marine Corps garrison gave the Japs the surprise of their lives by repelling the December attack. All America

135

was watching to see what the next move of the heroic leathernecks would be." Some people were comparing Wake to Davy Crockett and the Texans holding off the Mexicans at the Alamo or the Spartans holding off the Persians at Thermopylae.[1]

On December 12, a lone Jap patrol plane attacked shortly before 5:00 AM. Because of the low visibility at that time of day, the antiaircraft guns couldn't do much. By now, with only two planes operating, there was only one scout plane in the air. Captain Tharin was on patrol and went after the plane repeatedly till the Jap flipped into a dive and crashed into the sea. Later in the day, at their usual time, shortly before noon, the bombers came again. This time there were forty of them.[2] It was no surprise that the Japs decided to up the ante by increasing the number of bombers. After the beating they had taken the previous day, they had learned a lot about the Americans' courage and resolve. In one of John's typical understatements he would say, "They were sure anxious to get that island."

Though the number of bombers increased, according to John, the day was "uneventful." It's almost surreal for me to write that—when forty planes had just blasted the island with bombs. Nevertheless, that was John's perspective and that of his fellow Marines. One can only surmise that the definition of what is rational or normal in people's minds changes dramatically, based on the circumstances.

December 13 would be a special day. The Japs took a day off, and the defenders of Wake got a respite from the bombings. By now, all were on high alert at dawn each day and also close to noon. Those were the times when the Japs had previously attacked. That afternoon, John went over to the Officers' Club and had a chance to talk to some of them, including Captain Elrod. By now, word of Elrod's accomplishments had gotten around the atoll, but, like everyone else, he, too, was both humble and matter-of-fact about his accomplishments. John congratulated him, but just as John would say many times to me, Elrod's response to him was, "No big deal. It's what I was trained to do, so I did it." John told me, "There was no celebration or anything like that." While at the club, John picked up a bottle of whiskey that he planned to drink on Christmas Day with some of his buddies. He stored it with his gear that he was now keeping at Battery D and then continued to "do his job."

On the same day, Kay Kyser, a famous bandleader, dedicated a song to the men of Wake on his radio show. When Marine Captain Wesley M. Platt heard about it, he was reported to have said, "What did they play, 'Taps'?"[3] John shared another story with me that would be included in just about every book written about Wake and would also hit many major newspapers in the States, becoming a rallying cry for Americans. One of the regular messages from Wake to Pearl Harbor was misinterpreted to read, "Send us more Japs." The message was attributed to Devereux, who never uttered the words.[4] John said to me, "Geez, the last thing any of us wanted was more Japs."

On a more morbid note, the *Detroit Free Press* reported that Washington officials, including the president, assumed the Wake defenders would die, but their efforts would not be in vain. A *New York Times* headline read, "Marines Keep Wake." The report ended by stating, "Wake may be captured; its capture, indeed, had long been anticipated, but if its leathernecks add another glorious chapter to their history and inflict further losses on the enemy, they will not have died in vain."[5] John would tell me, "Yeah, for the longest time people thought we were all dead, including Alice."

Unfortunately, the day would not end without disappointment. As Captain Freuler was attempting to take off on a scouting run, his plane experienced mechanical problems and was unable to lift. Eventually it smashed into the brush. Freuler survived, but the plane was wrecked. The plane was moved next to the wreck of Elrod's plane, where they would act as decoys for the Japs, who wasted several bombs trying to hit them.[6]

Beginning on the fourteenth, the Japs would continue their bombardments for the next six days. The Marines kept damaging Jap planes that left smoking or leaking fuel after they attacked. It was impossible to tell, but Marines were sure some of the planes did not make it back to their base. However, on the 16th, John recalls an enemy plane crashing into the ocean that was also included on Captain Godbold's report[7] from the 3-inch guns on Peale. Yet, the Japs were relentless and kept coming, bringing from eighteen to forty planes each day.[8] As John often does, he had a positive spin about the next few days. He said, "Bombs were still doing damage when they hit, but the Japs were flying so high that many of them fell in the ocean or the lagoon."

No one on the atoll was getting more than a couple of hours of sleep. Between the lack of sleep and the daily physical exertion, the men would eventually reach a point of almost total exhaustion. John does not recall it affecting the men on Peale, but Devereux began to worry about the spread of diarrhea.[9] Some marines had reported suffering from it, and, if it persisted, it would make those afflicted even weaker.

On December 15, unbeknown to the men, Task Force 14 left Pearl Harbor to reinforce the Wake defenders. Commander of the Pacific Fleet Admiral Husband E. Kimmel had ordered the formation of the task force, centering on the aircraft carrier *Saratoga* under the command of Rear Admiral Frank Jack Fletcher. The task force also included three heavy cruisers, nine destroyers, two-hundred Marines from the Fourth Defense Battalion, and an ample supply of shells for the 3- and 5-inch guns as well as ammunition for the machine guns.[10] The men on Wake were all well aware that, without reinforcements, it would be a matter of time before the Japs would annihilate them. Some were vocal, complaining about why it was taking so long for reinforcements to arrive. Others, like John, pushed it out of their minds to maintain focus on what had to be done.

December 16 was the day John became eligible to be promoted to Second Class; that meant more than doubling his current pay. It wouldn't happen because of the inconvenience of the war. Though he had done very well on his tests and now had the seniority, he would not be granted Second Class rating till after the war.

On December 17, Commander Cunningham received word from his Commander, Rear Admiral Claude C. Bloch, to begin organizing for a possible civilian evacuation.[11] There was no mention by Bloch to Cunningham of reinforcements, but an order to get civilians ready to leave the island would surely mean that reinforcements were also on the way.

On the same day, two Japanese submarines that had been patrolling near Wake accidentally collided, both sinking instantly. Rear Admiral Matome Ugaki would write in his diary, "That island is almost bewitched."[12] As bad as the men at Wake had it, the losses of both men and materials were piling up for the Japs. Better yet, as Ugaki alluded to, it was playing on the Japs' psyche. Maybe they were not invincible after all.

December 19 brought a new level of fury from the Japanese planes. Up till then, the Japs had been dropping 132-pound bombs. On the nineteenth, they began dropping 1,000-pound behemoths.[13] When I asked John if there had been a noticeable difference on the ground, he first replied that "All the days were the same to me. There were bombs every day." Then he smiled, and, using his best gallows humor, he added, "Maybe that's why the island started shaking a little bit more." Devereux described the craters left by the bigger bombs as seven feet deep and thirty feet wide.[14] On a serious note, I asked John if he recalled his mind-set after being attacked for ten days and especially now that the Japs were using bigger bombs. He said, "You know, I was brought up 'rough,' you might say; my grandmother instilled in me being tough. I knew they were going to bomb us again tomorrow, and I didn't let it affect me much. It's just the way it goes. Some things are just the way they are, and there's not much you can do about it."

December 20 brought heavy rains to the atoll and prevented the Japs from making a bombing run. Once again, it was a welcome respite. That day also brought a PBY flying boat from Pearl Harbor. From his vantage point at Toki Point, John saw the plane first circle the island and then land in the lagoon, near what now were the ruins of the Pan Am Hotel.

The pilots, Ensigns J. J. Murphy and Howard Ady, jumped out of their plane, headed down the seaplane ramp, and then asked some Marines, "Where's the hotel?" The weary Marines, incredulous of the question, pointed at the rubble that remained of the hotel. As they walked to Cunningham's command post, they got a clear picture of how bad things were on the atoll. Neither pilot expected what they saw. They informed Cunningham of the task force that was sailing to Wake and told him to prepare the civilians to evacuate by December 24. Finally, they asked that Cunningham retain 350 civilians on the atoll to further fortify Wake's defenses.[15] The last directive to Cunningham—to keep hundreds of civilians on the atoll—struck me as a tall order. After twelve days of being under siege, who in their right mind would *choose* to stay? As I continued reading about Wake, I was pleasantly surprised to learn that many men did volunteer to remain at Wake. Unfortunately, it would become a moot point.

The news of the task force quickly spread around the islands and gave most of the men a much-needed boost. The pilots put the word out that they would take any letters that men wanted to send home. Many men wrote notes or letters to their loved ones, including John. But somehow his letter never made it to Alice. I asked John what else he recalled about the Clipper, and he jokingly said, "We all wanted to get on it."

Captain Elrod wrote a letter to his wife Elizabeth that included the following:

> *I'm writing this in something of a hurry and under some-*
> *what difficult circumstances. I'll think of a million things that*
> *I should have said after I've gone to sleep tonight. But now I'm*
> *going to say that I love you and you alone always and always*
> *and repeat it a million times or so. Give my love to Mary also.*
> *Between the two of you, you have it all—There isn't any room for*
> *anyone else. I know that you are praying for me and I have noth-*
> *ing more to ask than that your prayers be answered.*

> *"Your devoted and loving—Talmage"*[16]

Major Walter L. J. Bayler, who had been temporarily sent to Wake to set up the squadron's air-ground communications, would join Ady and Murphy on their return trip to Pearl. There, he would report in detail about the conditions at Wake.[17] Though the news about the task force had been welcome, some were concerned that the Navy would not risk losing more ships, especially after the beating it had taken at Pearl. Also, the risk of losing a precious carrier on a rescue mission had to weigh heavy on the decision to continue to Wake.

The PBY took off at 7:00 AM the next day with Major Bayler and the bag of letters. December 21 would be a memorable day for a variety of reasons. For John, it would include another near-death experience.

The Japs hit at 9:00 AM and brought an ominous message. The thirty bombers were now escorted by carrier-based fighter planes.[18] This meant that a Japanese task force was near Wake.

Before the attack and after his daily touch point with Chambliss, John was in his vehicle going between Battery D and Battery B. "When I got close, there was nobody moving around, and I thought, *Oh, there is something wrong.*" Suddenly, he heard planes and turned around to spot a much smaller one than the bombers he was used to seeing. Also, this one was flying awfully low. As he was nearing the bunker, John decided to ditch the station wagon, but he was still some distance away. The vehicle was a much bigger target, and he did not want to direct the Jap plane into his guys. Almost immediately, he heard one of the men at a machine gun position yelling at him, "Keep running, Doc—keep running." John said, "The Jap plane was so close that I could almost see the pilot's face. I was zig-zagging, with bullets landing all around me. He was so low that he was almost on the ground when he pulled up." John figured that he didn't get hit because the Jap was firing at the machine-gun position. It didn't make any difference, as he was close enough to be in the way of the bullets. When he reached the shelter, he dove in head first at such a high speed that the guys inside were screaming and stepping all over him in an effort to get out. "They thought I was a bomb and wanted no part of being there if it detonated." As John ran, there was absolutely nothing on his mind except making it to safety. Afterward, he sat down in the shelter and thought to himself that "The world had just come to an end." But luckily, it had not. He was still alive and breathing. Slowly, that realization set in. After figuring out that John was not a bomb that would send them to Elysium, the group around him laid low, waiting for the raid to end. I couldn't help but wonder when John shared that terrifying story, whether his mom and guardian angel Anna was on Wake with him that day. Upon further reflection, I'm sure she was.

John had been fortunate to escape injury and even death. Sergeant Wright was not as fortunate. Now bolstered by the carrier-based planes, the Japs attacked again around 2:30 PM.[19] It was the first time since the start of the battle that the Japs had attacked twice in one day. The big man who John so admired was killed near Battery D. The impact of a bomb propelled a tree right into Wright, killing him instantly. John presumed that Wright still had his lucky silver dollar but, on this day, its powers had run out. John recalls that, "We put him in a body bag and buried him nearby. However, the next day, the bombs shook the ground so badly, the grave opened up and pushed the body back above ground." Wright's death had a sobering impact on anyone who'd worked closely with the sergeant. It was a significant emotional loss for the Marines.

Whether it was the bomb that killed Wright or another one that dropped near Battery D that day, John's gear and personal belongings had been destroyed. The bottle of whiskey he was saving for Christmas, his marriage certificate from Tijuana, and, most tragically, Alice's letters, were all gone.

In the air, our last two planes had taken up the fight with Captain Freuler and Lieutenant Davidson at the controls. They focused on the Jap planes attacking Battery D. Davidson was last spotted chasing a Jap out to sea and never returned. Freuler engaged in a dogfight with the Japanese and was able to shoot one down before being overcome by the enemy's guns. He was seriously wounded but would survive. After three attempts to land his plane, he finally succeeded, but his aircraft would no longer fly.[20] The defenders of Wake were now without any planes to fight the Jap planes in the air. Also, any further raids by the Japs would be undetected till they were right on top of the Americans, as they no longer had scouting capabilities.

In the aftermath of Pearl Harbor, Admiral Chester W. Nimitz had replaced Admiral Kimmel as Commander of the Pacific Fleet. Prior to Nimitz's arrival at Pearl, Admiral William S. Pye was in command of the fleet. A cautious man, Pye dreaded losing more of the Pacific fleet before Nimitz was able to take command. He had allowed Fletcher to head west with the task force to reinforce Wake but was ready to recall the ships if the Japs suddenly appeared. To add to Pye's concerns, he had received word from Washington that Wake was considered a liability and that the decision to relieve the Marines was totally in his hands.[21]

There was one sliver of a silver lining on December 21. The Japanese bombardier Kanai, who had been credited with the bomb that exploded the *Arizona,* had been shot down at Wake during the raid. His death was a blow to the Jap Navy, which did not have an abundance of combat-tested airmen. Some in the Japanese Navy disapproved of the First Air Fleet's (of which Kanai was a part) involvement at Wake. Lieutenant Zenji Abe, who had flown with Kanai at Pearl Harbor, would say after the war that, "The Japanese could not inflict a decisive blow against the United States at such an isolated outpost. At that early stage (of the war), they could only give a valuable preview of Japanese strategy and tactics to the Americans, who could thus learn how to cope with them."[22]

The death of Kanai had achieved some measure of revenge against Nippon, though none of the men at Wake would know anything about the bombardier's demise till after the war. Some would never know. When I discussed it with John, he told me he was totally unaware of the story about Kanai, but it still brought a smile to his face and a, "Well, what do you know about that." John added that, after coming home, he had not read any books about the war. He would say, "I was done with it. I had no reason to read stuff that would make me relive it."

It had been a rough day on Wake for John and his fellow defenders. He would patch up the guys at Toki Point who needed it and try to get some rest for whatever was in store for him the next day. At some point that evening, he met with Chambliss at one of their regular touch points. After the rough day they had all experienced and expecting more of the same in the coming days, Chambliss was passing the word to all the corpsmen to prioritize the treatment of the wounded, with the goal of keeping the guns firing. Some of the guns had been knocked out that day, including the 5-inch guns at Toki Point. Accordingly, they had to optimize the guns they had left. Things were getting desperate. Though the number of deaths among the Marines was still relatively small, if reinforcements did not arrive soon, the prospects of survival were not good.

★ ★ ★

CHAPTER 10

"BULLETS WERE FLYING EVERYWHERE."

December 22 and 23, 1941

As dawn broke on December 22, it would be the penultimate day of the battle. The Japanese task force was getting closer to Wake and ready to deliver the final blow that would result in the capture of the atoll. The Japs executed another raid that, as John put it, "was another day of bombings, like all the others." The American guns that were still operating engaged the Japs with little notice. There had been no warning from patrol planes. For the second consecutive day, the carrier-based Jap fighters attacked the atoll. Eighteen dive-bombers, escorted by fighters, approached the atoll from the north[1] to deliver their pandemonium from the skies. There was no question now that the carrier or carriers nearby were there for the purpose of eliminating the American garrison at Wake. As John had said earlier, "the Japs really wanted the island."

Admiral Kajioka, who had suffered a humiliating defeat on the 13th, headed back to Wake with a much more formidable task force. He had nine vessels that he had brought from the Marshall Islands. In addition, the aircraft carriers *Soryu* and *Hiryu,* both of which had been involved at Pearl Harbor, had positioned themselves north of the atoll. To the east, six destroyers and six cruisers held vigil for any American ships that may approach Wake from Hawaii. The landing force had been beefed up from the 450 that had attempted to reach the beaches 10 days earlier, to 2,000 soldiers.[2]

Kajioka would not repeat the mistake of attacking at daylight. His plan was to get within striking distance of the atoll in the cover of darkness. He would then create a diversion off of Peale Island, with the intention of drawing the defenders' attention to the north. Shortly after, he would crash two patrol boats (converted destroyers) on Wake's southern beaches that would carry the landing force. Once on the beaches, the landing force would eliminate any pockets of resistance.

Lieutenant Robert M. Hanna, who was responsible for the machine-gun positions throughout the islands,[3] would receive welcome assistance from the surviving pilots. Captain Elrod took up a position on one of the machine guns at the airfield. Throughout the atoll the Marines and the civilians who were assisting them were preparing for the worst. Early on December 23, the defenders would experience the new hell that the Japanese had in store for them.

John will never forget how that day began at about 1:00 AM. He could see lights flashing in the distance off of Toki Point. "The flashes kept going and going, and for a while we thought there was a battle going on out there. That was wishful thinking that our guys were engaging the Japs." As they had on the 13th, the men at all positions had received word not to fire on enemy ships till they got the order from Devereux. Today, that order would not stand.

Devereux received a report that a landing had been sighted at Toki Point. He called Kessler to confirm it but was told, "There were lights but no landing as of yet." Kessler was ordered to double-check on the landing, which he did and reported back to Devereux that, "There are plenty of lights out there, but that is all." Devereux had a premonition that whatever was going on off of Peale was a diversion and that the Japs were about to hit them somewhere else on the atoll.[4] In line with his diversion plan, Kajioka ordered two cruisers to fire on Peale as the landing force approached Wake and Wilkes.[5] Once again, but for the last time, John and the men at Toki Point were being pounded with shells.

Fifteen minutes later, things began to move very fast. Two big ships (the converted destroyers) were spotted, coming in fast, at Peacock Point. Five minutes later, the machine guns on Wilkes opened fire on what was reported as two craft moving fast toward the beach.[6] John described it: "As I understand it, two transports came in on Wilkes and literally rammed into the reef and demolished their ships. I guess they thought that was the only way to get men on the island. I think one of those ships is still there today, where it rammed the reef."

Devereux would write of the invasion force: The Japanese plan was simple. The force from the destroyers would drive straight inland toward the airstrip. The next force, down the beach, would drive inland, turning the flank of any defenders attempting to hold the main group. The third landing party coming ashore near Camp 1 would swing toward the channel, rolling back the Marines holding that part of the beach, preventing them from moving to aid the defenders of the airfield.[7]

The previous day, the American task force from Pearl Harbor had stopped to refuel all of their ships, eating up valuable time. As the fight began on Wake on the twenty-third, Admiral Pye's conservative nature resulted in his order to the fleet to return to Pearl Harbor. He would not take the chance of running into Japanese carriers and losing more ships. He was also influenced by Washington, which now deemed Wake as good as lost. The recall resulted in angry reactions from Marine and Navy personnel aboard the ships. Some urged their superiors to ignore the order and steam ahead to rescue their brothers at Wake. Henry Frietas, aboard the *Tangier* (a cargo ship carrying troops), claimed that, "Every man on the ship would have voted to head into Wake, even though it meant placing ourselves in danger. It was war time; we would have gone in."[8]

On the *Saratoga*, Rear Admiral Fitch stormed off the bridge to avoid possible mutinous talk and being forced to react. One Navy officer on the *Enterprise* dejectedly wrote, "It's war between two yellow races." Even propagandist Tokyo Rose ridiculed the Navy with a biting question: "Where, oh, where, is the United States Navy?"[9] It was a question many of the men at Wake were also asking.

Back on the atoll, some of the 3- and 5-inch guns could not get into the fight because the ships had come in so close. Those that could, along with machine guns, opened fire. The first to be hit were the converted destroyers ferrying the landing force. As Devereux described it, "Lieutenant Hanna, who had taken over one of the 3-inch guns, blasted the vessels, made a slaughter pen of the crowded decks, and the destroyers burst into flame. Now the Marines could see the enemy. Japs were tumbling from the burning vessel into the water. The burning destroyers provided the light for our machine gunners to sweep the crowded water, to pin down the Japs who already had reached the shore."[10]

One of the officers aboard the ship that Lieutenant Hanna hit would write about his experience:

> *It was pitch dark. The enemy still seemed unaware of our presence. Suddenly the voice of the ship's commander rang out*

in the ominous silence. "Shore ahead!" We all fell flat on the
deck. With a loud crunching sound, the ship rode up on to the
shore. . . . As we started to rise to our feet, the enemy opened fire
all at once. Out of the darkness in front of us, shells came shriek-
ing like a thousand demons let loose.

One shell exploded the ship's bridge. Men fell where they
stood. Clambering down ladders and ropes, we disembarked in
great haste. But we were still not on land, as our ship had gone
on a reef. The water was so deep, we could hardly walk. Rifle in
hand, we desperately fought our way forward.

Artillery shells, machine gun bullets, rifle bullets—the
resisting fire of the enemy grew to a mad intensity. Lying flat
on our faces on the beach at the edge of the sea, we could not
wriggle an inch.[11]

As John and his mates were being shelled by the Jap ships off of
Peale, machine-gun and rifle fire was continuing on Wilkes, and it
had started at Wake. Literally hundreds of Japs from the landing force
poured into the water and were wading through the surf. They were
trying desperately to make it to the beach, to overcome the American
gun positions. Soon, communications began to break down among
the Americans spread out too thinly along the entire atoll.

Communications with Wilkes broke down shortly after the machine
guns there started firing. As the enemy moved forward with greater
numbers, they started shelling the Marines with mortars and small
guns from ships. Unfortunately, there were no targets for the 5-inch
guns. Though the Japanese were steadily advancing, the defenders were
inflicting heavy losses. Pockets of twenty or fewer Marines, some aided
by civilians, kept repelling hundreds of Japs.[12]

Marine Corporal Winford J. McAnally and Lieutenant Hanna's positions near the airport were both under heavy fire. By McAnally's position, two Japs wearing goggles and carrying tanks on their backs advanced on the Marines. None of them had ever seen anything like it. One Marine yelled, "What the hell is that?" but no one stopped to analyze the situation. A quick burst of fire caused one of the Japs to explode but the other hid behind a coral rock. The Marines went after that one with a steady stream of bullets aimed at the rock. After they had chipped away at the coral, they killed him, too. McAnally and his unit had just encountered the first flamethrowers of the Pacific War.[13]

West of the airstrip, Lieutenant Arthur R. Poindexter had received only occasional fire over a two-hour period. He decided that if the Japs were not going to attack him, he would attack them. Along with the men on Wilkes, Poindexter had lost communications with Devereux. Years later, he would explain his rationale to attack the Japs: "To hell with that old saw about 'a gallant last stand' like George Armstrong Custer at the Little Big Horn. The Marine Corps had taught me that the only way to accomplish anything is to take the offensive. If we were to fight to the very last man, we might as well die on the attack."[14] That was the prevailing feeling among all the Marines at Wake.

The fight raged on, and as dawn approached, John could now see ships all over, surrounding the atoll. As he put it, "There were ships galore." Most of the ships were out of range except off Toki Point, where Lieutenant Kessler opened up on a destroyer with the 5-inch guns. On the fourth try, the Marines scored a direct hit, causing the other Jap ships to sail away. The wounded destroyer would try to escape but would sink within sight of John and the men near Toki Point. After that, the rest of the Jap ships kept their distance beyond the range of the 5-inch guns.[15]

The fleeing Jap ships meant the end of shelling at Peale, and as John explained, "Somewhere along the line we got orders to head to Devereux's headquarters to reinforce that position. We took as many guns as we could carry and headed to Wake. Some men were on trucks while others ran as fast as they could to Devereux's command post. You could hear gunfire—the crack of guns being fired; as we got closer to the command post, bullets were flying everywhere." Devereux's command post was now north of the airfield, close to Cunningham's command post. The Japs were swarming all over Wilkes and Wake at that point. It was increasingly clearer to the defenders that they could either surrender or die trying to save the atoll. The Japanese forces and firepower were simply too overwhelming.

The Marines, along with some brave civilians, kept fighting. An exchange at Lieutenant Hanna's position was indicative of what was going on at all the gun positions. The Japanese pressed ahead, threatening to surround Hanna's 3-inch gun. The Japs were so close that the guns could not be lowered enough to have an impact. Since the gun emplacement offered little protective cover, they would all be dead in a matter of moments. He told his men, "We'll make our stand here. This is as far as we go." The officer admitted later that his order "was almost like telling the men this is where we are going to die, but I didn't quite put it that way."[16]

By the airfield, Captain Elrod, along with the other men, fired their rifles till they were out of bullets. They then lobbed hand grenades till those ran out. One civilian with the group, John Sorenson, then started throwing large rocks at the charging Japs. Elrod jumped up and shouted, "Kill the sons of bitches" and fired a submachine gun as the other men rallied around him. When a Marine nearby him ran out of bullets, Elrod handed him his weapon, grabbed a similar weapon from a dead

Japanese soldier, and continued to fight. He rarely sought cover as the battle raged around him.

The same Jap who had written about Hanna's guns decimating the landing force on one of the transports would also write the following:

"One large figure appeared before us to blaze away with a machine gun from his hip as they do in American gangster films."

He was most likely referring to Elrod. When Elrod ran out of ammunition, he, too, started lobbing hand grenades, but the odds caught up to him as he was cut down by a burst of Japanese fire and killed. For his actions this day and earlier over the skies of Wake, Captain Elrod was posthumously awarded the Congressional Medal of Honor.[17]

One of the Jap transport ships that rammed into the reef and a downed Japanese bomber on Dec. 23 (National Archives)

Shortly before 7:00 AM, dive-bombers approached the island and focused on Hanna's area near the airport. Soon after, Devereux reported to Cunningham that he had lost communications with the Marines on Wilkes and that there were reports of Jap flags flying on that island. Devereux had given Lieutenant Kliewer orders to blow up the airstrip when the Japs got within sight, but for some reason, the demolition had not occurred. Finally, the Japs were now within three hundred yards of his command post.[18] Cunningham had been communicating with Pearl Harbor about the conditions on the island. At 5:00 AM, he had sent a message saying, "Enemy on the island; issue in doubt." Later, he attempted to order a submarine he thought to be in the waters near Wake to join the fight. Instead, he received a transmission from Pearl Harbor that there were no American ships near Wake and none were expected.[19] The translation of that message was that the task force would not be arriving to provide reinforcements. The defenders of Wake were, sadly and tragically, on their own.

In books written after the war, Cunningham and Devereux gave conflicting accounts of how the decision to surrender was made—and who ultimately made it. One thing they did agree on is that they were in constant communication with each other during the attack on the 23rd.[20] Devereux would later write, "Cunningham's decision to surrender was inevitable, beyond argument. We could keep on spending lives, but we could not buy anything with them." He would add that Cunningham also had to think of the more than one thousand unarmed civilians.[21] Though Devereux had been in charge of the battle, military chain of command would suggest that Cunningham, the commander in charge of the atoll, would have made the final decision to surrender it.

Each passing day since December 8, everyone, including John, were becoming more and more fatigued. The combination of lack of sleep, the physical demands, and the constant tension over when the next attack would come wore heavily on all of the men, military and civilian alike. In addition, some of the men were sick and debilitated with diarrhea. Now, they were fighting against an overwhelming number of Jap ships, planes, and soldiers. John's coping mechanism throughout the ordeal had been to focus on doing his job to the best of his abilities, whatever that required. He logically concluded that everything else was beyond his control. For the Marines, it meant continuing to fight, but at unknown costs and an unknown end.

Meanwhile, John was once again dodging bullets and trying to keep himself alive, inching his way toward Devereux's command post. He kept getting closer and at one point, had to take shelter behind a rock to keep from being hit. When he could, he resumed toward the command post. John said, "I finally made my way into where Devereux was. There were a bunch of us there now, and pretty soon someone handed me a couple of candy bars and said, "Here, you better eat something." At about the same time, Devereux was beginning to spread the word that the Major (Cunningham) had given the order to surrender. According to John, "Devereux had been on the phone. As he hung up, he saw me and said, 'Come with me. You're wearing a red cross and they are not supposed to shoot you.' Hearing that, my mind immediately flashed back to the clearly marked hospital that had been blown to smithereens on December 9. Nevertheless, John did his duty and joined Devereux. They were accompanied by a third person John referred to as the "musician," who had jerry-rigged a pole with a white cloth to communicate the sign of surrender.

According to Devereux, the Marine carrying the flag was Sergeant Donald R. Malleck, who had volunteered to join them.[22] John explained what happened next: "The three of us started down the road, and we could see Japs coming right at us. As the Japanese were advancing toward us, a Marine hiding in the bushes opened fire and shot one of them right in the throat. The Japs returned fire, killing the Marine. Devereux then yelled to stop firing. One of the Japs saw the red cross band on my sleeve and motioned me over to the Jap who had been hit. I went over to the man and saw that he'd been hit in the neck and was bleeding out. I then made a motion across my neck as if to say, "He's dead—there's nothing I can do for him." At that point, the Japs grabbed John. "A couple of Japs came over to me and they stripped my medical pouch and just tore all my clothes off. They tied my hands behind my back with telephone wires. I also got a couple of blows, but I didn't feel them. I thought that was it for me—that I was done. As I was being taken away, I could see Devereux continuing to walk. You could hear that some Marines were still fighting." That would be John's first face-to-face encounter with the Japs. The seemingly interminable suffering was about to begin, but in the end, John and all our brave men would match the inhumane treatment by the Japanese and best them every step of the way.

It was several hours after John had met up with Devereux that all the Marines would finally stop fighting. Some of them were incredulous that they were being asked to give up their weapons. Devereux had to yell at one of them, "Major's orders! We are surrendering. It's not my order, Goddamnit!"[23] One Marine, Sergeant John Cemeris, managed to shoot down a Jap dive-bomber long after the surrender order had been issued. Devereux would write, "It made things a little ticklish for us because our Jap escort also saw it, but they only prodded us on."[24] Kliewer, who had been ordered to blow up the airfield, saw the white flags and was about fifty feet from Devereux when he heard the command to surrender. His men begged him to ignore the command. "Don't surrender, Lieutenant.

The Marines never surrender. It's a hoax." Kliewer briefly assessed the situation, put down his weapon, and raised his hands.[25]

At Wilkes, Marine Captain Wesley M. Platt had sixty men to defend an island one mile long and one-eighth of a mile in width.[26] The men fought throughout the night, repelling hundreds of Japs coming off the transports and killing scores of them. They had effectively eliminated enemy resistance on the island before advancing toward the channel between Wilkes and Wake, where they would see a white flag and a group of men approaching. As he got closer, he could see Japs smiling, which meant bad news. Devereux approached him to tell him the atoll had been surrendered. Bewildered, Platt said, "Who the hell gave that order?" Devereux calmly told Platt, "Trudy (a nickname for Platt), tell your men to lay their weapons down. It's an honorable surrender." Platt replied, "Major, do you know what you are asking me to do?" "Yes Trudy," replied Devereux. "Tell your men to lay their weapons down."[27] And so it went throughout the atoll.

John was taken to the airport, where all the military prisoners were being held. It would mark the first of 1,334 days—or almost 44-1/2 months—that John would be in captivity. All but the officers had been stripped down to their shorts while a lucky few had retained their shoes. John, not knowing that Kliewer had surrendered, described those first few moments of captivity. "As they were walking me to the airport, I kept thinking, '*Bang*—we are all dead.' I had heard rumors that the airfield had been mined and thought it was going to blow up. Then, as I got to the airport, I could see a bunch of Japs lined up with machine guns, so we started thinking that they are going to shoot us."

John's instincts about being shot by the Japs had merit in that, shortly after, Admiral Kajioka, dressed in his white uniform to accept the formal surrender, rushed to the airfield and ordered the Japanese to halt. He engaged in a heated debate with the Army officer in charge, and, after fifteen tense minutes, Kajioka prevailed. The Army officer reluctantly ordered his men to secure their guns and leave the airfield.[28] Before Kajioka and the task force left Wake the afternoon of the twenty-third, he claimed the Wake Atoll for Japan and rechristened it *"Otori Shima"* (Bird Island).[29] He also presented Commander Cunningham with the following:

PUBLIC NOTICE

The Great Empire of Japan who loves peace and respects justice has been obliged to take arms against the challenge of President Roosevelt. Therefore, in accordance with the peace-loving spirit of the Great Empire of Japan, Japanese Imperial Navy will not inflict any harms on those people—though they have been our enemy—who do not hold hostility against us in any respect. So, they be in peace!

But whoever violates our spirit or whoever are not obedient shall be severely punished by our martial law.

Issued by
THE HEADQUARTERS OF JAPANESE IMPERIAL NAVY[30]

The formal surrender took place on the airfield, and John clearly recollects the feeling he had when our flag was lowered and the Japanese raised theirs. He described it this way: "I could see the flagpole; the Japanese lowered our flag, threw it on the ground, and raised their flag. That moment got to me, and it really hurt." He would go on to tell me when I asked him about his darkest moments during the war, that the

American flag being lowered at Wake by the Japs was the worst. "When you see someone taking down your flag and hoisting theirs, it's just hard to take. It made you think." It's a testament to John's dedication and patriotism that he would rank that as the worst of all his memories, including the gruesome ones he would experience as a prisoner of war.

The men who perished during the sixteen-day battle died as heroes and had not died in vain. During the battle, forty-nine Marines and Navy bluejackets were killed in action defending the atoll, and thirty-six were seriously wounded. Sixty-five construction workers were killed in addition to the ten Chamorros employed by Pan Am who were killed in the hotel. The Japanese losses proved extremely costly. Despite the Japs' propensity to conceal reality, it is estimated that seven hundred or more enemy deaths occurred on December 11. An additional five hundred to six hundred were killed on the twenty-third. The submarine that went to the bottom of the sea carried about sixty crew. Losses aboard Japanese aircraft, most of them twin-engine bombers with five-man crews would result in another 100 to 150 fatalities. Yet more Japs were killed on destroyers.

The Japs raising their flag at Wake after lowering Old Glory on Dec. 23, 1941. (digitalarchives.broward.org. The picture is from a Japanese Propaganda leaflet entitled "Victory on the March," December 1942)

Altogether, the Wake campaign cost the Japanese 1,500 or more dead or about thirteen enemy fatalities for every American killed. In addition to the material losses they had suffered on the eleventh, the two Japanese converted destroyers that ferried the landing force on the twenty-third were shelled into oblivion and at least five other Jap ships were disabled. Finally, between twenty-one and twenty-nine planes were shot down over Wake.[31] More importantly, the Japanese timetable for expansion in the Pacific had been delayed by two weeks. The delay gave the U.S. valuable time to recover from Pearl Harbor and assemble men and materiel for a counter-offensive. It forced the Japs to delay their advance on Midway, giving the Americans time to reinforce the atoll, rebuild damaged ships and bring additional vessels over from the mainland to the front lines. All those factors would contribute to dealing a resounding defeat to the Japs at Midway.[32]

John remained tied up all night and got nothing to eat. At some point, he and the other men got some water that was tainted with gasoline. Apparently, the Japs had filled empty fuel tanks with water without sanitizing them. He was glad he had enjoyed a couple of candy bars earlier in the day. The heat was stifling, and the bunker where he'd been taken was grossly overcrowded with men. It's humorous what we tend to recollect, even in stressful situations. Smiling, John recalled that sometime that first night in captivity, he was woken by a Marine who was rearranging his legs to use as a pillow. John's sense of humor and ability to put things into perspective continued to amaze me. He would tell me more than once that "Not taking things too seriously really helped me get through some of the worst times."

The next day was Christmas Eve. Regrettably, none of the Americans on Wake were in a holiday mood.

★　★　★

CHAPTER 11

"THEY WOULD HAVE DRAGGED ME ON THAT PLANE AND PUSHED ME OUT OVER MIDWAY."

December 24, 1941 to January 11, 1942

The previous night, John had made his way around the crowded bunker to see if there was anything he could do for the injured. Without medical supplies, there was not much he could do, but, at the very least, he had to try. The more seriously injured had been taken to an aid station that John referred to as the "Japanese camp." The morning started ominously at his bunker. "About a half a dozen Japs came charging in and strafed the concrete ceiling with bullets that ricocheted down, hitting and killing a couple of our guys." Dr. Kahn was in the same bunker with John, but there was not much either of them could do for the Marines who were hit.

At some point that morning, the Japs ordered all the prisoners to go out to the airfield and get some clothes on. All of their clothes, many of them torn, had been piled up. No one would get their own clothes, so they took what they could. John's clothing didn't fit well (too big), but he was happy to be dressed again. Later that morning, the Japs came to the bunker again, this time asking for anyone who spoke German. Dr. Kahn pointed to John and told the English-speaking Jap that John spoke German. All the Japanese doctors and some of their officers spoke German, and they were looking for an American who could speak it, to assist with the injured. In John, they would get both a bilingual speaker who, fortuitously, happened to be a Corpsman.

John was brusquely taken away to a makeshift hospital that included all the Americans' medical supplies that had survived the attack. John described what happened next: "When I got over there, I was assigned to a Jap pilot who had been wounded pretty bad in one of his runs over Midway. He had injuries all over him. They wanted me to be his private nurse, you might say. One good thing was that I had access to all the medicine on the island, and eventually, they let me move between the Japanese and the American wounded."

Gunner John Hamas, who spoke some Japanese, risked being bayoneted by the Japs to call out to a Jap officer. He asked the officer if Dr. Kahn could attend to the wounded and one man who was dying. The Jap officer ordered the sentries to free Dr. Kahn and Hamas. Again, there was not much that could be done, except prevent some of the men who had passed out from the heat from choking to death.[1]

Though John would stay confined with the Japs most of the time, "I was able to go where our wounded were and was in contact with Dr. Kahn. At some point, I started stealing medicine for Dr. Kahn to treat our guys. Since I was allowed to go to the American wounded, I was able to sneak some medicines over there." It's not clear what the penalty would have been if John had been caught, but, based on the

Public Notice that Kojioka had given Cunningham, it's safe to say it would have included "severe punishment." John felt it was the least he could do, as he was better off than the other guys, who continued to be housed in the overcrowded bunkers or made to stand in the searing heat. Many of them were still bound. Some had their hands tied behind their backs and were noosed around their necks. It made any kind of movement virtually impossible. Also, the men were being fed almost nothing and were continuing to drink the fuel-tainted water. It was a portent of things to come.

After a couple of days, most of the men were put to work repairing things around the atoll or cleaning guns. Surreptitiously, they sabotaged anything they could. For example, when they were asked to clean the 3-inch guns that were still operable, they polished them bright and shiny and then slipped sand into the recoil mechanism. The same with rifles. The Marines would shine them up and then pour salt water down the barrels to make them useless.[2] Like John stealing medicines, the men working on the guns were risking severe punishment from their captors, but it gave them a sense of fighting back.

John shared another act of mischief that could have gotten him in big trouble. The Japanese commander came to him one day and told him he couldn't sleep. He asked John if there was anything he could give him. With a smile on his face, John said to me: "I had some phenobarbital that we used as a sleeping medicine. The regular dose was one-and-a-half grains. We measured things in grains at that time. I gave him six grains." My wife Randi and Jacki and Brian Unger were all in the room with me listening to John, and we all burst out laughing. John continued, "He took the dosage I gave him, and he came back the next day with a big smile on his face and thanked me. All I could do afterward, was shake my head. I think I could have gotten anything I wanted from him, he was so happy."

At the White House, Secretary of the Navy Knox would break the news to President Roosevelt that the Japs had landed on Wake. Roosevelt was devastated and called the news "worse than Pearl Harbor." The president castigated the Navy for its failure to save the men at Wake and demanded that the military figure out a way soon to strike back at the Japanese. Public figures lambasted Admiral Pyle and the Navy for the bungled relief effort. Admiral William F. Halsey said the task force could have caused severe damage to the Japs had it continued toward Wake. Respected journalist Clark Lee wrote that the Navy, still feeling the pain of the Pearl Harbor disaster, seemed more intent on not losing ships than with saving the men at Wake.[3] It seemed like, among civilian and military leaders alike, there was little, if any support, for Pyle's timid decision to order the task force to sail away from the men at Wake.

On an upbeat note, throughout the country, the men at Wake had energized the nation. An example of Americans' feelings about the Wake defenders was captured in an editorial by the *Washington Post* on December 24:

> *From what we hear by the grapevine, Santa Claus is going to give you boys on Wake Island the go-by this year.*
>
> *We hear he is afraid to take a chance on getting his whiskers singed if he comes sailing in over the island with his reindeer. In the heat of the battle you are putting up, it would be risky.*
>
> *We are sorry about this, pals.*
>
> *If you could only be reached by Santa Claus and all his helpers who would like to remember you, there wouldn't be room on that coral fly speck you are holding down to stow it all.*
>
> *It may be you will be too busy even to remember that it's Christmas Eve. . . .*

*But some of you will remember. And some of you will
think of other Christmases at home. . . . the folks, the snow, the
Christmas tree with the family, the happy grins on the kids' pans,
the smells from Mom's kitchen, the general gaiety . . .*

*You may get a little tight in the stomach for a minute or two,
thinking of this.*

*But we want you to know that you are the best
Christmas present this old U.S. ever had.*

Because of you, we all stand straighter. Eyes ahead.

*Because of you, there is new hope in the faces of liberty-
loving people.*

*Because of you, the American flag seems to give a special
prideful flirt as it snaps in the breeze these days.*

*Because of you, American boys are storming recruiting
offices, young soldiers in camp are on the double quick, sailors
live for their ships, factories are working day and night and the
President and Joe Doakes in the street are busting their buttons.*

*For all we know, because of you, that a Christmas will
come when there will be Peace on Earth, Good Will to Men!*

Merry Christmas Marines . . . and give them HELL![4]

John would not know about that editorial or any articles written
about Wake till after the war. He would learn of the impact they had on
the spirit of the country only after his return. As we were talking during
one of our interview sessions, John beamed and took particular pride
in the rush of men who had wanted to enlist in the military because of
the Wake defenders.

Another significant impact of the war at the home front was the number of women who entered the workforce, including Alice. During the

war, the number of women in the workforce would grow by 6.5 million.[5] Between 1940 and 1945, the female percentage of the U.S. workforce increased from 27 percent to nearly 37 percent. By 1945, nearly 1 out of every 4 married women worked outside the home. Some 350,000 would serve in the U.S. armed forces at home and abroad.[6] Alice would go to work as a keypunch operator at Mare Island, where over the years, she would rise through the ranks to a management role. At home, Alice's mom, now Granny Julia, Alice's brother Leon, who was 12, and sister Julia, 10, helped to take care of Johnny. Alice's youngest brother Richard, a toddler, at 3, was Johnny's primary playmate.

Back at Wake, there were about twenty Marines who'd been seriously wounded who were being cared for, as best possible, at the makeshift hospital. As the days passed, John was asked to care for three of the seriously injured Japs and two Marines who were severely wounded. John helped Dr. Kahn with one Marine, who literally had a hole on the side of his head where a bullet had passed through. John said, "You could actually look through it. I didn't have much to treat him with. I think I fixed up a stick with whatever bandages we had, swabbed some alcohol on it and ran it through the hole, to at least keep it clean. There wasn't anything else I could do for him. At times, the guy was pretty hard to handle, and the Japs were expecting me to keep him under control. The poor guy was delirious." Fifty-five years later, John, along with his grandsons Johnny and Tim, would meet that Marine at a POW reunion, and he thanked John for keeping him alive.

Christmas and New Year's came and went without any recognition or celebration. The POWs' diet was rice that was not fully cooked and had the consistency of gruel. John remembers that, at first, it was difficult to get that stuff down. He recognized that was all they were going to get, so he forced himself to eat it. He was able to supplement his diet somewhat, by wrestling with some of the Japs. Just as most of the Americans had never seen any Japanese, the same was true of them. Most Japs had never seen white men. As John explained it, "When I was not working, a few of the Japs would always want to wrestle me. They weren't very big, so I had no problems pinning most of them down. They wanted to test me to see how strong I was. I think they thought they were pretty strong, you know. It was usually the younger guys who wanted to challenge me—guys who were about my age. After a while, I figured out that, if I let them win, they would reward me with a candy bar or even some sake." If that's all it took to assuage their egos, John was happy to comply and get some more nutrition in the process. Not that candy bars and liquor made a wholesome diet, but "it filled the belly."

Besides the meager diet, the prisoners had to follow Jap rules that were initially unclear, resulting in a dangerous process of learning by trial and error. For example, if a prisoner yelled, it would result in a beating. In some cases, if a prisoner said anything at all, they could be beaten. At times, a truculent Jap would flog a prisoner because they didn't understand an order spoken in Japanese. The prisoners had to accept it and hope that the beatings would not incapacitate them. Initially, the men tried to do what they could to deflect the blows, so the Japs adjusted their technique by positioning another soldier with a bayonet on the back of the POW being beaten. That way, any movement would result in a cut or even being impaled.

As John was getting to know the Japs, he started to learn some words in Japanese, and communications improved a little with those who didn't speak German. John had learned from the pilots that they were going on bombing raids over Midway on almost a daily basis. A couple of times, he asked some of the Jap pilots if they would take him along on one of their raids. "I told them, 'Next time you go, take me along.' One morning at four o'clock, two pilots in their flight suits came in and told me, 'We take you to Midway.'" John's logical mind kicked in to hyper gear. He said to me, "Do you think they would have given me a parachute to jump off the plane. . . . nah. And even if they had, our guys would have probably shot me as I was coming down, thinking I was a Jap." The Japs started pulling John out of the hospital, and "if it wasn't for the officer I had been taking care of, they probably would have taken me." Luckily, the officer woke up and ordered the young pilots to leave John alone, "otherwise, they would have dragged me on that plane and pushed me out over Midway." In retrospect, John had no logical explanation as to what motivated him to ask the pilots for a ride to Midway. "Just one of those crazy things, you know."

On January 5, Roosevelt issued a Presidential Unit Citation recognizing the achievement of the First Defense Battalion and their commanders Major Devereux and Major Putnam, which would cause a bit of controversy. The citation did not include the Army and Navy personnel at Wake, including Commander Cunningham. The original citation recognized the following:

> *The Wake detachment of the 1ˢᵗ Defense Battalion, U.S. Marine Corps, under the Command of Major James P. Devereux.*

> *And*

> *Marine Fighting Squadron 211 of Marine Aircraft Group 21, under command of Major Paul A. Putnam, U.S. Marines.*

Once again, no one at Wake was aware of the citation, and, as far as John was concerned, when he did learn of it, he thought it was much ado about nothing. In his mind, Devereux and Putnam had been in charge of the battle, not Cunningham. As far as him personally, he had been with the Marine 1st Defense Battalion for two years, wore the Marine uniform and was proud of his contributions at Wake. He did not feel at all slighted.

THE WHITE HOUSE
WASHINGTON

Citation by

THE PRESIDENT OF THE UNITED STATES

of

The Wake detachment of the 1st Defense Battalion, U.S. Marine Corps, under command of Major James P.S. Devereux, U.S. Marines

and

Marine Fighting Squadron 211 of Marine Aircraft Group 21, under command of Major Paul A. Putnam, U.S. Marines

and

Army and Navy personnel present

"The courageous conduct of the officers and men who defended Wake Island against an overwhelming superiority of enemy air, sea, and land attacks from December 8 to 22, 1941, has been noted with admiration by their fellow countrymen and the civilized world, and will not be forgotten so long as gallantry and heroism are respected and honored. They are commended for their devotion to duty and splendid conduct at their battle stations under most adverse conditions. With limited defensive means against attacks in great force, they manned their shore installations and flew their aircraft so well that five enemy warships were either sunk or severely damaged, many hostile planes shot down, and an unknown number of land troops destroyed."

Franklin D. Roosevelt

The amended Citation, including Navy and Army personnel (From the personal collection of John I. Unger)

In the U.S., the men at Wake continued to be recognized. A radio broadcast on January 12, trying to bolster the enlistment of Marines, claimed that because of Wake Island, the nation had a new rallying cry and a new war motto that rang from one end of America to the other across our far-flung possessions—that cry is "REMEMBER WAKE ISLAND." Later that year, Ray Frank created a popular comic-book version of the battle targeting the youth of the nation.[7] Hollywood also got in on the praise of the defenders with the release of the motion picture *Wake Island* in August of 1942. The movie starred Brian Donlevy, Robert Preston, and William Bendix. Since little was known of the fate of the defenders or the last few days of the battle, it's no surprise that the movie was fraught with inaccuracies. One significant flaw in the movie was that the ending led the audience to believe that all the defenders had fought to the last man. I had a chance to sit with John to watch the movie, and after it was over, he looked at me, smirked, and said "Pure Hollywood." Despite John's tongue-in-cheek review of the film seventy years afterward, the film had been a hit and helped raise the awareness of the heroism of the men at Wake.

The unknown fate of the men at Wake would be a source of grave concern and frustration for families and loved ones. There was little or no communication from the government other than that their loved ones had been in the battle and that they were most likely prisoners of war. That was scant comfort for Alice and others, who would wait and hope that more definitive news would soon be forthcoming.

As the days passed, John and the rest of the men were getting into a routine. Harsh as it might be, they were adjusting to life as POWs. John didn't know what was in store for them, but he knew for sure he did not want to get any further from home. On January 11, that wish would be shattered when the Jap officers notified the POWs that, the next day, they would be transported across the Pacific. No one knew what that meant, but the men assumed if would be Japan. That same day, the captors posted what they called the Regulations for Prisoners. Listed below are the ominous rules that were much more specific than the Public Notice that Kajioka had issued on the twenty-third of December.

Regulations for Prisoners

1. *The prisoners disobeying the following orders will be punished with immediate death.*
   a. *Those disobeying orders and instructions.*
   b. *Those showing a motion of antagonism and raising a sign of opposition.*
   c. *Those disordering the regulations by individualism, egoism, thinking only about yourself, rushing for your own goods.*
   d. *Those talking without permission and raising loud voices.*
   e. *Those walking and moving without order.*
   f. *Those carrying unnecessary baggage in embarking.*
   g. *Those resisting mutually.*
   h. *Those touching the boat's materials, wires, electric lights, tools, switches, etc.*
   i. *Those climbing ladder without order.*
   j. *Those showing action of running away from the room or boat.*
   k. *Those trying to take more meal than given to them.*
   l. *Those using more than two blankets.*

> *2. Since the boat is not well equipped and the inside being*
> *narrow, food being scarce and poor you'll feel uncom-*
> *fortable during the short time on the boat. Those losing*
> *patience and disordering the regulation will be heavily*
> *punished for the reason of not being able to escort.*
> *3. Be sure to finish your "nature's call" evacuate the bowels*
> *and urine, before embarking.*
> *4. Meals will be given twice a day. One plate only to one*
> *prisoner. The prisoners called by the guard will give out*
> *the meal quick as possible and honestly. The remaining*
> *prisoners will stay in their places quietly and wait for*
> *your plate. Those moving from their places reaching for*
> *your plate without order will be heavily punished. Same*
> *orders will be applied in handling plates after meal.*[8]

The Regulations were posted around all the places housing the POWs but not at the facility where the seriously injured were being housed. Since John had been confined to that area, he was not aware of these new regulations.

When he learned about the voyage, he asked the Japanese doctor if he could remain on Wake to care for the seriously wounded Japs and Marines who were too weak to make the trip. John figured that "The Americans were going to liberate Wake long before they would reach Japan, so why not stay?" In addition to the wounded, the Japs would hold back more than three hundred civilians to help with construction projects on the atoll. The Jap doctor agreed to keep John on Wake, but the Japanese Commander would reverse that order the following day. It was a decision that might have saved John's life but would also introduce him to a new kind of hell.

* ★ * ★ * ★

CHAPTER 12

"OUR LIVES MEANT NOTHING TO THEM."

January 12, 1942 to January 24, 1942

On January 12, the *Nitta Maru*, a converted Japanese passenger liner, arrived at Wake to transport the almost 1,200 Marines and civilians. John thought he was staying till one of the Jap officers "came in to the sick bay and says he's (John) military and he's got to go now. One soldier grabbed me, and I was on my way. When they told me I had to go, I grabbed whatever I had, which wasn't much, and they escorted me to the gangway of the ship."

The *Nitta Maru* was originally built for the Nippon Yusen Kaisha (NYK) Cruise Line and launched in May of 1939. It was designed to rival European luxury liners that carried passengers from Europe to the Far East. Her passenger capacity was 283.[1] After Roosevelt had frozen Japanese assets in 1941 and in an effort to ease tension with Japan, Secretary of State Cordell Hull and Japanese ambassador to the U.S. Nomura agreed that three Japanese passenger vessels could make voyages from Japan to the United States as long as they carried no commercial cargo. Three ships from the NYK Cruise line, including the *Nitta Maru,* were approved to sail from Yokohama to different ports in the U.S. The *Nitta Maru* would cruise to Seattle on October 20.[2]

When the Japanese Navy needed military transports, the *Nitta Maru* was among the first to be drafted. She would continue to be used as a cruise liner, ferrying men. In October of 1942, it was converted to a carrier escort and renamed the *Chuyo.* The *Chuyo* made numerous voyages ferrying aircraft supplies and passengers from Japan to the Caroline Islands in the South Pacific. As part of a large task force on the morning of December 4, 1943, she was torpedoed by the U.S. submarine *Sailfish* and sunk. She had more than 1,400 passengers on board, including 21 American POWs. Only 160 survived, including 1 of the POWs.[3]

The *Nitta Maru* docked at Honolulu (World War II Database)

Due to the confusion about whether he'd stay or go, John was one of the last men to board the ship. "As I was going up the gangway, there were Japanese soldiers lined up on each side with bats and sticks, beating everybody as they came up into the hold. I got hit pretty good a couple of times but managed to get through the gauntlet. You could say those were my welcome blows." He added, "We didn't get any of the nice rooms on the ship. We got the stinking hold instead."

The hold or cargo area, is where the Japs would cram the 1,200 men for the entire trip. The civilians were kept separate from the military, but the conditions for all of them were abominable. "There was not enough room for anyone to lie down. To do so, guys had to stand to allow room for others to lie down. Most of us were standing. The heat down there was oppressive. The Japanese soldiers came down once, sometimes twice a day, with bayonets, and they'd make you stand up and hit you hard." Again, the men would try to sway when they were hit, but the Japs would position a soldier with a bayonet behind the man being hit so he wouldn't move. As John described the daily beatings, it struck me as the epitome of cowardice and ruthlessness on the part of the Japs. Their only aim was to inflict pain and invoke helplessness in their prisoners.

There were other reasons for the brutality that the Japs exacted on Allied POWs. *Bushido*—or the "Way of the Warrior"—was the ancient Japanese code of honor developed by Samurai. The code consisted of eight virtues or acceptable behaviors, including justice, courage, benevolence, honesty, honor, politeness, loyalty, and self-control.[4] Over the years the Japanese military in the twentieth century apparently warped the original virtues into a predominant belief that the Way of the Warrior is to die with honor, regardless of the costs. They would also warp the spirit of the code to rationalize exacting atrocities on Allied POWs.

General Hideki Tojo's instructions for servicemen declared that, "The man who would not disgrace himself must be strong. He must remember always the honor of his family and community and try to justify their faith in him. Do not survive in shame as a prisoner. Die, to ensure that you do not leave ignominy behind you."[5] The concept of honoring community and family also included honoring the emperor. Countless Japanese servicemen would commit suicide when a battle was lost or sacrifice themselves for the sake of honor.

American and British servicemen came from a culture that considered it natural to surrender when resistance was no longer rational.[6] It is stunning that Allied forces surrendered at a rate of 1 prisoner for every 3 dead while the Japanese surrendered at the rate of only 1 per 120 dead.[7] The *Bushido* mentality and proclamations added up to one inescapable notion: the Japanese simply could not understand why Allied soldiers chose surrender over death. Accordingly, the Japanese mind-set dictated that POWs should not be treated in an honorable way. John had a different theory about the Japs' ruthlessness: "Their sergeants beat the corporals; the corporals beat the privates, and the privates beat the POWs. Everybody beat somebody; it was their way. Our lives meant nothing to them."

After the war, Guy Kelnhofer Jr., PhD, USMC, and a Wake survivor, would share his views on the Japanese mind-set and cruelty. "I was listed as MIA, missing in action. From December 1941 to September 1945, I was listed as a POW. However, that was a misnomer, because I was not really a POW. That term connotes a certain legal status. We had no status, no rights, no privileges, and no protections of any kind. We lived at the whim of any Japanese military person who wished to do us harm. Wherever a Japanese commander chose to condone or encourage his troops to do so—and many did—we could be stabbed, shot, beheaded, starved, beaten, crucified, burned, disfigured, suffocated, frozen, drowned, electrocuted, hanged, buried alive, or tortured. The Japanese had been taught that we were their racial inferiors, that we were enemies, and that we were keeping them from pursuing their God-ordained destiny as rulers of Asia. In their view, we had disgraced our families, our country, and ourselves by surrendering. They could not understand such cowardice."[8]

To add to the inhumane overcrowding on the ship, there was little food and almost no water. In the oppressive heat of the hold, water was critically important. John explained: "Lots of people were dehydrated, and some got a bit delirious. There were some Marines who were really suffering. People must have their water. Not me—I'm like a camel and need very little water, so I shared mine with guys I thought needed it the most." Another deplorable factor was that there were only two waste buckets for the more than four hundred military men, one at either end of the hold. Naturally, some men would not make it to the buckets in time and defecated where they stood. It made the overall conditions even more oppressive. John tried to get out of the hold as often as he could, but there was only one way to do it. "I volunteered to take the buckets topside, to dump the waste overboard just to get outside. They always escorted us with bayonets to our backs. Others wanted to do it, too, just to get out of that stinking hold. I did it quite often."

In addition to the unsanitary conditions, there were the selective beatings every day. John explained: "If we were selected, they really hit us hard. Especially at night, I tried to change positions to avoid being picked for a beating. They would pick a bunch over here, then over there, so I kept moving, trying to outguess them."

John shared another story about a situation that took him by surprise. He had not seen the regulations for prisoners that had been posted back at Wake. A few days into the trip, one of the Japanese officers who spoke German sought him out and told John to remind all the military men of the rules. He acted as if he knew what they were and went on to do as he was asked. As he reviewed the rules, he thought to himself that he had been guilty of several of the violations he was now sharing with his fellow servicemen.

As the days passed, John tried to do what he could for the Marines who were in bad shape. Mostly, that meant sharing some of his water or trying to make room for the weaker men to lie down. "Luckily no one died in our hold, but that didn't surprise me. Those Marines were in good shape. I don't know if any of the civilians died on the trip."

The ship arrived in Yokohama, Japan, on January 18. As John and many of the men feared, they were now in Nippon's nest—the last place in the world they wanted to be. Yokahama is one of the largest port cities in Japan, located twenty-five miles southwest of Tokyo. It would not to be their final destination.

John remembers the Japs coming into the hold and carting away a few of the officers and enlisted men. At the time, no one knew why they had been selected. As it turned out, the men selected to disembark in Japan had been chosen for their specialties. The men included Major Putnam and Lieutenant Kliewer. Devereux would later write: "We never knew why these officers were picked out, but later we guessed it was because they represented a cross-section of the Wake establishment— the defense battalion, VMF 211 (the twelve-plane squadron), the naval air station, and naval communications. Most of the enlisted men were in communications, an indication of the Japs' interest in our radios."[9]

For the next couple of days, John and his fellow Marines remained in the hold, and the daily routines continued. Specifically: "There were the beatings, a lot of thinking, and no talking. The beatings, I guess, were to try to subdue us. Some of the guys were starting to have problems. The level of delirium was increasing. They didn't know if they were coming or going. Good thing I was a bullheaded German, and it didn't bother me that much. I was there to take care of the men when they needed it, and that is what I did."

After a couple of days at Yokohama, the ship began to move again, and still, no one knew where they were headed. The possibility still existed that they would still end up somewhere in Japan. Then, one of the worst things that John remembers about being in captivity would come to pass. "On the day we sailed away from Yokohama, the Japs came down into the hold, picked five of our guys at random, took them topside, and beheaded them. As far as I know, there was no reason why those five guys were chosen." The guard's explanation, as John was led to believe, was that "They were practicing cutting heads off. Can you imagine?" I talked to John many times in the course of writing this book. When he shared that story about the ruthless execution of the five Marines, it was the only time I could detect a palpable bitterness in his voice and in his demeanor.

The five men who were executed were Seamen Second Class John W. Lambert, Theodore Franklin, and Roy H. Gonzalez, Master Sergeant Earl R. Hannum, and Technical Sergeant Vincent W. Bailey. The official explanation that the Japs provided to rationalize the barbaric executions was revenge for the Japanese killed at Wake. After they were killed, the men were dumped overboard.[10]

The beheadings on the *Nitta Maru* were calculated, and it would be a form of death that would befall the Allies throughout the South Pacific. One of the most horrifying tales of mass murder that included numerous beheadings by the Japanese would take place on the infamous "Bataan Death March." On April 8, 1942, seventy-eight thousand Filipino and

American troops would surrender on the Bataan Peninsula on the main Philippine Island of Luzon. It was the largest surrender in the history of the U.S. Army. The men, many of them sick or starving, were forced to march from forty-five to sixty-five miles to different prison camps. During the march, prisoners who could not keep up were beheaded, shot, or beaten to death. Some were killed simply for the sport of it. The total number of deaths varies, as many more would die in the POW camps, but it is estimated that about 750 Americans and as many as 5,000 Filipinos perished on the march. Among the Filipinos, 300 to 400 were rounded up one day during the march. They were tied together and then beheaded or bayoneted to death. That killing spree went on for two hours.[11] The enmity of the Japs toward Allied soldiers and their wanton barbarity would continue throughout the war.

The *Nitta Maru* would travel almost another 1,100 miles further west in the Pacific, before arriving in Shanghai, China, on January 24, 1941. Shanghai is one of the busiest ports in the world, located in the Yangtze River Delta, on the eastern coast of central China. John does not recall the exact temperature that day, but he does remember that it was very cold. "The weather was like San Francisco weather, cold, damp and rainy. It was quite a difference from the temperature we'd endured in the hold for so many days. Everybody was taken off the ship, and we were told to march. There were plenty of Jap guards along the march to make sure no one got any ideas about running off. We didn't know where we were marching to, but after about five miles, we arrived at what we would soon learn was the Woosung Shanghai War Prisoners Camp." During the march, the prisoners had seen many curious Chinese, who were considered friendly to the Allies. Hopefully, there was a silver lining to being in China instead of Japan. Many of the men were weak from malnutrition, dehydration, or illness. Sometime during the march, freezing rain started to fall, making things more challenging. All the men were dressed in tropical clothing. John recollects, "There is one thing with the Japanese—you'd better be healthy, because if you couldn't take care of yourself, they would just shoot you or bayonet you. We were told to just do it (march)."

John recalls that when they arrived at the camp he was "tired to the bone." In addition to the weather conditions, none of the men knew whether the march would be one mile or one hundred. They were simply told to march, and if they were going too slow they were told to speed up. Mercifully, the march had been only a few miles. Had it been longer, some of the men may not have made it. John's first thoughts when they walked through the gates of the camp were: "As we arrived, I thought, *Okay, the march is finished and we'll get a place to sleep.*" Due to the cramped conditions on the boat, neither John nor anyone else had gotten much sleep in the past twelve days. Before they could find out what their new accommodations would be, they had to listen to Colonel Yuse, the camp commander, for more than an hour. There they stood in the cold and rain, listening to the Jap Colonel spout off, and none of them understood a word he was saying. John assumed he was ranting about all the violations that would result in death, but he had no idea. John eventually got some clarity when, "an interpreter made some things clearer. He warned us about not touching the fence surrounding the camp because it was electrified and would kill us. He went over some camp rules, like bowing and being respectful to the guards, learning how to line up and count off in Japanese during morning reveille and the evening roll call. Failure to obey the rules was punishable by a beating or worse. One of the warnings that I particularly heeded as a Corpsman, was not to drink the water unless it was boiled, or it could also cause death."

A coincidental irony of the Camp at Woosung is that it would also house the crew of the *USS Wake* gunboat. When it was originally built, the ship was named the *USS Guam*. In 1928, it was renamed the *USS Wake*, and the boat patrolled the Yangtze river prior to the war. It was moored at Shanghai on December 8, when the war broke out. It had the distinction of being the only U.S. Navy vessel to be captured intact during World War II. The boat survived the war and would be transferred to the Chinese in 1949 and be renamed again to *Tai Yaun*.

The camp was an old army facility consisting of seven barracks. Six of the barracks were 210 feet long by 50 feet wide and were divided into 6 sections, each holding up to 36 men. Each barrack housed about 230 men and the military continued to be separated from the civilians. The men slept on raised platforms on bare boards. The roofs were constructed of metal, and the windows were made of glass. When windows broke, they were not replaced. The officers had separate rooms with two to four in a room, depending on their rank. The latrines were behind the barracks about ten feet away. There were two bathrooms, one for officers and one for enlisted men.[12]

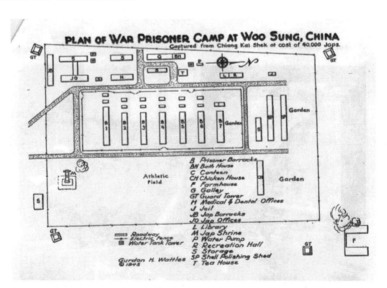

A sketch of the Camp at Woosung by Gordon Wattles, one of the civilians captured at Wake (North China Marines Website)

John settled in that first night in Woosung, in barracks number two. As he tried to get some sleep, he thought about what might come next and told himself, "Don't take any of this too seriously, and do your job." He also thought about his family and when, if ever, he would see them again. Alice and John were now 6,125 miles apart from each other across the vastness of the Pacific Ocean. John would spend another 1,302 days in captivity.

★　★　★

CHAPTER 13

"WOW, DID THEY BEAT ME! I WAS SO MAD I DIDN'T FEEL IT."

January 25, 1941 to December 6, 1942

After the first night of sleeping in the cold at Woosung, the guys quickly figured out that they would need something more than the three blankets each that they had been given. John described them as "not being good at all. We slept close together, side by side, to take advantage of our body heat. I slept next to Artie Brewer. We also figured out that, by putting newspapers between the blankets, it helped to keep us warmer but still not good. I don't remember where we got the newspapers, but they came in handy."

John thought the sanitary conditions were pretty bad. "Trying to keep clean was a challenge. There was a trough to bathe but not something you could get into. The water was not clean. You had to cup your hands, to scoop it out. Toilet paper was pretty much nonexistent. For the first few months, we didn't get soap, but after the Japs allowed Red Cross packages to be delivered to us, we started getting some. We would also get some cigarettes in the packages. I wasn't a smoker, so I would trade mine for more soap." He also recalls that "the waste from the latrines was carted off by Chinese farmers, supposedly to use as fertilizer. Some of the men called them 'coolies,' but I think they were just dirt-poor farmers."

This sketch of the barracks at Woosung was drawn by Joseph Astarita, who was among the civilians captured at Wake (North China Marines Website)

"Soon after we got to Woosung, a couple of our guys figured out how to make a radio that would pick up English-speaking stations from China. None of the news was good." The Japs were advancing all over the South Pacific. One piece of good news that would shock the Japanese and energize Americans was the "Doolittle Raid" on Tokyo. President Roosevelt asked the military leaders to figure out a way to send the Japs a message about American resolve. In response, a plan was conceived to fly sixteen B-25 twin engine bombers off a carrier to bomb the heart of Tokyo.

The raid was led by Lieutenant Colonel James H. Doolittle, a world-famous daredevil airman and seventy-nine other Army pilots who volunteered for the mission. When the men volunteered in December of 1941 and started extensive training, the only information they were given was that the mission would be, "dangerous, important, and interesting."[1] Doolittle addressed the volunteers on March 3, 1942, for the first time, and they still did not know where the mission would take them. Doolittle told them: "My name's Doolittle. I've been put in charge of the project that you men have volunteered for. This is the toughest training you'll ever have. It will be the most dangerous thing any of you have ever done. It is inevitable that some of you will fall into the hand of the enemy." Doolittle then gave all the men the opportunity to drop out, and not a single one considered it. They were all in.[2]

They continued training and on April 1 boarded the carrier *Hornet*. The next day, when the *Hornet* sailed, they would learn for the first time that their target was Tokyo.[3] The plan was for the *Hornet* to ferry them to within five hundred miles of Tokyo, but after being sighted by a Japanese fishing boat on April 18, the bombers took off from the carrier, more than 650 miles away from their target. They did not have enough fuel to return to the *Hornet*, so the plan, after bombing military and industrial sites, was to keep flying and try to land their planes in China. The mission was a huge success. The level of material damage inflicted on Japan was minimal compared to what our bombers would do later in the war. However, the impact on Japanese military leaders and American morale was inestimable. Years later, Doolittle would, in an understated way, say:

The raid had three advantages. First, was to give the people at the time a little fillip. The news had all been bad till then. The second advantage was to cause the Japanese to worry and feel that they were vulnerable, and third and most useful was that it caused a diversion of aircraft and equipment to the defense of the home islands which the Japanese badly needed where the war was actually going on.[4]

Eleven of the crews bailed out over China, and one plane landed on a rice paddy. Three of the crews ditched in the waters off the China coast and one bomber landed in Russia. Of the eighty men, three were killed exiting their aircrafts, and eight were captured by the Japs. Of those eight, three were executed, one died of malnutrition while a POW, and four would be captive till after the war.[5] The other sixty-nine would find their way back home after the raid.

Meanwhile at Woosung, John continued his duties as a Corpsman supporting Dr. Kahn, tending to the sick and wounded. "We had some serious cases. Malnutrition, malaria, and dysentery were common, but we also had cases of beriberi and typhoid fever. Of course, we saw a full array of injuries—men who were totally exhausted and a handful of men who were electrocuted by the fence we were told to avoid."

About a week after the men from Wake arrived at Woosung, a bunch of Marines from North China were brought to the camp, including two doctors: William T. Foley and Leo C. Thyson. Those Marines were from the U.S. Embassy detail and were in good shape. They walked in with their dress uniforms and their gear. According to John, "They were good guys; they shared some of their clothing with us, which really helped. They had hats and coats that came in handy for some of our men. They also had hand-held radios, which were better than the homemade ones our guys had put together."

A group of American Officers at the Camp in Woosung meeting with the Japanese. Dr. Thyson is on the table on the left, third from the left. To his left is Major Devereux. Dr. Kahn is at the center table second from the left. (North China Marines Website)

I asked John how often he thought about Alice and Johnny and getting back home. He said, "At first, almost all of us thought about families or women, but after a while the thoughts turned to food and eventually, just surviving from one day to the next. I was hungry, but I never felt that I was starving. I think my upbringing in Austria and having so little to eat as a child helped me with that." For some, in times of great stress, thinking of loved ones or earthly pleasures beyond their reach can do more harm than good. John continued to focus on doing his job, his faith in God, and his belief that America was too powerful to fail. About once a month, a priest was allowed into the camp and conducted mass for the men. John recalls the priest giving the men communion and telling them, "Go to confession when you get home. There were quite a few Catholics there, and it made us feel better to attend mass. So, yes, religion, my faith, really helped." He also believed in his heart and mind that the Americans would come sooner or later. It did not help him or the others that some of the more boorish guards cherished telling the POWs, "This is your life—this is how you are going to spend the rest of your lives."

One individual in particular who spoke English and was the primary interpreter was universally hated by the men. He was a civilian known to all as the "Beast of the East," and if he had any conscience at all, it did not intrude on his savagery. His name was Isamu Ishihara. John described him as "sadistic in the extreme. He was infamous for beating us. He expected every prisoner to bow to him respectfully, and if it wasn't to his liking, he'd hit us in the head with his stick." On one occasion, at formation, John and Artie Brewer stood on either side of a Marine sergeant and had to restrain him by holding his arms down by the wrist. The sergeant was literally shaking to get a shot at Ishihara. "The Beast" was administering a beating to a fellow Marine, and the sergeant wanted to go to his aid. Had John and Artie not restrained the sergeant, he, too, would have been beaten or bayoneted by one of the other Jap guards. As John talked about Ishihara, the picture that came to my mind was of a cruel misanthrope. During beatings, most of the men tried to be as stoic as possible to show the Japs that they would not be defeated by their brutality.

The "Beast" was also known for torturing men with the "Water Cure" and the "Finger Wire." The "Water Cure" consisted of a POW being strapped to a board or a ladder with his head lower than his body. Water was forced into him till he vomited, and the process was then repeated. At times, when his stomach was bloated, he was beaten across the stomach. The Finger Wire was slowly bending a finger back using a wire contraption till the finger broke or became disjointed. The Beast constantly harangued the POWs about surrendering and how they were men without honor.[6] After each Water Cure or Finger Wire, John and his fellow Corpsmen would do what they could to get those men healthy again and back on duty.

One of the men who was subjected to the "Water Cure," Private First Class Leonard G. Mettscher, USMC, shared his story after the war. "In 1944 I was nearly beaten to death. I was in charge of a horse that was used for hauling away debris. The guard made me overload the cart. I protested, to no avail. The horse stumbled and fell, hitting his head against a post. The fall paralyzed him. Later it died. They blamed me and gave me the water cure. They put a tube into my throat with a funnel attached and poured liquids down it. You could either swallow it or drown. When my stomach distended after much liquid, they beat me with a rubber hose till I was unconscious."[7]

Being slapped in the face or suffering a beating with a bat or a stick could happen at any time, for any reason. For example, at reveille if you did not shout out your number in line, in Japanese, it would result in at least a slap in the face and, if you were a repeat offender, much worse. John explained: "You had to learn how to count in Japanese—not just memorize your number. Any given day you might be a different number in formation because one of the guys before you might not be there because of illness or any number of reasons. I learned to count pretty well but have forgotten it over the years." Not bowing to the guards or providing a response to a question that was not to their liking could also elicit a beating. Some of the beatings were so severe that the man would lose consciousness. John added that, "not all the guards were sadists, but there were some you had to watch all the time." The worst, by far, was Ishihara, who looked for the smallest infraction or disrespect by the POWs to administer his cruelty.

The days usually started around five thirty in the morning, and the work details would return about twelve hours later. Some days were even longer. There were usually three meals a day, if they could be called that. The meals were the regular rice gruel and an occasional fish head. Meat was rare, and, when you got some, it was a meager portion. John was cautious about anything that looked like meat. "I tried to avoid cat or rat meat because it was an almost guaranteed cause of dysentery. I was lucky that I got dysentery only once, which may have been from eating some meat from a feral animal. Cats in particular did not last long in the camp. You'd see one running around, and almost immediately they'd be gone and on somebody's food bowl. The only liquid was tea, because you didn't dare drink the water." Most of the POWs worked outside the camp building or repairing roads. Those who were too weak due to illness would wash clothes. Others cooked the horrible meals that were served to the men, and the officers had light duty, like tending the gardens. The gardening was mostly for naught as the Japs would take most of its harvest.

John and his fellow Corpsmen worked in the POW hospital. The hours at the hospital coincided with the work details, but the Corpsmen would often be there much longer hours tending to the sick. "They kept me busy. I had to check the guys who didn't or couldn't go on the work detail. They had to go through me. I'd check them out to see if they were okay, and if there was any doubt, I'd refer them to one of the doctors. If they couldn't work, I had to write a slip for the Japanese to approve for the man to stay in the barracks or, if need be, the hospital. When I said they couldn't go, the Japanese pretty much took my word for it." On any given day, there may be upwards of twenty-five men in the hospital, and if any of those men needed overnight attention, one or more of the Corpsmen would stay at the hospital with them.

When Dr. Thyson arrived from China, he had been able to bring a supply of medicine with him, but it was all gone by the summer. Because of John's bilingual skills, he could communicate with the Japanese doctor who also spoke German. Accordingly, John was given an armband that had Japanese *kanji* characters on it. He had no idea what the characters meant, but he wore it at all times while he was on duty. The armband let the Japanese guards know that he was allowed to go to their hospital that was outside the perimeter of the POW camp. John laughed and said, "Sometimes, when there were new guards and they saw the armband, they would actually bow when I came by." All medicines were kept at the Japanese hospital. John was sent there mostly by Dr. Kahn, but all three doctors could request medicines for the POWs. "For months, the doctors themselves were not allowed to go to the Japanese hospital. I was the only one who could go over there because I could tell the Japanese doctor what medicines our doctors needed. When the Japanese doctor wasn't there, I used hand signals or pointed to what medicine I needed to communicate with their Corpsmen."

The primary illness among the prisoners was malaria. John said, "Probably 80 percent of the guys had it at one time or another. Whenever I was over at the Jap place and I could try to sneak some quinine pills, I would pop a couple in my mouth and swallow or chew them as fast as I could. I never got malaria. Unfortunately, I couldn't bring any back for the other guys unless it was requested by one of the doctors. What I could steal, I had to take right on the spot. One day, Dr. Kahn needed some medicine urgently for one of our guys, and the Jap hospital was closed. I checked the door, and it was locked, so I climbed up over the door and got inside through a transom window. I knew where the medicines were kept, so I grabbed what I needed, and, as I was coming out, three Japs were waiting for me, bayonets and all. One of them accused me of stealing; then the three of them lined up and took turns beating me. Wow! Did they beat me! I was so mad I didn't feel it. Dr. Kahn had to tend to my cuts and bruises, but I'd be okay." Regardless, John got the medicine for the sick Marine.

There was a library at the camp that some of the men, including John, appreciated. Reading allowed them brief respites from the daily grind. John joked about a book he was reading. "I can't remember the name of the book, but it was really thick. I was worried that we would be liberated before I had a chance to finish it." That recollection of the thick book was indicative of one of John's coping mechanisms: "Don't take anything too seriously, and keep doing what you need to do."

For the first few months, the priest continued to come into camp once a month to conduct mass for interested men. John attended, whenever he could get away from the hospital. Some men played baseball or football on Sundays with makeshift equipment. Since John's athletic interest was swimming, he did not participate. "There was very little downtime at the hospital, and that's where I spent most of my time."

In March, Commander Cunningham, along with Artie Brewer and a couple of other Marines escaped from Woosung. John relayed the conversation he had with Brewer. "Since we worked together and slept next to each other, Artie tried to talk me into going with them. I didn't think there was much of a chance that they'd succeed, so I said 'No.' My sixth sense told me to stay put." John was right. All of the escapees were captured within a day. "They were taken back to Woosung for a short time, and then they were sent to other camps. I didn't see Artie again till after the war." As a punishment to all the POWs for not alerting the Japs about the planned escape, they were placed on half rations of food for thirty days.

Cunningham would attempt another escape in October of 1944 by sawing through bars in his cell window at the Ward Road Jail in Shanghai. He was recaptured again and returned to his cell within ten hours. One escape that did succeed involved Lieutenants Kinney and McAllister and two other non-Wake Marines. As they were being transported between prison camps, the four men jumped off a train and were fortunate to run into friendly Chinese forces, who helped them to safety. Bill Taylor, a civilian, would do the same and also succeed in escaping.[8]

The Japanese did not allow the Red Cross to visit the Camp till September of 1942. The first Red Cross boxes with food and medical supplies—were looted by the Camp commander and the guards—were not delivered till Christmas of 1942. By that time, the men had been transferred to another camp five miles away in Kiangwan. Colonel William W. Ashurst of the North China Marines was the senior officer, and he refused to sign for Red Cross boxes that had been looted. Eventually the Japs relented and allowed the full delivery of the boxes.[9]

In September of 1942, a group of seventy men, consisting of laborers, technicians, and specialists were transferred to a POW camp in Fukuoka, Japan. In November, another group of twelve civilians and fifty-eight Marines, including a couple of the Corpsmen, were transferred to the same camp. In December, the entire camp at Woosung was moved to Kiangwan, China.[10] John told me that, once again, they "were told to march. The new camp was about five miles away, but now we were not in as good a shape as when we'd first arrived in China. It was a hard march, but there were no incidents." In September, the Japanese camp commander Yuse had passed away. No one knew what caused his death, but, according to John, "the Japs stopped the work details for three days and gave everyone a little extra food to honor the Colonel's passing." He added, "I wish more of their officers would have died so our guys could benefit from some rest and extra food." Yuse was succeeded by Colonel Satoshi Otera, who the men nicknamed "Handlebar" due to his flamboyant mustache.

During that first year of John's captivity, the American Pacific Fleet, the Army, and Marines would score significant victories against the Japs. Among the most notable was the "Miracle at Midway" and the Guadalcanal Campaign that marked the beginning of the Pacific Island battles that would eventually lead our troops to Japan. At Midway, our fleet scored a decisive victory over the Japs between June 3 and June 7, 1942. The Americans deceived the Japanese into attacking Midway and then hit them with everything they had. The Japanese were anxious to capture the island for its airport. More importantly, they wanted to strike a crippling blow to the Americans' Pacific fleet by destroying the carriers that they had missed at the attack on Pearl Harbor. Where Admiral Pyle had been timid and reserved, pulling back the task force to reinforce Wake, Admiral Nimitz was bold and daring in taking on a superior Japanese force at Midway.

Nimitz's plan was elegantly simple: He would hide his three carriers till Admiral Nagumo's planes hit Midway. He'd then attack the unprotected Japanese carriers. The Japanese sailed and flew themselves right into the ambush.[11] The Marines and Navy personnel at Midway knew the Jap fleet was headed their way, and, not being fully privy to Nimitz's plan, were resigned to "another Wake." However, one and all were determined to continue to work on Midway's defense to the end.[12] In the end, Midway would not be another Wake because Nimitz's plan would work out. The Japanese lost four of their mighty carriers: The *Hiryu, Kaga, Soryu,* and *Akagi,*[13] while the Americans lost only one, the *Yorktown.* In addition, Japan lost 322 aircraft while the Americans lost 147. The Japanese carriers had been caught while refueling and rearming their planes, making them especially vulnerable.[14]

Arguably, the devastating blow to the Japanese at Midway turned the course of the war in America's favor, only six months after Japanese attack on Pearl Harbor and Wake. Hideki Tojo would say after the war: "Basically it was lack of coordination. When the Prime Minister, to whom is entrusted the destiny of the nation, lacks the authority to participate in supreme decisions, it is not likely a country will win a war." This was a self-serving half-truth. But it was, indeed, hard for a nation's chief executive to control its destinies when, for instance, he was told nothing of the Navy's defeat at Midway till weeks after the battle.[15]

The battle of Guadalcanal, an island in the Solomon chain, would mark the first major offensive by the Americans and would be fought on land, sea, and in the air. The battle began in August of 1941 and continue till February of 1942. The Army and Marines suffered 6,300 casualties, including 1,600 killed. The Japs suffered 21,000 killed—that represented about two-thirds of those who fought on the island. The remainder of the Jap troops were evacuated between December and February.[16] It was another humiliating defeat for Japan. The Japs would be frequently wrong about the Americans' courage and resolve but seldom doubted that they would defeat them. It was a mind-set that would doom the self-proclaimed Great Empire.

Back at Wake in late 1942, the injured Marines that had been too weak to travel to Woosung were taken to prison camps in Japan. In September, 200 civilians had also been transported to Japanese camps. Only 98 civilians remained on the atoll to complete work projects. Among them was Dr. Shank, who refused to abandon his fellow civilians.

John and the rest of the men at Woosung arrived at Kiangwan Prisoner of War Camp on Sunday December 6, 1942. He would spend his second Christmas away from Alice and would endure still another 986 days of captivity.

★ ★ ★

CHAPTER 14

"I TORE IT UP AND THREW IT IN THE LATRINE."

December 7, 1942 to December 31, 1944

The new camp at Kiangwan was similar to the layout at Woosung. It, too, was an old Army barracks, and this one had hot and cold running water, which made cleaning up better, but the men still couldn't drink the water that came from a well. There were two airports near the camp, one civilian and one military. The barracks were similar, and as was the case at Woosung, civilians and military were in separate quarters. John had been assigned to Barrack 1, Section 8. Drs. Kahn, Thyson, and Foley continued to care for the military personnel and worked with a Japanese doctor, Lieutenant Shindo, to care for the civilians. John mentioned that Shindo "was okay. He did what he could to help us out."

Brewer's attempted escape and the two other Corpsmen transferred to prisons in Japan left only three Corpsmen to assist in the infirmary. A fourth, Pharmacist Mate Second Class Laurence Atwood, whose specialty was dentistry, focused primarily on the dental care of the men. There were plenty of dental issues given the diet, unsanitary conditions, and the lack of toothbrushes or powder. John never had a toothbrush in his years of captivity. "I'd use my fingers or at times a cloth to try to clean the grime. Occasionally, we'd get some cleaning powder, but most of us swallowed it because it tasted so good." One of the maladies that John suffered in captivity was "a tooth that was driving me crazy. Atwood pulled it without any local anesthesia. It hurt like hell, but after a while, the pain was gone, and it felt good to stop the constant ache. We did what we had to do to get by."

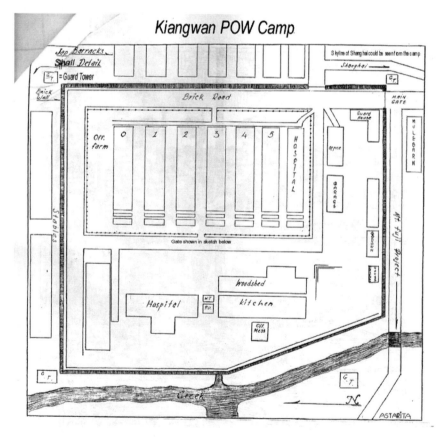

A sketch of the POW camp at Kiangwan by Joseph Astarita (North China Marines Website)

The new Commander, Otera, was more accommodating than Yuse had been, especially as it related to Red Cross boxes. John can't recall exactly how many Red Cross packages they received at Kiangwan; he believes it was at least three or four. The Japs still took some of the contents but not as much as they had from the first shipments. Regardless, whenever they received them they were a welcome sight. It boosted morale a bit, and they could use as much of that as they could get. John particularly appreciated the candy, but, unfortunately, it never lasted very long. Meals at the new camp continued to be the rice gruel, fish heads, and tea. The occasional mystery meat continued to concern him, so for the most part, he avoided it. On Christmas of 1942, the men received an unexpected gift. An American restaurateur living in Shanghai, who was known to all the men as Jimmy James, was allowed by the Japanese to deliver a Christmas dinner to the POWs at Kiangwan. The men luxuriated on turkey and sweet potatoes. John said, "It was the only decent meal we ate during our captivity. I don't know how that guy pulled it off, but we were grateful."

In late 1942 a couple of the officers were allowed to go on a radio broadcast and send messages to their families. John guessed that the Japs thought it might generate some good public relations for them. John believed that "Most people in the U.S. thought we had fought to the last man at Wake, including Alice." In addition to their personal messages, the officers were allowed to share a list of names of the men who had survived the Wake attack. John's name was naturally on the list, and the word got back, through what John believes, were short-wave radios that picked up the broadcast. When Alice reported to work on Friday, January 14, 1943, she got the surprise of her life. She had been working as a Keypuncher for the Navy. Captain Bruce Pierce from the Ordnance Department at the Headquarters of the Benicia Arsenal had received notice that John was alive and a Prisoner of War in Kiangwan, China. He was asked to inform Alice about John's status. On the fourteenth, he wrote her a note that was delivered to her department. It read:

Memorandum for: Mrs. Unger
Key Punch Room

Lt. Knight, wants to see you after 8 o'clock AM tomorrow relative to speaking over the radio in a special broadcast to our troops overseas with several other people from the arsenal. Please see me before you leave.

Bruce Pierce. Capt. Ord Dept.

Alice was confused but soon learned that the reason she was being asked to be part of a broadcast was that John was alive. After the shock came the elation that her one and only love had survived the battle at Wake. John does not recall if Alice spoke on the broadcast that was supposedly meant to be heard by the POWs. If she did speak, he didn't hear her.

In addition to the broadcast, POWs were now allowed to receive and send letters to their loved ones. However, anything received or sent was subject to censorship by both the Japs and the Americans. John shared that "You could only write things that did not depict the Japs in a bad light. Our letters home had to be brief, and we had to print them because they couldn't decipher cursive. If you wrote something they didn't like, they'd literally tear it up in front of you and sent you away." One of the things the Japs ordered them to write was that they were in great health. John wrote his first letter to Alice since becoming a POW in January of 1943. He had not been able to write to her since December of 1941, but that letter was never delivered. The last letter Alice had received from him was on the fifteenth of November, 1941.

If you received a letter from home that they didn't like, the Japs would destroy it. "Sometimes they would tear it up in front of you. You would be notified you received a letter, and then you'd go to the office. Once there, you'd salute whoever had the letter; almost always it was the interpreter and heartless beast Ishihara. Then, he'd read it and destroy it or just tear it up without reading it to you."

Wake survivor, Major Robert M. Brown USMC, provided his perspectives about Ishihara and the letters after the war. "The 'Beast' lined us up and leaned back in his chair. He had several letters in his hand. He stared at us for a while before he erupted. 'You are the cause of an insult to the Japanese empire,' he screamed. 'You have your cheap, common women at home, and they dare to write you here. Your whores dare to speak of love. This is not a time for love. This is a time for war. Maybe you Marines think first of love and then of fighting. Maybe that's why you now live in this camp.' He went on and on. When he subsided, he smiled at us. One by one, he tore the letters into tiny pieces and threw them in our direction. 'Here,' he said. 'Take them and be ashamed.' I doubt that I will ever recover from the hatred I felt and feel still for Mr. Ishihara. It doesn't help to know that he died a very painful death from cancer in prison. He still lives on in my nightmares."[1]

John wrote a letter to Alice in January of 1943 that read as follows:

Dearest wife and son,

I'm hoping this letter reached you in the best of health and spirit. I'm thankful for this opportunity to be able to inform you

that I'm in best of health and can say we have adequate food sup-
ply here and entertainment.

Daily I'm occupied working at the hospital which makes
the time pass quicker and keeps me occupied and useful. Please
inform my parents and do not worry about me.

Hoping to see you soon

Your loving husband
John

The letter was far from the detailed letters John had previously written, but it served the purpose of letting Alice know that he was coping with his situation and, more importantly, that he loved her and Johnny.

Now that John had limited contact with Alice, it made life more tolerable. However, it didn't change the conditions at Kiangwan, nor did it change the demands on him and his fellow POWs. The primary work duty for the Marines was what they all called building Mount Fuji. The Marines labored long hours every day building a hill. According to John, the men were told they were building the hill for a recreational park but soon surmised that the purpose of the hill was to be used as a wall or barricade for a firing range. As the hill grew in size, the work got harder, as the men had to go higher and higher hauling bags of dirt. John could see the results at the hospital each day when the number of men asking not to work started increasing. He did what he could to relieve the most fatigued, by keeping them at the hospital.

In June of 1943, he was allowed to send Alice a letter. Johnny had turned two in May and still had not met his father. John wrote:

Dearest wife and son,

When you receive this letter, our Wayne will have been two years old. I am certainly hoping that he will have a most content and happy birthday. After sixteen months of imprisonment I'm still healthy, without a single day of sickness, except I've lost weight, I had a tooth extraction and had my hair cut close. I only hope it grows out before I see you.

Darling, I hope that you are again in best of health, and there should not, or rather must not be a single cause for you to worry. I'll close now with hope of seeing you and Johnny soon.
  Till then.

Forever Yours
John

Ironically, John suffered his only bout with dysentery after that letter, but luckily, he overcame it. He recalls that "The doctors had come up with a creative way to treat the condition without the appropriate medicines. They'd have us scrape the burnt rice or the charcoal on the bottom of the pots used to make the gruel. That's how we treated guys with dysentery, and that's how I treated myself. It was a homemade medicine, but it seemed to work pretty well."

He got a chance to write another brief note on July 12. This was unusual in that the rule was no more than one letter home per quarter unless you got special permission. This letter didn't say much more than the last one, but it felt good for John to write.

Dearest Wife and son,

Another brief opportunity to inform you of my well-being
and a reminder that I'm always thinking of you and Wayne.
Camp facilities still include an adequate library, hospital,
sports and with everyone well occupied, it makes the time pass
more quickly. Closing with love to all and hopes of seeing you soon.

Devotedly
John

John continued to be the only Corpsman to shuttle back and forth from the Japanese hospital for medicines, though now the doctors were also allowed to go. Two Marines came down with typhoid fever, and John was asked to take care of them. With an incredulous look on his face he said to me, "Two of our guys were diagnosed with typhoid fever, and guess who they picked to take care of them? Me." Typhoid fever is caused by bacteria in food or water and is highly contagious. Infected people can pass the bacteria through bodily fluids. In short, the men had to be quarantined, and someone had to be with them to attend to their needs. That meant that John literally cared for them night and day, including sleeping in the same room with them.

Those two Marines would recover, but other men would not. John considered it very fortunate that under the care of the three doctors he supported, only three Marines died on his watch. A total of 28 military personnel from Wake would die in various camps over the years of captivity. The three John regretted losing were a case of tuberculosis that required quarantine, one Marine with typhoid fever, and one that electrocuted himself. I asked him about that third one, and his response was, "It could have been an accident or it might have been a suicide; it was hard to tell. However, it's hard to believe he didn't know about the danger of the hot fence. It was a well-known fact that if you contacted the fence, it would kill you, and other guys had already died accidentally." John vividly recalls working with Dr. Kahn to try to save that Marine's life. "Dr. Kahn and I worked on him for an hour trying to resuscitate him, but we couldn't bring him back."

After the war, Wake survivor Gunnery Sergeant John J. Johnson, USMC shared a story about a different electrocution. "I had been writing notes of what happened since the start of the war. After the war, I was briefed by the U.S. military in Yokahama; they took some of my notes for evidence. I'd kept a record of some of the men killed in prison camp. One Marine was an old hand from earlier China service; he was ordered to cut the grass under the fence. He had a scythe and was doing it when the Japs turned on the electrical current on the fence. He didn't know the juice was on, and he touched a wire with the scythe; it electrocuted the man in an instant."[2]

Of the 1,593 military and civilians that had been captured at Wake Island 244—or more than 15 percent—would perish in captivity.[3] Of the more than 300 civilians who had initially stayed at Wake, 45 had died by December of 1942. The Japanese had pushed them so hard and fed them so little that they died from malnutrition and exhaustion.[4] After the transfer of some of the civilians to Japan, the remaining 98 were slaughtered by order of the Japanese Commander and Rear Admiral, Shigemitsu Sakaibara. There were three potential reasons for the killings. The Americans had started bombing Wake as early as February of 1942 and intensified their attacks in the spring of 1943. On October 5, the assault by the Americans was particularly fierce, and it so angered Sakaibara that the next day he retaliated by killing the Americans.[5] After the war, John had also heard that the Japs were themselves starving to death at Wake, and ninety-eight fewer mouths to feed was a convenient excuse to kill them all. A third theory posited that after the assault by the Americans, Commander Sakaibara feared a landing on the atoll and that the civilians would take up the fight against his troops. Regardless of the demented rationalizations, it was a wanton and cowardly murder of innocents.

The American civilians were blindfolded, taken to a trench along the beach, and shot. For those who survived the shooting, a bayonet finished the job. One civilian managed to crawl away and hide for two days in the brush; he was then captured and beheaded. Lee Bong Moon, a Korean cook that the Japanese had brought to the atoll, described the execution after the war. "He was kneeling with his hands tied behind his back. We recognized each other, and tears came to his eyes. Shortly

An American fighter plane on a bombing raid over Wake in October of 1943 (National Archives).

after, a sword thrust ended the civilian's life." The men were buried but later were exhumed and spread throughout the atoll. It was an attempt by Sakaibara to make it appear as if they had been killed by American bombing raids.[6] Who knows what would have happened to John if he had stayed on the atoll as he had requested?

He may have been dispatched with the injured Marines when they were healthy enough to be transported to China, or he may have been on that beach with the civilians when they were shot and bayoneted.

Other than the civilians killed at Wake, I asked John why a higher percentage of civilians died in captivity. "Marines were overall considerably younger than the civilians and in much better physical fitness. The training and attitude of the Marines also contributed. Those guys were tough, and, like me, many of them were bullheaded, which helped."

As 1943 was coming to an end, the Americans engaged in one of the bloodiest battles of the war at Tarawa Atoll in the Gilbert Islands. Between November 20 and November 23, the Marines fought the Japs for control of the atoll, resulting in 3,000 casualties for the Americans, including more than 1,100 killed or missing.[7] Of the 4,700 defenders, only 17 survived.[8] The losses to the Americans were similar to the fighting at Guadalcanal, but that campaign lasted six months compared to Tarawa's three days.[9] Though costly, the Marines continued their Pacific island battles on their way to Japan. *Life* magazine wrote about battle: "Tarawa proved again that the famous tenacity of the Japs is not equal to the tenacity of an American roused. Tarawa was a proof that we are now on the way to certain victory. Two years ago, on Dec. 6, America spent its last days at peace. In two years, the country, while dedicating itself to the defeat of Germany first, has nevertheless moved from the unawareness of Pearl Harbor, from the crushing loss of Guam and Wake, through the nightmares of Bataan and Guadalcanal, to Tarawa."[10]

Captain Forrest P. Sherman, Chief of Staff to Vice Admiral John H. Towers, Commander of the Air Forces of the Pacific, had proposed a plan to recapture Wake and use it as a springboard to then assault the Marshall Islands, which lay about five hundred miles to the south. However, Admiral Raymond A. Spruance favored attacking much further southeast in the Gilbert Islands, where greater land-based air support from rear bases in the South Pacific could support our troops.[11] Spruance prevailed, and the focus would be on Tarawa. The Americans eventually blockaded Wake, preventing the Japs from getting much-needed supplies, but Wake would remain under Japanese control till after the war.

John was allowed to send another letter on November 1, 1943 that was testimony to the limitations that the Japs placed on what could be written. The holidays were around the corner but he would not mention them. The letter, or more accurately, the note, read as follows:

Dearest wife and son,

Just a few words to let you know that I am still in the best of health and spirit and thinking of you always and hoping that you are the same.

Still passing the years away in my work and reading a great number of books of which we have quite a variety.

Please give my love and best wishes to all and pardon my absence.

Forever,
John

In addition to the propaganda that the Japs expected in the letters, that note also struck a tone of melancholy. But John would prevail; his faith and his work would keep him going. He, along with his fellow Corpsmen, continued to do their part to keep the men in captivity as healthy as possible. Among the memories of procedures that he performed on behalf of his fellow captives were "two appendectomies that we did with a little bit of ether to sedate the guys and crude operating tools. We did not have regular surgical tools, so the doctors had to improvise. Those two fellows would be okay, and they would make it through the war."

Yeoman Third Class Glenn E. Tripp, one of the Wake defenders, also wrote to John's nephew Jim Kelly after the war. In his letter he talked about the great support he and the other soldiers received from the Corpsmen during the attack on Wake and especially in the POW camps. Specific to John, Tripp wrote, *"John did a hell of a job in caring for us sick. He had very little to work with* (referring to medicines and medical instruments)." He added: *"Our lives we owe to God and those Corpsmen. John was one good man, and if you see him, tell him that the defenders of Wake think they* (referring to the Corpsmen*) were the greatest."*

John had a couple of opportunities to care for Major Devereux. He clearly remembered one situation: "Devereux came to me one day and asked if I could do something to alleviate a bothersome sty that he had on his eyelid. I removed the thing, and I surprised myself that I did such a good job. I had never done that before. The major really appreciated it."

As the days turned into months and the months became years, the horrendous conditions in which John lived and operated could have destroyed many men, but John kept going; "Just doing my job." John continued to be assiduous about administering to his mates, and his efforts would not go unnoticed by either the Japs or the Marines. One day, in early 1944, the Japs called all the men to formation and brought John up front and center. He described to me what transpired: "There we were in formation, everyone standing at attention, and the Jap commander read off a paper for a few minutes, and then handed it to me, and that was that. It was a citation recognizing the care I had been providing to our men. I took it, and the first chance I got, I tore it up and threw it in the latrine." John broke out into a hearty laugh and added. "You know, it felt good to throw it away. That helped me to get through another year as a prisoner. It was good to be able to fight back, even if it was only in a small way." I asked John if there was any resentment on the part of the men that he had been recognized by the

Japs. "Oh, no. I really felt that the Marines really appreciated what I was doing for them."

Though proud of what he was doing to help, John felt that he needed a change, and a few months later, he asked Devereux if he could transfer from hospital duty to the work detail with the Marines. John explained, "After about three years, the stress and strain was too much for me to handle. Patients dying, chronic illnesses, and no hope in sight. I contacted Devereux and told him that I could no longer endure the work and asked that I be allowed to work outside the hospital like the other men. He advised me to please remain, that I was doing an excellent job, had a good relationship with the Japanese medical personnel, and that after the war was over, if I needed anything, he would do anything in his power for me. So, I stayed working as a Corpsman." After the war, in 1946, based on a recommendation from Dr. Thyson, John would receive a citation from then Secretary of the Navy, James Forrestal. The citation read, in part:

The Secretary of the Navy takes pleasure in commending

John Ignacious Unger
Chief Pharmacist's Mate
United States Navy

For service set forth in the following Citation:

For your heroic and meritorious devotion to duty for a period of forty-four months as a prisoner of the Japanese in China, Korea and Japan. With officers of the medical department and other pharmacist's mates, Unger helped organize and maintain a hospital for the shifting internment center which administered to the medical needs of American military prisoners of war. Without thought of rest or his own welfare Unger labored incessantly, tirelessly and devotedly in the care of the sick and injured during the entire internment period. When the position of the internment center was shifted and prisoners were forced to travel under the most loathsome and unsanitary conditions possible—crowded in filthy cattle cars and jammed in the dirty, foul-smelling holds of prison ships, Unger remained devoutly at his task. His conduct in the face of these most trying conditions was an inspiration to all and was in keeping with the best traditions of the United States Naval Service.

James Forrestal, Secretary of the Navy

But, that citation was to come later. For now, John had to find a way to persevere, and things would not get any easier. "Early in 1944, they brought an American pilot into camp who had been shot down. When we asked him how the war was going, he told us that we were having success against the Japs but that he thought the war was never going to end." Not what anyone wanted to hear. Around the same time, John and the other Corpsmen were transferred from Barrack 1 to Barrack 2. Barrack 2 housed the officers, so his sleeping quarters were a bit better. He has no idea why they were transferred; he simply went along. He also received a typewriter from the Japanese to help with the recording of treatments the POWs were receiving and the deaths that occurred in the camp.

Another helpful addition to the infirmary is what John called a "Hibachi Pot." He explained its usefulness. "It was meant for heating a room, but we eventually used it to cook stuff. One day, one of the guys brought over a snake, and we cooked it on the pot. It was good meat. Better than the rats and cats. Mostly, it kept my hands warm so I could type when I had to."

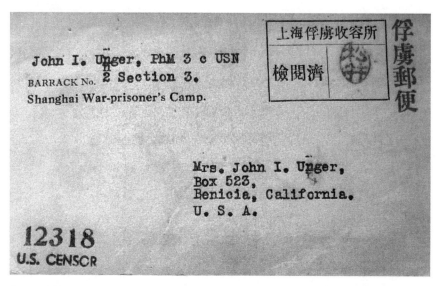

A sample letter envelope stamped by the U.S. military indicating the letter had been reviewed by the censor's office (From the personal collection of John I. Unger)

In addition to the experiment with cooking the snake, there were others that wouldn't turn out as well. Both the Marines and the Corpsmen tried to use alcohol to mix a brew for drinking. John drank the concocted alcohol once, and "I woke up the next day with a broken finger. I couldn't remember anything. I don't know how I did it, but I had a broken finger. I didn't drink that stuff again."

One of Seaman First Class Cassius Smith's USN jobs at Kiangwan was "to go to the racetrack where the Japs had us bury sixty-five-gallon drums of alcohol. They used the alcohol for fuel for their cars and trucks. Yes, I drank some of it, even though it was 180 proof. The alcohol got me in trouble. The Corpsmen in the camp asked me to bring back some of the alcohol so they could use it in the clinic. Some of the guys got tire inner tubes and melted ends together and made water bottles out of them. I filled some of them and carried them back to the medics. One day I got caught. The camp guards inspected every prisoner in the camp. They found the alcohol. They stripped me naked and threw me in solitary confinement for three weeks. I had half rations of a cup of rice and a cup of water a day. They also beat me up every day."[12]

John could now compose letters to Alice on the typewriter. He sent the longest letter from captivity on February 10, 1944. It was a surprisingly long and candid missive, given the Japs' limitations on what and how things could be written. In the letter, John's foresight about his future with Alice would, indeed, come to be.

Dearest wife and son,

As I write this letter to wish you joy on this day, my heart is so full. My thoughts go back to the old days with you, when you were so charming and sweet. It is now my deepest regret that I did not spend my whole time with you. You can think of me now as poor and lonely, but with my heart full of the warmest desire for God's richest blessing upon you and my son.

It is quite impossible for me to tell you how much I miss you and Wayne, who by now must be a most enchanting and loveable youngster. God bless you two dear people.

Dear Alice, I feel convinced that a bright and happy future lies before us, and my heart is longing to be with you both to enjoy the bright future together. I am longing greatly some news and pictures from you as I have not received any for a long time now. I heard that there are some letters for me at the office which I expect daily and the thought of receiving them makes me happy.

Please give Wayne my love, and at the same time my warmest wishes for a long, bright and blessed life for both of you.

Your loving Husband,
John

John would be limited to typing short postcards for the remainder of his captivity. On June 6, days before his twenty-fourth birthday, he wrote:

Dear Wife and son,

Have again received some letters from you but still no pictures.

Am hoping that you are still in the best of health and enjoying life. As for me, I have no complaints except perhaps that I could be just a little less lonesome and not altogether happy. But still in best of hopes health and spirit.

With Best Wishes to All. Love,
John

John wrote to Alice and John Wayne again in August and September. In April, Alice had written to John but he had not received it till August with a picture of his son. It was the first time John saw a likeness of his son.

During 1944, the war was raging all over the world. In Europe, the Russians had prevailed over the Germans in the Siege of Leningrad.

John Wayne Unger at around two years of age (From the personal collection of John I. Unger)

The siege had started in September of 1941 and had mercifully ended in January of 1944. It is estimated that between 600,000 and 1,200,000 died by August of 1942. The total losses were inestimable.[13] On June 6 of 1944, the long-awaited invasion of France took place along a stretch of 56 miles of beaches at Normandy France. A total of 175,000 American, Canadian, and British troops entered Normandy by air or sea at the cost of approximately 4,900 casualties.[14] Two thousand of the casualties occurred on Omaha Beach.[15] By December of 1944, the Battle of the Bulge would begin in the Ardennes Forest (located mainly in Luxembourg and Belgium but also extending into France and Germany) .

In the Pacific, the island battles continued. George Herbert Bush, who would become our forty-first president, flew his first mission as a Navy Pilot off the light carrier the *USS San Jacinto* on May 21, 1944. His target was Wake Island.[16] In June, the Marines landed on Saipan in the Mariana Islands for what would be a three-week battle, resulting in more than three thousand Americans killed. The Japanese would lose approximately twenty-seven thousand. The battle marked the end of Hideki Tojo as prime minister as he had boasted that the U.S. would never take Saipan.[17] The battle was also notable for the grisly carnage that took place at Banzai and Suicide Cliffs, where hundreds of civilians were either killed by Jap soldiers or jumped to their deaths. Warned by the Japanese soldiers that Americans were beasts that would kill any survivors, Japanese soldiers killed themselves with grenades often with a group of civilians surrounding them. Others pushed women and children off the cliffs and then committed suicide themselves. Many of the women jumped themselves, after throwing their children off the cliffs.[18] Approximately fourteen thousand Army and Marine personnel were killed, wounded, or went missing in action. Almost the entire Japanese garrison of thirty thousand was wiped out.[19]

In September, another bloody battle took place at Peleliu in the Palau Islands, where Americans suffered more than three thousand killed and thousands more wounded. The exact number of Japanese killed has never been determined, but the total ranged from eleven thousand to thirteen thousand.[20] Another notable occurrence of the Pacific war that demonstrated the fanaticism of the Japanese was that Lieutenant Ei Yamaguchi and thirty-three other soldiers would not turn themselves in till April of 1947, twenty months after the war had ended. The men had held out in the intricate underground tunnels in the Umurgrobol area of Peleliu.[21] Finally, in October of 1944, the Americans landed on Leyte Islands to mark the beginning of General MacArthur's commitment to return to liberate the Philippines from the Japanese.

As 1944 drew to a close, John typed one final note for the year in November:

Dearest Wife, Son & all:

Wishing you all a Merry Christmas and a Happy New Year. Hope to be home next year at this time.

I am still in best of health, so do not worry about me, as all is OK & Love,

John

All was not okay, but John and his fellow POWs kept pushing from one day to the next, trying to survive and hoping for the liberation that could not come soon enough. Three years of gross malnutrition and the long hours of work were taking a heavy toll. Everyone had lost significant weight, and though the rumors of the Americans' success in the Pacific were more prevalent, the POWs could not know if any of them would survive to see the end of the war. That Christmas of 1944 marked the fourth one that John and Alice had been apart. He had not held her, run his fingers through her hair, or kissed her since Christmas of 1940. John Wayne was more than three-and-one-half years old and had not yet met his father. John would still endure 230 more days of captivity. Part of that time would be spent in Japan—the place he and all his fellow POWs had dreaded since leaving Wake.

★ ★ ★

CHAPTER 15

"DUE TO THE ATOMIC BOMB, WE SURRENDER."

January 1, 1945 to August 18, 1945

Among the many ironies of World War II were the number of prisoners of war killed by friendly fire. Most notably, in the Pacific, around ten thousand died on ships sunk by American submarines. The submarine captains had no way of identifying ships carrying POWs till near the end of the war, when code-breaking efforts identified some convoys carrying prisoners. As the Japs kept losing battles and territory, they were moving thousands of prisoners from China and other camps in the South Pacific, to the home islands. Prisoners were primarily used as slave labor. Regardless of the occasional decrypts of Jap messages, the U.S. Navy adopted a ruthless position: destroying the enemy took priority over attempts to safeguard POWs.[1] I asked John if he was aware that other POWs were being killed during transport to Japan, and he said, "We had heard some rumors of it from some of the new POWs who had been brought into the camps, but it was not something that was top of mind for us."

To make matters worse, some Japs, in their customary barbarity, would threaten prisoners on the transport ships to Japan. An example played out on the *Shinyo Maru* in September of 1944. The Japanese commander informed prisoners enroute from Mindanao in the Philippines that if the ship was attacked, he would kill them all. The *Shinyo* was, indeed, sunk by the U.S. submarine *Paddle,* and, as promised, the Jap guards shot all of the prisoners who tried to flee the wreck. About twenty were mistakenly picked up by other Japanese ships on the convoy, and they, too, were shot and killed.[2] In rare instances, American ships picked up POWs left in the ocean by the Japanese, but they were able to save only a fraction of those who were shot or left to drown. The sinking of ships transporting Allied military would matter to John and his friends, as in a few months, they, too, would be transported from China to Japan.

By the beginning of 1945, the men at Kiangwan were wearing down. Illnesses and injuries added to the deteriorating conditions of the POWs. Tuberculosis, malaria, beriberi, and dysentery were ubiquitous. John described the mind-set of most of the men: "You always had to be cognizant that today might be the day you suffer a crippling injury, succumb to illness, or whatever malady you already had would get worse." Other constant worries included being bayoneted by an overly eager guard or the ever-present danger of being subjected to a brutal beating by the "Beast of the East." Ishihara's appetite for humiliating the POWs and inflicting pain had not abated one bit. The Americans were now bombing Japan on a regular basis, and John describes an incident that transformed joy into pain. "One day, an American fighter, I think it was a P-51, shot down a Jap plane in clear view of many of us at the camp. We all started cheering and jumping up and down. What did the

Japs do? They bayoneted three of our guys. I had to fix one up who'd gotten bayoneted in the butt. The other two were more serious." John continued to immerse himself in doing his job to the best of his ability, but it was getting harder each passing day. "The number of guys who were sick or near death was discouraging." The one silver lining that he clung to was that, if American fighter planes were flying over the camp, it meant they were getting very close.

On January 4, 1945, unbeknown to John at the time, he would write his last note to Alice and Johnny from a POW camp.

Dearest wife and son,

Another line to let you know that I'm still in best of health and thinking of you two. Hope you both had a Merry Christmas & a Happy New Year, and may the next one see us together again. Give my love to all.

Yours,
John

On the war front, the Battle of the Bulge in Europe came to a merciful end in January of 1945. More than a million German and Allied soldiers had engaged in the battle, often in freezing conditions, sometimes reaching below-zero temperatures. Nineteen thousand Americans lost their lives to the enemy or the weather conditions, 47,000 were wounded, and 15,000 had been captured. The Germans had suffered more than 100,000 casualties. The battle was the costliest ever for the U.S. Army. General George Patton's Third Army had played a key role in turning the fate of the battle in the Allies' favor. When asked about how he succeeded in overcoming the elements and the enemy, he said: "To tell you the truth, I didn't have anything much to do with it. All you need is confidence and good soldiers. I'll put our goddamn, bitching, belching, bellyaching G.I.s up against any troops in the world."[3]

On the Pacific front, the Marines would go ashore on Iwo Jima on February 19, 1945, and fight another incredibly costly battle that would not conclude till March 26. Iwo was strategically important for the American bombers that were based in Tinian and Saipan, making bombing raids on Japan. The bombers' almost 2,500-mile roundtrips were met both ways by attacking Japanese fighter planes based in Iwo Jima. Our bombers were unprotected because our fighter planes did not have the range to make the long round trips. The American crew and pilot casualties were mounting and not sustainable. In addition, Iwo Jima could be used for the American bombers to change crews, discharge wounded, take on fuel,[4] and make emergency landings when necessary. Finally, the taking of Iwo Jima would deliver another blow to Nippon's psyche. Iwo was part of the homeland and a mere 760 miles from Tokyo. At the same time, the iconic photo of the Marines raising the American flag on Mount Suribachi would prove to be a great morale booster for Americans.

Beginning on December 8, Iwo Jima would be bombed for seventy-two consecutive days, setting the record as the most heavily bombed target and the longest sustained bombardment in the Pacific War. Prior to the Marine Invasion of Iwo Jima, one of the pilots making regular bombing runs on the island told one of the Marine flamethrowers, "All you guys will have to do is clean up. No one could survive what we've been dropping."[5] What the pilots could not see was that General Tadamichi Kuribaya had ordered his troops to build an intricate system of caves to protect themselves from both bombs and Marines. As a result, the casualties at Iwo for both the Japanese and the Americans were significant. An estimated 20,000 to 22,000 Japanese were killed. Only about 1,100 were captured. Almost 7,000 Americans were killed, including 197 Navy medical personnel. The wounded totaled more than 19,000, including 541 Navy medical personnel.[6] Though the roles were reversed, similar to the Battle of Wake Island, the invading force suffered more casualties than the defenders.

April of 1945 proved to be a momentous month in the course of the war. President Franklin Roosevelt passed away on April 12 and was succeeded by Vice President Harry S. Truman. The president's death was mourned by Americans all over the world, military and civilian alike. In yet another of the war's ironies, Roosevelt had not lived to see the end of the war that he had tried so hard to avoid and, eventually, had fought so hard to win. On April 30, Adolph Hitler's mistress Eva Braun swallowed a cyanide pill, while he put a gun to his head and shot himself. Both were cremated in the garden of the bunker where he hid from the advancing Allies. A week later, on May 7, the Germans unconditionally surrendered to the Allies.

News of Germany's surrender meant little to the POWs in the Pacific. They were still living a day at a time, trying to survive the Japanese brutalities. At the camp in Kiangwan, the Japs were preparing to move the POWs to Japan. Moving to Japan, in essence, meant moving further into the belly of the war-mongering Nipponese beast. Especially troublesome was that it was now a foregone conclusion that Japan was being beaten everywhere in the Pacific, making the Japs even harder to deal with. On May 9, without any notice, John was thrown into an overcrowded boxcar and, along with the POWs remaining in the camp, was transported more than seven hundred miles to Fengtai, near Beijing, China. As had been the case on the *Nitta Maru*, the men were packed together so tightly that no one could lie down. Once again, the conditions were abhorrent. The only good news about leaving China was that the "Beast of the East" had been left behind.

The train arrived at Fengtai on May 15, 1945. After almost a week in the boxcar, some of the POWs were near delirium. Unfortunately, the conditions at the temporary camp in Fengtai would offer little reprieve. The men were confined in large warehouses with dirt and brick floors and no sleeping accommodations. To add to their misery, they were getting less to eat. After a month in Fengtai, they were once again herded into boxcars and taken to Pusan, Korea, where they had to march several miles in the mud to the harbor. John described the condition of the men. "Some of the guys were bordering on insanity. Guys just lost it, walking around talking to themselves. They had to keep us in Pusan a couple of days to allow the men to recuperate a little bit." The conditions over the previous month had taken a toll. Without medical supplies, John was doing what he could to help the men. He recalls how he spent his twenty-fifth birthday. "When we arrived at the Port of Pusan, we were in an open area. Some distance across from us, on the other side of a muddy field, there was a faucet which was the only source of fresh, drinkable water. I remember going back and forth most of the day. I walked a couple of hundred yards in ankle-deep mud hauling water back and forth for the guys who were too weak to make the trek by themselves." John looked at me with his now-familiar smile and said to me, "Hell of a way to celebrate a birthday, huh?"

From Pusan, there was another boat ride across the Sea of Japan in submarine-infested waters. A ferry took the men to Japan's northernmost Island of Hokkaido. Again, they were all packed in like sardines. The men disembarked on July 5 in the port city of Hakodate and were taken by rail to an area called Nishi-Ashibetsu. It was the first time John recalled hearing American bombs. "You could tell our guys were close. As soon as we got on the train, we could hear the bombs falling. We were all smiling and celebrating, and pretty soon, the guards came over, hit a few guys with their sticks, and closed all the curtains to the train. They told us we that we didn't need to see that. It was funny because we couldn't see the bombs dropping, but we could sure hear them." When the train stopped, the POWs were split up into different camps. John ended up at what was referred to as Hakadote POW Camp #4. He was interned with a group of men from Wake, Australians, British, and some of the North China Marines. He was assigned to a barracks with officers and a couple of other Corpsmen. Dr. Thyson was in charge, as he was the highest-ranking officer.

Other than individual and sporadic acts of kindness, John had not experienced the Japanese guards collectively doing anything to help the POWs. John explained the situation as the POWs were being marched to camp #4. "When we started marching, there were Japanese women on either side of us trying to hit us with sticks and stones. I was with the sick and wounded, so we couldn't go very fast, and pretty soon the stones started flying, and the ladies would come as close as possible so they could swat us. I figured that they knew that they were losing the war, so they were really upset with us. It was almost all women, but there were some children and some older men. All the young guys were dead or fighting the war. The guards walked alongside of us and stayed between us and the civilians who wanted to harm us."

Drs. Foley and Kahn had been sent to other camps. John learned later that, while in Japan, "Doctor Foley had been water-tortured over something he had said to one of the Japs." Though the "Beast" was no longer with them, the Japs' treatment of the POWs had not changed much. John continued to care for the wounded and sick. Most of the men worked in a nearby coal mine. In addition to cuts, bruises, broken bones, and sickness, the men in the mines now had to worry about cave-ins that might bury them alive. The rats ran freely throughout the camp. Overall, the conditions were worse than the camps in China. For example, the latrines were not emptied regularly and overflowed with waste, creating an awful stench. Worst of all was that the men were no longer allowed to send letters home to their loved ones.

The POWs had no idea how much longer they'd have to fight for survival but, thankfully, the war was coming to an end. In the Philippines, the battle that had started in October of 1944 came to an end on June 19, 1945. Once again, the casualties were staggering. In all, the liberation of the Philippines cost the U.S. Army 13,884 killed and 48,541 wounded. Japanese military and civilian dead numbered more than 250,000, and 114,010 others still remained to surrender at the end of the war on August 15, 1945.[7] More than 100,000 Filipino civilians died from American bombings and Japanese atrocities in Manila alone. Among the Jap atrocities in Manila were setting hospitals on fire after strapping patients to their beds, raping women of all ages before killing them, and gouging out babies' eyes and smearing them on walls.[8] In total, about 900,000 Filipinos would lose their lives during the war.[9]

Closer to Japan, the Americans landed on Okinawa on April 1, 1945 and fought the Japs till June 22. It would mark the last major battle of the Pacific War. Americans paid a heavy toll, with 12,510 killed or missing in action and 36,613 wounded. The Japanese suffered 107,539 confirmed dead, but there were thousands more that were not counted who were sealed in caves throughout the island.[10] The commanders on both sides of the battle perished at Okinawa. American commander General Simon Bolivar Buckner was killed by a shell, and Japanese

General Misomu Ushijima committed ritual suicide along with nine of his staff in their headquarters cave on the last day of the battle.[11]

July brought more horror with the sinking of the *Indianapolis.* Named in honor of the capital city of Indiana, the heavy cruiser had been hit by a Japanese bomb near Okinawa in March 1945. The plane that dropped the bomb then crashed into the ship. The ship was damaged but made its way back to Mare Island in California for repairs. When it was ready to sail again, the *Indianapolis* was assigned with a top-secret mission. At Hunters Point in San Francisco, under the command of Captain Charles B. McVay, the ship picked up the components of the atomic bomb that was to be dropped on Hiroshima. The crew was not aware that they were transporting the bomb, known as "Little Boy." The bomb would be dropped by the *Enola Gay,* piloted by Colonel Paul W. Tibbetts. The *Indianapolis* delivered the bomb to Tinian Island on July 26. She then sailed to Guam, before receiving new orders to head to Leyte in the Philippines without an escort. On July 30, she was hit by multiple torpedoes from a Jap submarine commanded by Lieutenant Commander Mochitsura Hashimoto. Approximately 300 men went down with the ship; 900 more leapt into the ocean, some badly burned. Of the 1,197 men on the ship, some died of their injuries, others drowned, and hundreds were killed by sharks. Only 317 survived, making it the worst tragedy at sea in our Navy's history. Living with the tragedy for years became too much for Captain McVay, who took his own life in 1968.[12]

At the end of July, in Potsdam, Germany, President Truman, British Prime Minister Clement Attlee (who had replaced Winston Churchill), and Russian leader Stalin, met to discuss peace settlements and called on Japan to surrender unconditionally. The Russians did not take part in the declaration since they were not yet at war with Japan.[13] The Russians had lost millions in their war against Germany and had not been anxious to join the war against Japan. However, the Russians would declare war on Japan on August 8, two days after the atomic bomb was dropped on Hiroshima and one day before the second atomic bomb was dropped on Nagasaki, Japan.

After Okinawa, the Americans were planning the invasion of Japan, to begin in November of 1945 on the island of Kyushu. The island is the southernmost and third largest of the four main islands of Japan. The plans called for taking Kyushu first, before moving on to Honshu and Tokyo in 1946. The operation would be larger than Normandy, with MacArthur commanding the ground troops and Nimitz leading the naval forces. President Truman had been advised that 25,000 of our men would die in the first 30 days, and there was also concern that the Japanese would slaughter POWs in the event of an invasion.[14]

The concerns about POWs proved to be very real. In August of 1944, the Japanese government had issued a directive to commanders of POW camps that came to be known as the "Kill-All Order." The order instructed the POW camp commanders to take "extreme measures" when the military situation became "urgent. . . . Whether they are destroyed individually or in groups, or however it is done, with mass bombing, poison smoke, poisons drowning, decapitation, or what, dispose of the prisoners as the situation dictates. . . . It is the aim not to allow the escape of a single one, to annihilate them all, and not leave any traces.[15]

The "Kill-All Order" appeared to be used in December of 1944 on the Philippine Island of Palawan. Under attack from the Americans and in an attempt to keep POWs from falling into enemy hands, the Japs slaughtered 150 men. The men were placed into an air raid shelter, doused with gasoline, and set on fire. Some men managed to escape the shelter and were gunned down or finished off by bayonets. Miraculously, a few escaped to tell the story of the massacre.[16] One of the men who escaped the atrocity was Private Eugene Nielsen, who shared his story with Army intelligence. "The trench smelled very strongly of gas. There was an explosion, and flames shot throughout the place. Some of the guys were moaning. I realized this was it—either I had to break for it or I die. Luckily, I was in the trench that was closest to the fence. So, I jumped and dove through the barbed wire. I fell over the cliff and somehow grabbed on to a small tree, which broke my fall and kept me from getting injured. There were Japanese soldiers posted down on the beach. I buried myself in a pile of garbage and coconut husks. I kept working my way under till I got fairly well covered up. Lying there, I could feel the little worms and bugs eating holes in the rubbish, and then I felt them eating holes into the skin of my back."[17] Nielsen eventually got to the water and swam across Puerto Princesa Bay to his escape.

At Camp #4 in Hakodate, the men continued to work in the mines. By August 15, things began to change. According to John, "Things began to improve. The guards started to let us get away with things like not bowing to them. Then the food rations improved. More rice and a couple of fish heads with each meal. Nothing special, but you could tell something was going on." Though the Japs had formally surrendered on the 15th (August 14th in Washington D.C.), they would not let the prisoners know till August 18. The combination of the two atomic bombs dropped on Hiroshima and Nagasaki, causing more than 100,000 deaths, and Russia declaring war on Japan had finally convinced the Japs to accept an unconditional surrender.

Not widely known or recognized is that the last Battle of World War II was fought by Japan and the Soviet Union in a place called Hutou. Hutou means "tiger head." This desolate town in China stands beside the Ussuri River on the eastern frontier of Manchuria.[18] It is fitting that the fighting would end in China, as some scholars have argued, the beginning of World War II started with the Japanese occupation of Manchuria in 1931—the year that John moved to the U.S.

At noon on August 15, Emperor Hirohito had arranged for a national radio broadcast to inform his people that, "After pondering deeply the general trends of the world and actual conditions obtaining in our Empire today, we have decided to effect a settlement of the present situation by resorting to an extraordinary measure. We have ordered our government to communicate to the governments of the United States, Great Britain, China, and the Soviet Union that our empire accepts the provisions of their joint declaration."[19] Specifically, the emperor was referring to the Potsdam Declaration requiring a total, unconditional surrender. At the last minute, President Truman consented to one condition: Allowing the emperor to retain his sovereignty. That was largely window dressing, since Hirohito would submit to the authority of the Supreme Allied Commander in Japan.[20]

Hirohito's lame message to his people would be repeated at Camp #4. John explained it: "A couple of days after the food rations improved, the guards told us we didn't have to work anymore. By that time, we knew something was going on, but we did not want to get our hopes up. The last day, by midmorning they called us together and said that, 'due to the atomic bomb, we surrender.' They dropped their guns and walked out of camp. Even the Jap officers were gone. We were stunned. We had no idea what an atomic bomb was, and we didn't care. The Japs disappeared, and the camp was ours." There had been no contrition on the part of the Japs, just as there had been no repentance on Hirohito's part. There was no humility, no asking for forgiveness, and no offer to help the prisoners. They simply left the POWs to fend for themselves.

The Japs had been thoroughly beaten and their self-proclaimed "Great Japanese Empire" decimated, but one had to wonder if they had learned anything from their reckless inhumanity. That spurious claim of greatness had resulted in the loss of millions of lives and unspeakable suffering. Several times since the end of World War II, Japanese government officials made statements that they regarded as an apology for their conduct in the war, but other nations did not accept it as a full, direct, and unambiguous apology. It was not till 1991, on the fiftieth anniversary of the Japanese attack on Pearl Harbor, that Japanese Prime Minister Kiichi Miyazawa apologized to the United States by expressing his "deep remorse . . . that we inflicted an unbearable blow on the people of America and the Asian countries."[21]

Regardless, the heinous cruelty of the Japs was over. More importantly, the Japs' defeat marked the beginning of a new chapter for the POWs, who had suffered so long. John, like many others, had put their youth on hold. For John it had been at the age of twenty-one. Now twenty-five, he could renew his dreams and aspirations, rather than focusing on surviving one more day.

Though the war was over for John, it would be almost two more months (fifty-six days) before he'd see his beloved Alice again and meet his son John Wayne for the first time. John Wayne was now almost four-and-a-half years old. John had survived sixteen days of bombings and the Japanese landing force at Wake, including his close encounter with a Jap fighter plane on December 21, 1941. He had survived the harrowing trip from Wake to China on the *Nitta Maru* and 1,334 days of captivity on Wake, China, and Japan. He had also survived a vicious beating by the Japs because of his sense of duty to do his job. Just as John had kept "doing his job" throughout the war, so, too, had his Guardian Angel Anna. John was grateful to be alive on August 18, 1945.

★　★　★

CHAPTER 16

"ARE YOU MY DADDY?"

August 19, 1945 to October 12, 1945

Four hundred and forty-two military personnel had been taken prisoner after the battle at Wake. Twenty-eight were not going home. Nineteen Marines and nine Navy personnel had died in the various POW camps.[1] Throughout the Pacific, 27,465 U.S. military personnel were captured by Japan, of whom 11,107 died in captivity—more than a 40 percent death rate. A large number of those who died were from the infamous "Death March of Bataan." The death rate of U.S. prisoners interned by Japan stood in stark contrast to the number of Americans that died in German POW camps. A total of 93,941 American military personnel were interned in German camps, and 1,121 died, representing a 1.1 percent death rate.[2] As ruthless as the Germans had been to Jews, Poles, Russians, and others, they had not shown the same level of barbarity to American POWs.

In addition to "The Beast" Ishihara's death in prison, the Japanese soldiers who had beheaded the five servicemen from Wake on the *Nitta Maru*, received life sentences for their crimes. Lieutenant Toshio Saito, who had ordered the murders, committed suicide before the end of his trial.[3] Rear Admiral Sakaibara, who had ordered the massacre of the ninety-eight civilians on Wake in 1943, was sentenced to death for the killings and for other war crimes. He was hanged on the eighteenth of June 1947. Several Japanese officers in American custody after the Japanese surrendered Wake had committed suicide over the incident, leaving written statements that incriminated Sakaibara.[4] At various tribunals after the war, more than five thousand Japanese were found guilty of war crimes, and more than nine hundred were executed.[5] Among those executed were Prime Minister Hideki Tojo and Koki Hirota, Prime Minister during Japan's most vicious atrocities against the Chinese; General Iwane Matsui, who commanded troops involved in the Rape of Nanking; and General Akira Muto, commander of the troops in the Philippines. None showed any sign of repentance. They dropped in the gallows to their deaths shouting *"Banzai"* (the traditional Japanese battle cry).[6] It was grim evidence that these key Japanese leaders had learned nothing from their reckless actions.

Estimates of the number of deaths during World War II are just that: estimates. The National World War II Museum in New Orleans estimates that approximately sixty million people (including military and civilians) died during the war.[7] Some Chinese scholars have claimed the number of Chinese deaths alone was as high as fifty million.[8] If those numbers are accurate, it would push the overall number of deaths during the war to ninety million. A couple of things are certain: China and Russia each lost more than twenty million people. Poland lost more than 5.5 million military and civilians. The primary aggressors, Japan and Germany, lost between 2.6 and 3.1 million and 6.6 and 8.8 million, respectively. The United Kingdom lost 450,700 souls, and the number of dead Americans was 418,000.[9] By any measure, the numbers were mind-boggling.

There had been no wild celebration by the POWs on the first day of their liberation at Camp #4. There was no cheering, laughter, or merriment of any kind that John recalls. At a time when most would expect unbridled joy, John's reaction and that of his fellow servicemen was one of stunned disbelief and then reflection about the realization that they were free again. The hell of being POWs for so long was finally over. John recalls, "No one really said much. I was thinking, *What happens next?* There had been no contact with our troops. The next day we started wandering outside of the camp. We didn't know when the Americans would come to get us." He and Ernest C. Vaale ventured outside the camp and into the nearby village. John did not know the name of the village, but it was most likely Nishi Ashibetsu. "We walked out the gates of the camp and into the village. We walked around for about an hour and ran into civilians. They were staring at us, but we had no contact with them. We were not armed. The guns the Japs had left behind had been gathered and stored in one of the barracks. The civilians, who were mostly women and children, made no attempt to harm us like they had done when we got off the train. They were probably just as stunned as we were."

Over the following days after their liberation, the various camps in Japan were close enough to each other that some men traveled between camps. In early September, Colonel Ashurst, who was the highest-ranking commander, assigned other officers to take command at the various camps in Hakodate till rescue arrived. Major Devereux was assigned to take command of Camp #3. Dr. Thyson was in charge of Camp 4. On August 21, American B-29 planes dropped the first shipment of supplies to the POWs. John said, "It was great to see the planes overhead. The supplies included radios that allowed us to communicate with the planes, canned food, shoes, candy bars, and other things. I don't know who opened the can of peaches that I had, but it was good. I think it was the first fruit

I had eaten since Wake." Unfortunately, the supply drops had a tragic downside for some of the POWs. John explained, "It did not happen at our camp, but I heard a few days later, that some of our guys had been killed by the supply containers. They were so eager to get to the food that they got crushed by the containers parachuting down on top of them. Those planes were coming in pretty low, and the parachutes were coming down fast. It was unbelievable that guys survived the war and the camps and then got killed by our own guys trying to help."

Two other Wake survivors at other camps shared their stories about the supply drops. Sergeant Norman Kaz-Fritzshall, USMC, said, "I was too sick to work for quite a while. I had malaria, beriberi, and dysentery and was so sick I couldn't walk. When the American planes came over dropping food, I was too sick to go out and get any of it. I remember that one of the torpedoes they dropped, filled with food, hit close to the men, skidded, spun around, and killed three of the POWs."[10] In another camp (apparently in the Japanese section), Gene A. Fleener, USMC shared his experience. "B-29 bombers dropped food for us and kept us well supplied. Then, later on, torpedo planes began bringing in supplies. They'd cut a torpedo in half and stuffed it with food and things and then dropped it. One of them fell right on a little shack where we got our lamps. There were 11 Japs inside, and the "food bomb" killed nine of them."[11]

On September 4, 1945, more than two thousand miles away on Wake Island, the Japanese were surrendering to an American Marine unit commanded by Brigadier General Lawton H. Sanderson. General Sanderson refused to acknowledge a Japanese offer to shake hands. The General then warned Sakaibara about Japanese sabotage. The admiral assured him not to be concerned as almost 1,900 of his men had already died from American bombings and disease. They were too weak from malnutrition to mount any resistance. At the time, the Americans were not aware that Sakaibara had ordered the slaughter of ninety-eight of their countrymen.[12]

There was a brief ceremony to once again raise "Old Glory." When the Japs had taken down the flag on Wake on December 23, 1941, it had been John's lowest point in the war. Though he would not witness it directly, he could now take comfort in the fact that our flag was, once again, flying over Wake.

General Sanderson officially gave control of Wake to Navy Commander William Masek. Masek summed up the emotions of Americans at the atoll and back home when he said, "I accept this island proudly. Because this is Wake Island. Not just any island. It was here the Marines showed us how."[13]

Rear Admiral Sakaibara signing the surrender of Wake. General Sanderson is seated in the middle. (National Archives)

In Hakodate, John and his fellow ex-POWs did their best to eat as much as they could hold. Some ate too much or consumed foods that would make them sick. Most of the men, including John, were regaining some of their weight. However, for many, it would take a long time to return

American Flag being raised at Wake after the Japanese surrender. September 4, 1945. (National Archives)

to normal eating habits, and some would face challenges from which they would not recover.

In a medical report prepared shortly after the war, a doctor who examined many of the POWs from Japan wrote this: "After the intake of a high-caloric diet when they were first liberated, glossitis (inflammation of the tongue), stomatitis (inflammation of the mucous membrane of the mouth), and edema (an accumulation of an excessive amount of watery fluid in cells) reappeared or became more pronounced. The losses of weight ranged from 20 to 110 pounds. There was a noted remarkable ability to regain weight without corresponding improvement in the fundamental nutritional state. Many patients had protuberant abdomens, commonly called "rice bellies," while their shoulder girdles and extremities showed very marked wasting. Almost without exception, the patients had suffered from attacks of diarrhea at some time during their imprisonment. It is necessary to distinguish between diarrhea that most individuals have from time to time in normal life and true dysentery, consisting of prolonged periods of watery or bloody stools. Of the first 1,500 prisoners examined, 1,359 had one or more attacks of dysentery.[14]

On the same report a physician who had himself been a Japanese prisoner of war wrote: "It is my opinion that the average physician in a VA (Veterans Affairs) hospital has no conception what three-and-one-half years of starvation can do to a man and has no idea how to evaluate the disability. This statement is not intended as a criticism of VA physicians, as it also holds true for the average physician out of the VA."[15] Another physician also interned by the Japs provided this perspective: "Since my return to the United States and since the war, I have had occasion to observe many men who were confined in the Japanese prison camps. These observations were oftentimes casual conversations and oftentimes professional in nature. It is my opinion that no one who suffered the prolonged starvation, degradation, and physical suffering experienced by this group has been able to make a full recovery, either physically or emotionally. It is also my opinion that no one who has not experienced such a situation has a concept of the problem presented by these men."[16] The list of physical and mental issues among the POWs was long, and many would live with the consequences for the rest of their lives.

A few days passed that John described as a time when "we did more thinking than talking. Everyone was anxious to get home, and no one knew what to expect. It had been a long time, and who knows what had changed." On September 12, the American military finally began arriving at the camps, and on the 15th John began his long-awaited trip home. The men were told to march a few miles to the train station, where they would be taken to Chitosi airfield. The sick and wounded and the Corpsmen taking care of them would go first, with the more able-bodied men to follow. From Chitosi, they would be flown to Tokyo, where the USS Rescue hospital ship would conduct physicals and triage the men as appropriate. Some would be admitted to the ship and be taken home; others would be assigned to other ships or planes to ferry them home.

John explained what happened to him as he arrived at the train station in Hakodate. "As we were getting close to the train, I doubled over in pain. I couldn't even walk any more. Dr. Thyson, who was with us, came over and talked to me for a while trying to figure out what was going on. He poked around a while; then he told me I had appendicitis. The guys took me into the train and laid me down; when we got to the airfield, they rushed me to the plane, where they put me in an area where I could lie flat. On the way to Tokyo, the pilots called ahead and had an ambulance waiting for me that rushed me to a dispensary where an American doctor did an appendectomy. I was lucky, you know, that the doctor had the right surgical tools. Not like the appendectomies I had assisted on the guys in the prison camps. They kept me in the dispensary for a day, and the next day they put me in an ambulance again to take me to the *USS Rescue* hospital ship that was docked in Yokohama, not far from Tokyo. When they were taking me up the gangplank of the ship, the first guy I ran into was Dr. Foley, who I hadn't seen since we got to Japan. He made the trip with me to the U.S."

The *USS Rescue* had been built as a passenger liner in Newport Beach News, Virginia, and launched in 1932 as the *SS Saint John*. The Navy acquired it in 1941 and converted it first into a submarine tender, renaming it the *USS Antaeus (AS-21)*. As a tender, it resupplied the subs with food, water, spare parts, and other provisions necessary to keep the submarines at sea. The vessel was converted again in January of 1945 to a hospital ship and renamed again to the *USS Rescue (AH-19)*. As a hospital ship, it had a crew of more than four hundred and a patient capacity of almost eight hundred. It served during the battle of Okinawa before being tasked to ferry POWs from Japan to the U.S. and being decommissioned in April of 1946.[17]

John had survived again, but it would take him much longer to get home than most of the guys from Wake. The *USS Rescue* spent a few more days triaging POWs and then started the long sail to the U.S. It made stops at Guam and Pearl Harbor before arriving in Oakland on October 8, 1945. "When I got on the ship, they put me to bed right away. At that time, they wanted to keep you in bed for a week." He described his first memory, after settling in. "This lady nurse came by and told me that the next day she was going to give me a bath, but I said to myself, *Oh, no*. So that night I got out of bed and took a shower by myself. I was pretty grimy, you know. I hadn't had a real bath in years, and in the Japanese camps the facilities were worse than in China, so all we did was to clean ourselves with a wet cloth every once in a while." As is still the case today, John's modesty was without question.

John continued his story about the trip home. "I was a patient on the ship for about six or seven days; then they put me to work again as a Corpsman. At first it was light duty, like getting bandages ready for the doctors or nurses." Eventually, he did whatever was necessary to take care of the wounded. "There were wounded guys on the ship who needed a lot of care, but mostly it was taking care of lots of guys with malaria and dysentery." When he was put to work, it marked the first time since joining the Navy that he had served as a Corpsman on a ship. All his other times on ships had been as a passenger and not on official Corpsman duty.

The *USS Rescue* hospital ship that brought John home from Japan. (Navsource.Org)

I asked John if there was much talk about the war on the ship, and he responded, "No. There was no talk at all about it. We were done with the war. We talked about food. I remember guys eating a lot of bread. Some would eat a whole loaf. The captain of the ship had to order the cooks to make more bread or whatever the guys wanted to eat. I was eating as much as I could, but I knew I had to be careful not to overdo it. I remember a funny moment when we had a table full of food and the ship was rocking back and forth in some weather; a few of us were scrambling to make sure none of the food hit the ground. We didn't want to waste any. During the trip, I didn't do much other than work, eat, and sleep. I was putting on weight and feeling much more fit. I even started helping to move the bedridden guys. Toward the end, in the camp, I'd been losing my strength. I would lose my breath with any kind of exertion, so it was good to be getting my strength back."

John had not been able to communicate with Alice. The note he had written in January of 1945 was the last contact she had from him. She knew the war was over and that POWs were headed home, but she did not how or when John would arrive. There was also the possibility that John had not survived. She simply did not know. The ship arrived on Monday, October 8, 1945, but John did not contact Alice for another four days. As the *USS Rescue* had been getting closer to home, John got more anxious. "The ship docked in Oakland. I could see the shore, and I was getting so anxious that I thought about diving off. They kept us there for two more days for processing. It seemed like a lifetime. That was the hardest time after being liberated. You know you are that close but can't do anything about it." John finally got off the ship and had to check in at the Naval hospital because he was technically still a patient. After a day there, still not having been in contact with Alice, he got a new uniform and some money, and on Friday, October 12, 1945, after not seeing each other since Christmas of 1940, he headed for her house.

John explained the long-awaited meeting. "I got into a cab and asked the guy to take me to Benicia. The cabbie and I got to talking, and I told him I had been a prisoner and gone for almost four years. He asked me what was in Benicia, and I told him, 'My wife. My wife and son.' The cabbie then asked me if I had called ahead of time, and I told him 'No.' Then he said to me, 'You'd better stop and call. Women have changed, you know. A lot of them have gotten remarried or have some other guy. You don't want to just barge in. You don't know what you may walk into.'" John explained that, "He had me worried there for a minute." According to John, he would later learn that, indeed, some of the married woman had remarried, believing their husbands had died at Wake. He continued his back-and-forth with the cabbie. "The cabbie was really insistent that I call Alice before showing up at the house, but I told him to keep driving." In an interview he would do seventy-three years later for *Aging Tree*, the newsletter for the Senior Living Company where he lives, John said, "Some of the ladies got remarried, because we were all supposed to be dead." He added, "I didn't worry about Alice remarrying because," he joked, "I'd left her barefoot and pregnant."

John continued to tell me about going home. "When I got there, I knocked on the door, and this young lady answered. At first, I thought it was Alice. She hugged me and said, 'Welcome. I'll call Alice.' When she said that, I realized it was Julia, her younger sister, who was now almost sixteen and looked a lot like Alice when I had last seen her. She had long dark hair just like Alice. So for a minute there, I was confused. As Julia went to call Alice, a little boy came up to me and asked, 'Are you my daddy?' I told him, 'Yes.' That was the first time I met my son, John Wayne."

Alice was at work on Mare Island and had carpooled to work so she had to wait till her shift ended before she could get home. When she walked into the house, John and Alice hugged, kissed, and told each other, "I love you." John told me, "It felt like I'd never left."

★　★　★

CHAPTER 17

"I HATE TO WAKE UP, BECAUSE YOU ARE NOT THERE."

October 13, 1945 to December 2, 1947

After the brief greeting with his son, John began the process of trying to get to know him and trying to reconnect with Alice and the rest of the family. John Wayne recalls meeting his dad like this. "I heard a knock on the door, and I saw a man in a uniform standing there, and, after asking if he was my daddy, I showed him around the house. I showed him where Mom kept her perfume and her makeup and just walked around showing him stuff." Like a typical four-year-old, after showing his dad around, John Wayne ran off to play. I asked John how John Wayne figured out who he was, and John explained. "There were a couple of pictures of me around the house, so maybe he put things together. He might also have had some premonition that I was coming home." In any event, for the first time in their respective lives, the John Ignacious Unger family was now together.

John Wayne explained what life was like the first few weeks with his father; it wasn't all good. Throughout his short life, he had had no father figure. That said, he got plenty of attention and love from his mom, Granny Julia, Alice's sister Julia, and her brothers Richard and Leon. John Wayne said, "Even the neighbors pitched in to take care of me." He was the center of attention in the family. By his own admission, he confessed, "I was spoiled rotten." On the second day that John was home, John Wayne was throwing a tantrum in the garage. As he explained it, "Mom was taking Granny home in Leon's car, and I wanted to go with her. I always did, but today they wouldn't let me. Dad proceeded to pick me up by the back of my pants and gave me a spanking that I've never forgotten. He left no doubt in my mind that there was a new sheriff in town." Though John had put on weight, John Wayne explained that, "Dad was all skin and bones, especially after the years as a POW and then, the appendectomy. Granny was doing all she could to fatten him up." John was eating as much as he could but also feeling a bit guilty. "At the time I got back there was still some rationing going on in the country. For example, car tires, sugar, and good steaks were not always available. When they were, you could only get a limited amount. Well, Granny bought steaks when she could, and she made them for me. While the rest of the family was eating something less appetizing, I was fattening up on steaks. But gee, I hadn't eaten one in over four years."

For the next couple of weeks, John shuttled back and forth from the naval hospital on Mare Island to their rented home in Benicia. At the hospital, he was undergoing a series of physical and psychological tests, to determine his overall health. He had exams on almost a daily basis. Some of the men were being tested, to determine their fitness to continue to serve in the armed forces, while others were being assessed, simply to be able to successfully function in society. Because the armed services now needed significantly fewer men, many who wanted to stay in the military were not allowed to do so. John explained what happened to guys who did not pass their physicals. "When someone was determined to be unfit and still needed care, the military would try to send them to a hospital or mental facility as close to their home as possible."

John with Johnny and Alice in 1945 (From the personal collection of John I. Unger)

After World War II, General Omar N. Bradley, who had served in Europe, took over leadership of the Veterans Affairs (VA) Administration. At the time, the VA was operating 97 hospitals with a bed capacity of 82,241. Hospital construction was already in process, and capacity would increase by another 13,594 beds. But World War II had mobilized more than 15 million men and women. Hundreds of thousands had been injured, and over the years, millions would require medical treatments. Soon after the war, the existing hospitals were filled to capacity. There were waiting lists for admission at practically all hospitals.[1] Untold numbers of service personnel, including John, were declared fit and not require immediate medical assistance. However, they would eventually need help to deal with either physical or mental conditions resulting from their years of service during the war.

After all his medical tests and a psychological evaluation, John was pronounced fit but given three months of convalescence leave. I asked him what was involved with the psychological evaluation, and he said, "I sat down and talked to a doctor for a while, he asked me a bunch of questions, and that was it. Later, after three months, a panel of doctors evaluated me further, and they told me I had some stress from the war but also said I was okay, so I moved on." John told me several times that Alice never asked him about the war. He added, "Alice did not feel sorry for me, and that helped. When friends or relatives started asking me questions about the war, she would always find a way to change the subject right then and there. Eventually, people stopped trying to raise the topic."

However, Alice knew early on after John's return that he was not the same person she had known before the war. She knew John was fighting demons in his mind that would haunt him for decades. Carol Fisher, the daughter of George H. Lewis, a Wake survivor who died in a car accident in 1947, videotaped an interview with John and Alice around 2008. Carol, who was in her mother's womb at the time of the accident, was the only one to survive the accident. Her request to talk to John and Alice was to learn what she could about the father she'd never met. At one point in the interview, the topic changed to John and what it was like after the war. Alice told Carol, "The first three months after John came home, he'd drink a pint of whiskey every night to get himself to sleep." John shared that, "The nightmares didn't start till I was home for a couple of weeks but then lasted for months after that. And it wasn't just bad dreams. I would scream and thrash around and scare Alice and Granny and anyone else in the house. Alice always calmed me down. The nightmares eventually stopped as a nightly occurrence, but I had them on and off for years."

In addition to the nightmares, he'd go through periods when he did not want to be around people. He recalled one incident shortly after he returned. "I remember being in the car with Alice, driving to a party with some of her friends, and I turned the car around and went back home. I did not want to be with a bunch of people in a crowded place. She didn't like it, but she always supported me."

John recognized he had problems. In August of 1946, when it was time for him to leave the Navy after his original six-year commitment, he decided to stay in the service. He explained his logic

Alice and John, shortly after his return from Japan. (From the personal collection of John I. Unger)

for the decision. "I got three hundred dollars to recommit for another six years, which was pretty good money, but my other reason for reenlisting was that, as a Corpsman, if there was anything wrong, I would be around a lot of doctors." I asked him if he had nightmares on Wake or as a POW, and he said, "No. It was crazy. I never had nightmares at all during the war, but when I got home, I guess I didn't want to be back in the war, so that's when they started. I was afraid that it would all happen again." Another byproduct of his years as a POW was getting used to sleeping on a bed. For a time, he was more comfortable sleeping on the floor; that was more familiar to him.

Going back to the Civil War, doctors have documented mental disorders in soldiers and made attempts to treat them. Over the years, the terms used to describe a serviceperson suffering mental anguish from experiences in battle included an "irritable heart," "battle shock," and "shell shock." In 1945, toward the end of World War II, the terminology changed to "combat exhaustion." Seven years later, the American Psychiatric Association included "gross stress reaction" in its *Diagnostic and Statistical Manual of Mental Disorders*, which it later dropped. It was not till 1980, several years after the Vietnam war that the Association added "Posttraumatic Stress Disorder" (PTSD) to the manual.[2] Today PTSD is commonly recognized and treated. In 1945, the stresses caused by war and captivity were recognized, but accurate diagnosis and treatment were limited. John learned to control his psychological challenges like many other participants in the war—by not talking about it. However, controlling it did not mean curing it. It would not be till almost the turn of the century that his nightmares would stop.

On a lighter note, adjusting to his new life also meant catching up with a society that had changed in his four years away. John explained. "Things that used to cost a dime now cost a dollar. For example, milk shakes, which I really craved when I got back, were way more expensive." Regarding Granny's attempts to fatten him up, he recalls Alice's little brother Richard, who was about seven at the time, complaining to her. "Granny, how come he gets steak, and all we get are potatoes?" John had a rapacious appetite that would not abate any time soon.

As John was adjusting, he thought it was time to get more serious about getting reacquainted with Alice. On October 30, 1945, with lots of back-pay in the bank, Alice and John went off to Reno, Nevada, to rekindle the torrid love affair they had started and then put on hold in 1940. Their first time alone in more than four years started with a renewal of their marriage vows at the courthouse in Washoe County, Nevada. This time, instead of a cabbie, two of Alice's friends acted as witnesses and then left the couple to enjoy their second honeymoon. This one lasted a few more days than the first and resulted in Alice's second pregnancy. John had lost their first marriage license at Wake, and he wasn't sure going down to Mexico to get a new one made much sense. Ergo, they simply got married again.

Alice and Johnny (From the personal collection of John I. Unger)

Back home after Reno, John bought a car for the family and eventually purchased the home that Alice and Granny had been renting in Benicia. A couple of years later, they moved to Vallejo, California, where they would live till 2014. One of his first experiences with the car is still fresh in his mind after seventy-two years. "I was planning to wash the car, so I had to get it out of the garage. I started the car and put it in gear. The car had a throttle on the dashboard to control the gas. As I pulled, it came all the way out, and the car took off. There was a muddy ditch in front of our house, and the car went right into it. The wheels were spinning like crazy, and this whole time, the car radio is blaring. The noise must have been terrific, because the whole neighborhood came out. I'm sure people were saying, "Who is that crazy guy?" So anyhow, as I'm getting out, the car takes off again and goes across the street into another ditch that was full of water. They were building a house there, and the hole for the foundation was fairly deep. The car plunged right into that ditch and all you could see was the roof. The rest was under water. As I was getting out, the door hit me on the side, and I had some bruises but I was all right. So, a tow truck came over, and people were watching, trying to figure out how we were going to get the car out of that ditch. I said, "No problem." I took the tow truck's hook, dove under the water, hooked it to the car's bumper, and the guy pulled it out." I asked John what he thought after that incident, and he laughed and said, "There I was. I got through the war in good shape and now I'm limping around and almost drowned. But, heck—I was the talk of the town in Benicia." To save money, John ended up doing most of the repairs on the car. He needed new tires for the car, and because of the rationing, he could not find a garage that would sell him any. One of his

Alice and John 1945 (From the personal collection of John I. Unger)

service buddies asked, "Have you told them you were a prisoner of war?" He hadn't. "I went back to one place and told them I had been a POW and got my tires right away. People treated us ex-POWs pretty nice."

On November 24, 1945, John received a letter that still hangs on his wall today.

Dear John Ignacious Unger,

It gives me special pleasure to welcome you back to your native shores, and to express, on behalf of the people of the United States, the joy we feel at your deliverance from the hands of the enemy. It is a source of profound satisfaction that our efforts to accomplish your return have been successful.

You have fought valiantly and have suffered greatly. As your Commander in Chief, I take pride in your past achievements and express the thanks of a grateful nation for your services in combat and your steadfastness while a prisoner of war.

May God grant you happiness and a successful future.

(signed) *Harry S. Truman*

Shortly after getting home, John received his promotion to Hospital Corpsman Second class. He would have been promoted to that rank in December of 1941, had the war not broken out. Dr. Kahn wrote a letter to the Navy Command in support of John and Ernest Vaale, so they could get their promotions. The promotions were retroactive, but they did not get the pay raise that they would have received back in 1941. Navy Warrant Officer Ball and Petty Officer Schwartz, two men John had known prior to going to Wake, recommended John to be promoted to Chief Hospital Corpsman. John was also told that, because of his time in the Navy and his exemplary record, as soon as he returned to duty, he could make First Class the first day, acting Chief Petty Officer the next, and permanent Chief Hospital Corpsman the following day. He would have to pass some exams, but as usual, John worked hard, studied, and all his promotions came through in early 1946 and with them, a hefty pay raise. John told me, "I was happy with the way the Navy handled my promotions. I was free, and I was back with Alice. I was happy."

Unfortunately, tragedy would strike the Ungers again. After a short pregnancy, Alice lost the baby. With only one kidney since 1941, the pregnancy proved too difficult for her, and the doctor recommended that she end it. She did, and they would not have another biological child. It would have been their second boy, but it was not to be. Once again, their unconditional love for each other would get them through it. John was back on duty, and Alice was recuperating at the Naval Hospital on Mare Island. Though he was close enough to see her, he would write to her in case he worked too long and couldn't get to the hospital in time. In one of the letters he wrote:

Dearest I'm writing this awfully fast, so hope you can read it. But I'll try and see you tonight.

Sweetheart, I hope you are still feeling fine and miss me? I'm lost without you so please get well fast and hurry home. I do miss you greatly. I didn't see Johnny yesterday. He was asleep when I got there. Mom took him out three times yesterday with his bike so he got tired.

Darling wife hurry home. Love and kisses. Your ever-loving husband. John

John wearing his new uniform, including his Chief Hospital Corpsman patch on his left arm after his promotion in 1946. (From the personal collection of John I. Unger)

After Alice returned home, he would write to her from work in case he worked too late to see her.

> *I sure love you honey. It doesn't take long to miss you terrible. You know sweetheart don't ever change, you are a darling just as you are.*
>
> *I think I better go before my sentiments run away with me and if I wrote them you would probably be shocked.*

> *Forever yours.*
> *John*

> *P.S. Miss me adorable one?*

A couple of weeks later he again wrote to Alice fearing he would not get home in time to see her. He ended that letter with the following:

> *Did I ever tell you that I have the most-loveliest, craziest, wonderful wife for a sweetheart in the world? Really, she is you know, you ought to know her. And I love her with all my heart, as always and forever.*

> *Your devoted husband,*
> *John*

After the long separation during the war, even long work hours that kept them apart were a challenge. Over the coming years, John would do everything in his power to minimize the time away from Alice and Johnny. But Navy life would continue to temporarily keep them separated.

In March of 1946, he was assigned to New Orleans where they needed a Chief Hospital Corpsman. He worked in the detail office, where he was responsible for assigning other Corpsmen to wherever the hospital had a need. Alice quit her job, and they all moved east together.

On the way to New Orleans, something interesting occurred that has been shared with every generation of the Unger family. As John was driving his nonair-conditioned car through the bayou with his windows rolled down, a bee flew into the car. John explained what happened next. "The bee went right for my crotch and stung me. I stopped and jumped out of the car screaming and trying to swat it away. Alice didn't know what was going on and started yelling at Johnny to roll up all the windows and lock the doors. She screamed to Johnny, 'He's crazy! He's lost it!'"

John Wayne shared another story about his dad. "When we got to New Orleans, Dad was trying to secure a billet (a civilian's house or other nonmilitary facility, where soldiers are lodged temporarily). We went to the office that handled the billets, and the lady in charge said, 'We do have billets available, but they don't allow children.' Then, I remember my dad saying, 'I'll be back in a few minutes.' The lady asked him where he was going and dad said, 'I'm taking him (John Wayne) to the bayou and I'm going to throw him in.'" John Wayne didn't know how to take that. "I still didn't know this man very well, so I didn't know how to react. About that time, an officer came out who had overheard the conversation, looked at Dad's uniform and the POW medal, and said, 'Wait a minute. He is an ex-prisoner of war—we can make those arrangements.' And that is how we got a place to stay." John Wayne laughed and added, "I still don't know if Dad was joking or serious about throwing me in the bayou. Back in those days, he could be very blunt. Dad was also a disciplinarian to me, like no one else had been before in my life. I was a kind of a wild kid and would do some crazy things. One time, Dad found out I was selling mothballs to other kids telling them it was gum, and I got another spanking. It took me a while to figure out that if I kept doing crazy things, he's going to continue to spank me."

John was stationed in New Orleans till November of 1946. The hospital in New Orleans was unexpectedly closed, and he was assigned to the Naval Hospital in San Diego. Housing in San Diego was at a premium, so Alice and John Wayne returned to their house in Benicia. Granny, sister Julia, and Richard lived in their house any time John was assigned to duty in other cities. In San Diego, the ex-POW factor would help John get his family together again, which was his highest priority. He remembers talking to the officer in charge of housing. "I was told I had to live on base because there were no billets available, and I decided that, if the POW thing had worked in New Orleans, I'd give it a try. All of a sudden, I was asked, 'Do you want to live here or here or here?' It worked but I was getting really tired of telling people I was an ex-POW. But if it got my family together again, it was fine."

John continued to be bounced around from place to place wherever he was needed. In San Diego, he was assigned to personnel, and his duties were largely administrative. Shortly after arriving in San Diego, John asked to be transferred back to Mare Island. As long as they were in California, he wanted Alice and Johnny to be closer to her family. The executive officer (a captain) in San Diego told him they needed him there and didn't want John to transfer. He took John's transfer request letter and tore it up. John was not happy. He told the captain, "Sir, that is not addressed to you. It's addressed to the Chief of Navy Personnel." John typed up another request, and the captain wrote on it "disapproved" but sent the letter anyway. It soon came back "approved." John went to the captain, asked when he could leave, and was told, "You can get the hell out of here right now." John said, "Probably not the smartest thing I did, but sure enough, I was going back to the Naval Hospital at Mare Island."

Back at Mare Island, he took the opportunity to get his high school diploma. Though his education now far exceeded high-school level, he wanted to get it done. He explained, "I went to night school for a couple of weeks at the community college to get ready for the test, took it, passed it, and I had my diploma." October of 1947 brought an unexpected opportunity to serve in American Samoa in the South Pacific. Samoa was Alice's birthplace, so he saw it as an opportunity for her to reconnect with her homeland and for John Wayne to experience living in his mother's native culture. John traveled alone to Pearl Harbor and then to American Samoa. He then arranged for John Wayne and Alice to join him.

John left from San Francisco to Pearl Harbor on the *USS General W. A. Mann (AP-112)* the first week in November 1947. The *Mann* was a troop transport ship with 43 officers and a crew of 464. It could ferry more than 5,000 passengers. Built in 1942, it had served in Europe and Africa during the war and would serve in China and the Korean War.[3] Enroute to Hawaii, John was getting back his sea legs. The first couple of days were rough seas, but he did not get sick. He was hoping not to get sick because, "every time I sat down for a meal, I was starving." He wrote to Alice about an interesting experience at sea.

We just had a little excitement. Someone spotted a Jap mine, so the ship stopped and manned the guns. You should have seen the people run when the loudspeaker hollered to, "Man the guns." They used two big guns and exploded the mine on about the 10th shot. It sure made a big noise when they hit it. So, you see, it will be safe for you two.

Well honey, this is just a few lines to let you know that I'm think-
ing of you and love you very much. Good night darling and Johnny.

Your daddy,
John

The day before arriving at Pearl, he closed his letter with this.

Well goodnight sweetheart. I'll write you from the beach
tomorrow. Sure wish you were there. But I guess I'll just have to
wait for the most beautiful girl in the world.

My love to all of you,
John

As he had before the war, John was writing letters to Alice and Johnny every couple of days. Some days he'd write two letters a day. He stayed on the base almost the entire time he was in Hawaii. He complained about the cost of living but was really enjoying the weather and was able to get lots of rest. His waist size, which had been less than 30 inches after the war, was now a robust 36 inches. He couldn't stop eating.

He bought Johnny a toy dog and mailed it home. He wrote:

I bought Johnny a toy dog, you might have seen it, when you
press his tail, his eyes light up and when it burns out, all you
have to do is put in a new battery.

He went to movies almost every night at the submarine base and tried to keep himself busy to lessen the pain of not being with Alice and Johnny. His favorite time of the day was mail call at 3:00 PM. He was always there early, hoping for letters from Alice. She was writing as often as he was.

There were only two military flights from Hawaii to Samoa each month, and he had not been able to confirm when he'd leave. On November 14, he got his confirmation. An excerpt from a letter that day follows.

Darling wife and son,

I received a priority on a plane to Samoa, so I should be on the plane leaving here on the 25th. The first thing they do is make you fill out a chit with your next of kin. They sure must not trust their planes.

I haven't been ashore yet. I would like to go just once to see what the place looks like. OK by you if I behave myself?

You can get another dress but why not a swim suit instead. Or are you going swimming native style. I hope, I hope.

You can keep writing to me here till the 23rd and after that address the letters to Samoa.

Well baby darling, that's about all for today.

Your loving husband,
John

Hurry to me!

On a letter on November 23, John didn't just pour his heart out as he usually did. On this letter, he also shared some of his demons.

Dearest darling,

Sure hope that by the time you receive this I'll be on my way to Samoa. Sure wished that you were on the plane going out. It would be fun, well for me anyway.

You know honey, when a fellow has nothing to do, he does a lot of thinking.

For instance, I'm sure that I love you more than the way I act when I'm with you. Because now that I am away you feel strange to me.

Yesterday I saw the picture, "God is My Copilot." It had something to do with a Jap prison camp. Anyhow what I think is the matter with me, is that I'm afraid something like that might happen again. And well it kind of hurts. Of course, a lot of difference it would make now. I just love you too much, much too much. Or is that possible.

I hope that made sense to you. I hope you understand better. I talk a lot huh? I adore you darling.

Always yours,
John

John got on the bomber plane for the 2,600-mile trip and arrived in Samoa on Thanksgiving Day 1947.

His job in Samoa was health inspector for part of the island but also to perform basic medical procedures for any civilians in need of healthcare. He was given a jeep to get around during work hours, and he was assigned three nurses to help him. He described them to Alice in a letter.

"The nurses are Samoan; they're cute. One of them is fat, the other one fatter and the third one the fattest."

In a separate letter he told Alice.

"I don't think I've seen any of the three nurses wearing shoes since I got here."

As a health inspector, it was his job to ensure that sanitation was appropriate in his sectors of the island. He worked out of the Naval Station in the district of Pago Pago, and the village of Tutuila. Alice had a relative still living there who was a big chief. Ergo, between his role as an inspector and her family's clout, John carried a big stick. He wrote the following about his newfound power.

The people seem to be afraid of me. I can levy a fine, if they don't keep their places clean. My nurses take care of the sick. I supervise them and I inspect the villages. I even have the power to fire the Chief of Police and the Mayor if they don't do what I tell them.

John sent letters to Alice telling her about Samoa. There were no restaurants, you couldn't buy much except food, there were too many cars on the island, and most of the people didn't know how to drive. He also warned her about not bringing any clothes that required dry cleaning, because no such services existed on the island. On December 2, John wrote to Alice explaining what she should expect on the trip to Samoa.

Now baby darling. I want to tell you what to expect on your plane trip. The plane from Frisco to Pearl Harbor is usually a cushioned seater. You will get into P.H. the following morning. Usually, you have to stay at their hotel for about 2 or 3 days. Very seldom do they leave the same day to Samoa. The hotel is very nice and practically free. One woman said she only had to pay 75 cents for three days.

The plane for Samoa leaves at 8:30. It's a cargo plane, therefore, it has canvas seats along the side but it has 3 cushioned seats in the middle. So, if there aren't too many women, you and Johnny can take one of them. Be sure and put Johnny in one so the sailors won't grab it. They will issue you some blankets. You can make Johnny a bed on the floor and for yourself if it's not too crowded. Otherwise, you have to stay sitting up. You might not be able to sleep anyhow. I know I couldn't. Of course, every time a plane takes off or lands you have to fasten your safety belt in case the plane bumps a little so you won't fall out of your seat and hurt yourself.

The orderly on the plane is very nice. They help you quite a bit. And damn if they have all the coffee you want, any time. The plane will land at Johnston Island at about 11:30 PM and stay there for about 30 minutes. Right outside the plane is the mess hall. I think it costs about 25 cents for you to eat there. Of course, Johnny might not be awake but I want you to notice how small the island is.

Next, you will land on Kanton Island which is just to get some gas. Nothing to eat there. You will get into Samoa at about 1 or 2 and it really looks big after seeing those tiny islands. On that cargo plane, in case you need to go to the bathroom, it's up where the pilots are. It's in the back for the men.

The plane rides very smoothly. You hardly know you are in the air. It feels a little bumpy when it takes off or lands or when it goes through a cloud while it's raining. After you take off, I'm sure you'll feel quite safe. Hope I'm telling you everything so it will be more comfortable. If there is anything else you want to know just ask, I'm smart, I've been around.

That letter expressed the love and caring John felt for his family. More than anything, he wanted both of them to feel comfortable and safe. He ended that letter with this.

I would rather write you a great big love letter but honey I'm not so good at that. I'm getting to like Samoa better, getting used to it. But I refuse to be happy here till your sweet presence puts sunshine into this rock.

I'm getting a big campaign going so the natives will clean up their places. Besides, I want it to look good before you come. Well love of my life, I had better close. Please stay happy and keep smiling. I surely hope the next month passes fast. I dream of you often. I hate to wake up, because you are not there.

I love you and Johnny so take good care of yourselves.

Your darling daddy,
Johnny

It would be almost two more months before they'd see each other again. Once Alice arrived in Samoa, they would be together for twenty-two months. It would be the longest period of time they'd be together since they'd met in 1940.

★ ★ ★

CHAPTER 18

"I'M OKAY. IT WAS A LIZARD."

December 3, 1947 to April 1, 1959

As John waited for Alice and Johnny to arrive in Samoa, he contacted some of her family. In a letter to Alice on December 3, 1947, he wrote to tell her about a sad meeting with her grandmother.

> *Your grandmother is at the hospital with TB. I believe they*
> *tell me she is 80 years old. I went by and saw her this morn-*
> *ing. I used one of the Samoan nurses for an interpreter. She was*
> *quite happy to see me. Cried at that. She says she probably won't*
> *be alive by the time you get here. Robert Allen, who is a young*
> *member of your family, also helped with interpretation and said*
> *your grandmother's imminent death is the way God wants it. He*
> *also gave me the whole of your family's history.*
> *Someone in your family, I gather, must be a high chief on*
> *some village, but Robert doesn't seem to like him. Of course, he*
> *told me about your grandmother being a princess. He expects*
> *you to stay here on the land he says it's yours, as soon as your*

grandmother dies. I told him we already had a house and that he had better stay on the land.

Also, mom's brother is in the barracks right across from me. He is in the Fita Guard (U.S.N.). I'll probably see him tomorrow. I don't know if these people are happy to see me or whether they are anxious to see you. I guess they are trying to make a princess out of you.

The Fita National Guard is an elite group of native Samoans enlisted by the U.S. Navy to help patrol the islands.

John went to Alice's hometown to check on the family house, but he didn't feel it was in good enough shape for his family. He had also met Chief Unutoa, the relative. The chief told John he should become a chief in Samoa, and John told him thanks, but that he was already a chief in the U.S. Navy. John was amazed at how direct the Samoans were. "They'd ask you about anything they wanted to know regardless of how personal it was. They were not bashful. Also, if you give a Samoan a bottle of beer and they don't like it, they raise hell and ask you to buy them a different one."

After reuniting with Alice after the war, another three months apart seemed like forever. On December 9, he ended a long letter with the following:

Now my darling, it's time for me to go to bed. I like to wake up in the morning and say, one day less to wait for you. Sure, wish you would hurry. Slow Poke.

I love you darling, sure wish I had a moving picture of you. Night now sweetheart. See you soon.

Love,
John

The next day, he received six letters from Alice that made his waiting a bit more tolerable, but not much. John was planning to get Johnny enrolled in school. There were not many options. In the meantime, Alice was worried about how much weight her luggage was going to be. She wasn't just bringing clothing but also kitchenware and other things that were adding up. John told her not to worry as he had learned that another Navy wife had recently arrived with 350 pounds of luggage. In the meantime, the people in her native village of Aua were cleaning up their houses in anticipation of her arrival. John wrote in a short letter:

I believe the day you get here will be a holiday. Of course, it will be for me. They never have the brass bands for planes before, just for ships. But I wouldn't be surprised if they did when you come in.

Sure do love you honey. I hope the next month passes quickly. There are no toys here. Maybe Johnny will be satisfied with a Pau Pau (Samoan boat), and with his fishing gear, he should be all set. It sure feels like ages since I've seen you.

Love you darling forever,
John

As the weeks were dragging, John kept himself busy and read Alice's letters over and over, to make himself feel closer to her. He had met Tafasao, her uncle, and had learned that he was in a band and had eight children. He, too, told him, that Alice's family and others in her village were anxiously awaiting her arrival.

As Christmas approached, it would be the fifth in the past seven years that they would not celebrate together. John was questioning why he'd reenlisted and how many more Christmases he'd miss being with his family. One of the other Navy chiefs had a motion-picture camera and had shown some of his family's movies to John. He suggested to Alice that for Christmas of 1948 they could buy one for each other. It cost three hundred dollars, but he felt it was worth it. If they were separated again, he could take the film of her and Johnny with him and hopefully make the time away from them more bearable. On several of his letters from Samoa, John told Alice how much he wished that he had motion pictures of her and Johnny.

A ship was said to be coming with toys, and John planned on getting one for Johnny. He asked Alice to tell him at Christmas that Santa had left something for him in Samoa. John was missing the best years of Johnny enjoying the holiday as only kids who believe in Santa do. He ended up getting Johnny five toys and two books that, as he said, "were perfect for a six-year-old, and the works only cost me eleven dollars." On Christmas, he finally got confirmation from the Navy about Alice and Johnny's travel date. He wrote her the following:

Dearest Wife,

> *Darling I was going to send you a telegram wishing you all a very Merry Christmas but last night, I found out they wouldn't do it.*
> *Although Christmas will now have been over, let me wish you, or rather hope that you did have a Merry Christmas and may you have a very happy New Year.*
> *Please convey my wishes to all. Best wishes with love. Your darling husband.*

John
P.S. Only 34 more days to go

Later that day he received a package from Alice with his Christmas gifts. He wrote her another letter on the twenty-seventh. Below is an excerpt from that eight-page letter.

Dearest Darling,

Thank you and Johnny and mom for the Christmas presents. I received them at about 5 PM on the 24th. Of course, I opened them right away. The cookies are very good but most of them were broken. But that didn't change the taste any. The pen and pencil set is just what I wanted but I don't know about the funny books. After all I'm too big. But Superman was pretty good. Ask Johnny how come he didn't send Capt. Marvel! The picture came in good shape. You look pretty good. Beautiful.

One long month from tomorrow and I should be kissing and hugging you honey. Be sure to cure your cold. If you have a bad one, they won't let you go. Take a lot of salt gargles and every-thing else. OK?

Certainly hope you bought that formal you liked. Better go and get it now if you haven't. You just got to have one down here to be in style when we go to the dances.

You had better take advantage of the cold climate you are having or you might wish that you had brought some with you. Of course, when you get here, it might be OK as I will have someone cold to snuggle up to. Huh!!!!!!!!

Miss you and love you very much.

Always,
John

John was losing some of the weight he had gained. He wasn't crazy about the food, and he was swimming regularly again, which helped him to lose weight. In subsequent letters, he asked Alice to bring him swimming trunks and shorts, sizes thirty-four or thirty-five inches. He couldn't buy any in Samoa, and he kept borrowing them from a friend. He told Alice that he *"wouldn't stay in Samoa if he were not married but that anywhere with her was paradise."* He added, *"If you don't get here soon, I'm leaving this place."*

John found a housing compound that consisted of one main home and several smaller lodgings that were sitting vacant. The place was outside of town overlooking the ocean and had a cove where you could swim. It was flush with papaya, banana, and coconut trees. It had been a Jesuit monastery at one time, according to John Wayne, and had no electricity. He told me, "Whenever we could get Dad energized to go turn on the generator, we had electricity for a while." According to John, the place had been most recently used by the U.S. government for agricultural research. He struck a deal for his family to live there without paying rent, as long as he acted as the caretaker for the property. He was also looking for a "house girl" to help Alice with daily chores and taking care of Johnny. He was having to maneuver through some sensitive issues with Alice's family, because some of her young cousins wanted the job. He finally settled on a woman who had been the house girl at the property when it had been occupied. Her name was Sapienza. John described her as older, more reliable, and honest. With the money he'd save by not paying rent, John bought a Jeep for the family.

John still enjoyed his whiskey, and according to him, "It was really cheap and much better than the favorite local drink they call Kava. It acts as a sedative and doesn't taste very good. The only time I had it was with one of the chiefs. I took one gulp. Didn't think much of it but took another gulp to be polite. That was it. I threw the rest out, the first chance I got. Samoans really liked their beer, too. That young man Allen could drink eight or more in one sitting. Some guys would drink a whole can in one breath."

On New Year's Eve, John wrote Alice a letter that was part poem.

Sweetheart:

I do believe that God above,
created you for me to love.
And set aside from all the rest,
just you for me to love the best.
I swear to God who smiles above,
that you're the one I love.

There is no world while we're apart,
I find I'm lost without your heart.
I mean it all, each word I say,
my heart is yours both night and day.
So please be sweet and always true,
Just as much as I'm to you.

And darling when I think of you; so kind and true.
I often wonder why I dare, to claim a girl as sweet as you.
I wish so much that I could say,
that all the time I've been away.
That now I'm coming home to stay.
Coming home to roam no more,
and once there to lock the door.

But as I can't, I'll see you soon,
if things go right
and still try with all my might
to make things pleasant for you always.

So long, till then my fairest one.
Goodnight for now, the year is done.

Hoping darling, and I'll try my best to make this year the
happiest of them all.

Love you always,
John

Below his barracks was a hall that held dance formals every few weeks. The days of the formals were the worst for him. He wished Alice was with him so they could hold each other and dance the night away. His letters continued on an almost-daily basis. In one, he told her that he had written all there was to say about his job and about Samoa and then ended it by writing, *"I love you,"* twenty-five times. He continued losing weight and got a terrible sunburn that made him sick. He was close to hitting rock bottom, and it was still three weeks before Alice and Johnny would join him. In a way, those months apart had been harder than the POW years. As a POW, he did not know what tomorrow would bring and tried not to think about it. He worked and prayed and took it one day at a time. This was worse, because of the anticipation of reuniting with his family, which couldn't come fast enough. To add to his misery, he had a wisdom tooth extracted that caused him a sore throat and ear. He went past rock bottom a couple of days later, when the plane that brought the letters was quarantined. John explained, "The plane had stopped in New Zealand, where they had polio so, it had to be fumigated." Feeling lousy, lonely, and heartsick, and now he didn't have new letters from Alice.

On January 14, 1948, John wrote his last letter to Alice; it would be discovered in the attic of their home in Vallejo sixty-six years later by his son Brian and his wife Jacki. Though John and Alice would be separated again before he left the Navy, they would primarily communicate by phone. Also, John and Alice had bought that camera that would take motion pictures for John to watch while he was away. Since they'd met in the summer of 1940, John had written Alice almost six hundred pages of letters. Every single one expressed his steadfast love for her. Below is that last letter in its entirety.

My Dearest Darling,

> *I hope my darling that this is my last letter. The plane is leaving tomorrow, the last plane. You should be here on the same plane when it comes back. Nothing had better go wrong, as I'm just too anxious to see you. I only received 2 letters from you today and I never did learn whether or not you received the $150. Hope so. What mail service!*
>
> *Another Chief Pharmacist Mate came in today, though he is going home on the next plane, as he was here only to set up our new X-ray machine. He is in the same room with me. His name is Bissell, and he will be someone I can talk to till you come.*
>
> *Now darling, my final order. Be sure that you have your medicine for your sickness, and come healthy full of vim, vigor and vitality. You must be taking your vitamin pills the way you*

say wait till I get you by myself. But I feel like a very old man. So, take it easy. Huh.

So, my darling Alice and Johnny, here is hoping you have a very pleasant trip, and get a little sleep on the plane if you can. I'll be waiting for you.

See you both soon, very soon. I love you my darling. Always.

John

John Wayne and Alice's passport picture. (From the personal collection of John I. Unger)

By mid-January, he was going to their new house whenever he could and busied himself cleaning and painting. He wanted the house to be as nice as he could make it for Alice and Johnny. Their furniture was being shipped from the U.S., and he'd have to buy some things when Alice arrived.

Alice and Johnny arrived on January 29. When they saw each other for the first time, they hugged and kissed and John said to them *"Talofa"* ("Hello" in Samoan). The wait was finally over. Their time together in Samoa would allow Alice, John Wayne, and John to work on being a family. Other than the time John spent at work, they spent most of the time together. John took Johnny to the cove below their house to swim, and the three of them attended church at the Fagatoga Chapel, in the downtown area of Pago Pago. Alice and John went to formals whenever they could. They also visited her family and spent time with the Kirklands, a couple from the Navy base who became good friends. They were invited to family luaus several times, where they ate the traditional Kalua pig. Alice did get to see her grandmother before she died, though she could not be with her at the time of her passing.

John's job as health inspector created some interesting situations. He explained a particularly memorable one: "I was getting a lot of complaints about pigs running around, eating people's gardens. The pigs were not confined at all, creating unsanitary conditions. I asked the pig owners repeatedly to keep their animals penned up, but they weren't doing it. So, I talked to the chief of police, and we agreed that I would put up a notice that stray pigs would be shot and killed. A few days after I posted the notice, I went out with the chief to look for stray pigs. We came up on a few of them running around, and I told the chief to shoot them. The chief looked at me, horrified, and said, 'I can't shoot those pigs.'" John asked him why, and the chief said, "Those are *my* pigs!" John smiled and said, "Samoans sure have their unique way." The next time, John went out looking for pigs, we went by himself and carried a shotgun. He came up on one, and he shot it. He said, "The pig didn't die, and I ended up taking the shrapnel out of it. Maybe I was turning into a Samoan."

John was now questioning how much influence he really had with the Samoans. More than once he'd issue a sanitation order, and if the natives didn't like it, they'd say to him, "We are going to tell your wife." John added, "I was nobody; the Samoans thought Princess Alice had all the power." But John was not deterred. When something didn't sit well with him, he wasn't shy about being aggressive. John Wayne shared a story about an incident involving him. "Outside of our house, there was a large cement slab where I use to ride my tricycle, and our dog would chase me. When I was done playing, I'd leave the tricycle by the front door. One morning I got up, and the tricycle was gone—somebody had stolen it. So, Dad went around all the villages and told people that if he saw anyone riding that tricycle he was going to shoot them. Next morning, the tricycle was back."

John Wayne shared another story about adjusting to his dad's expectations. "One time, Dad was taking me to school, and he was in his dress uniform. He stopped to inspect some standing water on the side of the road that he thought might be a health hazard. As he was inspecting it, he slipped and went right into the mud. Everyone immediately went inside their huts, and no one would come out. By that time, I was smart enough to keep my mouth shut. I said to myself, *Don't talk, don't laugh, just shut up. Otherwise, there will be consequences.* Years later, Dad would tell that story and just laugh."

John Wayne shared another story about John, once again having an animated encounter with wildlife. It was also the second time John scared Alice out of her wits. John Wayne explained: "One of the buildings in the compound was a shed where the Jesuits kept a library. Dad was going to the shed to get a book, and he noticed there was a large lizard on the ground. He stomped his foot near the lizard, hoping it would go away. Instead, the lizard ran up his leg, and dad was jumping up and down, screaming and ripping his clothes off. That startled Mom, and she went around the house locking all the doors and windows. She was yelling at me, 'Don't open the door—your father has finally lost his marbles.'" John Wayne added, "Mom actually said something much more profane, but let's just say 'marbles.' Dad eventually got rid of the lizard, came to the door, and told Alice, 'I'm okay. It was a lizard,' but she wouldn't believe him. He had to convince her that he was okay, and she finally let him in. Mom always had this fear that Dad would have some issues left over from his time in the prison camps. In her mind, she always needed to protect me. Eventually, Mom got over Dad potentially flipping out because of his time as a POW."

Alice's love for John was unconditional, but she did not hesitate to put him in his place when she thought it was necessary. When John did something she didn't like, she was known to call him a "Square Head." When she thought he was being obstinate, she would tell him, "Your crazy German logic isn't working."

Life was interesting for the Ungers, but eventually they would have to say *tofa* ("Goodbye") to their friends and family in Samoa. In November of 1949, after almost two years in Samoa, John was reassigned for duty to Kansas City, where he supported doctors who performed physicals on prospective Navy officers. John described that duty as "one continuous game of canasta. There wasn't much to do. We would do only a couple of physicals every few days. There wasn't much need for new officers, so, it was very slow." Alice had not had a job since she left Benicia in 1948, and she was getting antsy to get back to work. John asked around to see if anyone needed a keypuncher, and he got a lead to have Alice apply at a cosmetics company. Alice went to the company and took a couple of tests. John called the next day to see how she had done. "The manager told me that she was the best keypuncher he had ever seen, and he ended up hiring her."

Unfortunately for Alice, John received orders to move again in May of 1950—this time, to St. Louis, Missouri, where he would get reacquainted with his father and stepmother. Once again, John was assigned to duty at a recruitment office, assisting the doctors conducting physicals on new recruits. According to Alice, John Unger Sr. spent lots of time showing off his son to all his friends, and the two drank a lot of whiskey together. They visited with his parents quite often, and John went hunting squirrels with his dad from time to time.

While he was stationed in St. Louis, John and Alice married for the third time. Though Alice had always been a practicing Catholic, she had never been baptized or formally confirmed by the church. They would go to church every Sunday but not take communion. One day, the priest, Reverend Francis Beykirch, asked them why they didn't take communion, and John explained to him that Alice had never gone through the sacraments. Father Beykirch arranged for Alice to, as John put it, "go through a crash course on the sacraments so we could be formally married by the Catholic Church." The church frowns on marriages during Lent, but Father Beykirch obtained special dispensation from the Archbishop, and John and Alice were married at Saint Martin of Tours Catholic Church on Saturday, March 10, 1951. This time, John's stepsister Theresa and her husband Thomas stood as witnesses.

The first month in St. Louis, John's work at the Office of Naval Officer Procurement was as slow as it had been in Kansas City. That is, till a month later, when the Korean War broke out. Beginning in June, John had more work than he could handle. John said, "All of a sudden, overnight, we were swamped with work." When before, they were doing a couple of physicals a day, now they were processing more twenty in a day. The Navy was once again in need of thousands of able-bodied men. A year-and-a-half into the war, John got new orders to report for sea duty on the *USS Kenneth Whitting (AV-14.)*. The *Whitting* was a seaplane tender, with a complement of 113 Officers and 964 enlisted men. It had served in Okinawa and off Japan during World War II.[1] John was ordered to report to the ship, which was at the Bremerton Naval Base in Washington State, where it was undergoing repairs and enhancements. Other than that brief time he had served on the *USS Rescue* after World War II, the *Whitting* was only the second time he'd served on a ship.

The family drove to Benicia, where Johnny and Alice would live till John returned. His orders indicated he would be on sea duty for as long as eighteen months, but they did not specify where the *Whitting* was being deployed. Once again, he would be separated from his family for an extended period of time. John drove to Bremerton, where he reported to the *Whitting* on November 10, 1952. To his anger and dismay, he learned that the ship was going to Japan. He argued with the captain that he could not return to Japan. The officer said there was nothing he could do. The ship needed a Chief Hospital Corpsman, and it was his assignment. John decided to drive down to San Diego to take the matter up with Chief Warrant Officer Bernhardt, who had assigned him to the *Whitting*.

John explained his state of mind and what happened next. "That's all I needed to hear—that they were sending me back to Japan. There was no way I wanted to do that. I drove all night to get to the duty office in San Diego. The Duty Officer was a guy I knew from my days at Mare Island, Chief Warrant Officer Bernhardt. I explained my situation, and he was really understanding but told me that the *Whitting* needed Chief Corpsmen, and I was the only one available. He asked me to please give it a try, and, if I found the situation too difficult, he would do everything in his power to get me out of there. I got back in the car and drove back up to Bremerton. So, I went to Japan."

The Korean War had started on June 25, 1950, and would last for three years. After World War II, the Americans and Russians agreed to split the country in two. North of the thirty-eighth parallel was occupied by the Russians and later ceded to China, and the South by the U.S. As the Cold War intensified, the chances of peacefully reuniting the country became increasingly unlikely. In 1948, the U.S. requested that the United Nations organize parliamentary elections in South Korea. The Soviet Union strongly opposed the measure. That led the Communists to set up their own government in the North. Neither the North nor the South recognized the legitimacy of the other's government. Relations continued to decline, and the North Koreans, with the support of Communist China, invaded South Korea in an effort to reunify the country.[2]

On the *Whitting,* John supported one doctor who had been recalled from the reserves, and he supervised five Junior Corpsmen. The ship docked in Iwakuni, Japan, where the U.S. had been using a naval base and airstrip since the start of the Korean War. The *Whitting* was part of Task Force 96, which served in direct support of the military effort in Korea. The seaplanes supported by the *Whitting* conducted reconnaissance flights but occasionally ran into combat situations, resulting in some injuries to the crews. John and his team supported the plane crews and the more than one thousand-member crew on the ship.

Though he was reluctantly going to Japan, John told me. "It was the best thing that could have happened to me. I found out that, during peacetime, the people were really nice. I think because of the time there, I came out of it better than most of the other Japanese POWs. Instead of hating the Japanese, I realized it was the fortunes of war. In peacetime, they were very friendly people."

John had an unexpected and profound experience during his time in Japan. He explained it to me: "For some reason, the commanding officer of the ship wanted me to go to Hiroshima. It was a short distance away, and he wanted me to look around and report to him." Iwakuni is twenty-six miles from Hiroshima, so John took the train. "I got up there in the morning. It was a sight to see. There was only one big building you could see; the rest of it was rubble and shacks. I went to the civilian hospital to see all the wounded people there." John choked up a bit and said, "It was pretty sad. There was lot of suffering in there. You could tell many people were in different stages of dying." The hospital included people with radiation wounds, severe burns, various types of cancers caused by the radiation, and saddest of all were the young children with birth defects. "I was there three or four hours and then got back on the train to return to the ship and, of course, I was in full uniform. The train was loaded with people, but there was an empty seat next to me. Nobody would sit next to me. I had the area all to myself. As I look back on it now, I can understand why they left me alone."

The Genbaku Dome as it appeared after the atomic bomb. (National Archives)

The dome as it appears today at the site of the Peace Memorial Park. (en-wikipedia.org)

The building John referred to seeing on his way to the hospital was the Genbaku Dome. Built in 1915, as the Prefectural Industrial Promotion Hall, it was one of the few structures that had survived the atomic blast. It is particularly symbolic because the building, which resides on the banks of the Ota River, stood only 150 meters from the bomb's epicenter. *Genbaku* means "atomic bomb." The building was reinforced and today is part of the Peace Memorial Park.[3]

Any time John got liberty, he went into town and walked around. He also went to restaurants and bars. Everywhere he went, he was treated very well by the Japanese. John smiled, laughed, and said to me, "The Japanese didn't have any guns, so I wasn't afraid of them anymore. But really, everywhere we went, the Japanese were very courteous. They would bow to me and treated me very respectfully. In some ways, they were nicer than our own people. That experience meant a lot to me. Till then, I was like most of the other POWs, thinking we hated the Japanese. I had shore leave almost every week, and I looked forward to going into town and interacting with the Japanese. I realized that war is war, and what happened to me when I went back really helped. I held no animosity toward the Japanese after that. That's no way to go through life—hating an entire race of people. I'm glad I went."

The Korean War resulted in more than 54,000 Americans killed. An additional 103,284 were wounded. The Republic of Korea (the South) military lost 59,000 soldiers. The Chinese and North Koreans lost an estimated 500,000 soldiers killed in action. Civilian deaths between the North and South exceed 2 million souls.[4] Of the 7,140 Americans taken prisoner, 2,700, or a rate of almost 38 percent, died. That was a POW death rate comparable to the Japanese POWs in World War II. In one notorious death march, in November of 1950, 130 of 700 POWs perished on a 120-mile forced march.[5] It had been another costly war for America, only this one had not achieved anything more than a stalemate.

After the war, John continued to serve on the *Whitting* till receiving new orders to report to the Naval Hospital in Hawaii in January of 1954. In Hawaii, he reunited with Alice and Johnny, and they enjoyed the beauty of the islands. They went swimming, enjoyed the beach at Waikiki, went to movies, and otherwise just spent quality time with each other. According to Alice, at times John still shied away from crowds and drank too much. The nightmares still persisted, but she'd always comfort him when they were at their worst. In a speech on Memorial Day 2014, John talked about going to the Punchbowl while he was stationed in Hawaii. John said, "When I saw the graves of all the men who had died at Pearl Harbor and other places in the Pacific, it brought back bad memories. It tears at you, thinking of all the guys who didn't make it back."

The Punchbowl National Cemetery is located in Oahu and was built in 1948. The cemetery is situated in an extinct volcano named *Pouwaina*, meaning "hill of sacrifice." It's the resting place for American armed forces members who served in World War II and Korea. Subsequent to John's visit, it would also include many soldiers who were killed in Vietnam. Seven-hundred-and-seventy-six casualties from the December 7, 1941 attack on Pearl Harbor were among the first to be buried at the Punchbowl.[6] The cemetery opened to the public on July of 1949, with services for five war dead: an unknown serviceman, two Marines, an Army lieutenant, and one civilian—noted war correspondent Ernie Pyle. Eventually, more than 13,000 soldiers and sailors who died during World War II were laid to rest at the Punchbowl.[7]

John, Alice, and Johnny enjoyed their time in Hawaii till 1957, when John received orders to report to the Naval Shipyard at Mare Island. They were going home, where they bought a house in Vallejo and lived in it for more than fifty years. Back at Mare Island, John was assigned to support the men and women working on building nuclear submarines. Among his responsibilities were caring for the men and women and taking regular radiation readings, to ensure no one was contaminated in the course of their work.

By 1959, John was coming up on twenty years in the Navy and, soon, he would be required to do another tour of duty at sea. As luck would have it, there was a civil service job at the Mare Island Shipyard that was also involved with the nuclear submarine program. The job was as a Physical Science Technician in the Medical Department. John inquired about it and was told he'd be a perfect fit. He decided that it was time to retire from the military. In April of 1959, he was transferred to the Navy Fleet Reserve and began working as a civilian. John had earned sixteen medals for his service in World War II and Korea, a Presidential Citation for his role at Wake, and a Citation from the Secretary of the Navy for his service in the POW camps. He had served the Navy and his country with distinction.

★　★　★

CHAPTER 19

"I WISH YOU COULD COME WITH ME."

April 2, 1959 to Present Day

John had no problem adjusting to civilian life. He said, "I had regular hours and didn't have to worry about where my next duty would take me. Best of all, I was with my family." I asked John what he thought about his overall experience in the service, and he said, "Notwithstanding what happened during the war, I enjoyed it, and I believe service is a good thing. Everyone should serve their country in some capacity. People don't have to stay in the service as long as I did, but it's a good thing for people to do for the country." John is proud that he had some influence in the decisions made by some in his family to serve. Jim Kelly, the son of his stepsister Theresa, shared his story. "When Uncle John was working at the shipyard at Mare Island with the submarines, he took me aboard one of the vessels and showed me around. I thought it was very cool. I was hooked. John encouraged me to join the Navy, and I did." Like John, Jim achieved the rank of Master

Chief Petty Officer. He did not serve on a submarine but did serve on a carrier during the Vietnam War.

Around the time John was adjusting to civilian life, John Wayne was graduating from high school. He had been a straight-A student, but his last year of school was another story. He said, "I got a bit wild that year and almost didn't graduate. I remember sitting down to eat breakfast, and Granny, Mom, and her siblings were all there. I was at one end of the table, and Dad was at the other end. Dad looked at me and asked, 'Now that you've graduated, what are you going to do?' I said, 'I have a job.' Dad said, 'Good. What are you going to do?' I told him I was going to work at the Mare Island filling station. Dad said, 'Great, my son is going to be a damn grease monkey.' So, that pissed me off, and I went down and joined the Navy that day. I had to forge his name on the documents because I wasn't of age yet." I asked John Wayne why he chose the Navy, and he said, "I don't know. I guess because I had been around Navy personnel most of my life, and most of the people Mom and Dad spent time with at the different duty stations were Navy people." I asked John Wayne what his dad's reaction was, and he said, "Dad was okay with it. He was happy I wasn't going to be a grease monkey. He didn't say much because that's just the way he is, but I knew he was happy with me enlisting."

John Wayne shared a story about his time in boot camp. "When I got to boot camp in San Diego, there was a man by the name of Clodfelter, who was a Chief Corpsman, just like my dad. He had known my dad for a lot of years. Clodfelter had a lot of clout. In boot camp, you were confined to the base for eight weeks. One day, Clodfelter walked in and told the First Class who was in charge that 'he needed to take me to a phone to call my mother.' The First Class said, 'He can't go,' and Clodfelter said, 'He can go. I'll bring him back in about an hour.' So, I went. Mom wanted to check on me to make sure I was okay. She wanted to know if I was minding my business and staying out of trouble. That was the first time I had been away from her. Dad had called Clodfelter and asked him to have me call Mom. Clodfelter became like a second father to me and influenced me becoming a Corpsman just like him and Dad. I figured 'Why not?' I'd learn something."

Prior to going to boot camp. John had said to John Wayne, "Once you leave, you are not coming back home. You need to be on your own." John Wayne took that to be gospel. However, he would come back home and live with his parents for about eight months after the Navy, when he was going to college. John accepted his son's return and didn't say anything. John Wayne laughed and added, "I think Mom had talked to him." I asked John what he was trying to convey to his son and he said, "I wanted him to take responsibility for his decisions and for his life." John Wayne added that, "At some point later, Dad told me that his father had told him the same thing he had told me. 'You are not coming back home.' You could say Grandpa was a full-blooded German and had some tough concepts that he passed on to Dad."

After boot camp in San Diego, John Wayne went through Corpsman training and was assigned to the dispensary at Norfolk, Virginia. There, he ran into Chief Warrant Officer Bernhardt, the man who had asked John to go to Japan. John Wayne explained what transpired: "Being a nonrated swabee, you literally swab decks till you achieve your first rate. I was swabbing the deck; an officer came by, and I accidentally got his shoe. So, I said, 'Excuse me, sir.' He said to me, 'That's all right, son. Are you by any chance related to Chief Unger?' I said, 'Yes, sir—he's my father.' He said, 'Come with me, son.' That was my last day of swabbing. He talked to the guy in charge at the Master at Arms office and told him, 'This man is going to be assigned to my division.'" John Wayne added, "No one but Bernhardt could tell me what to do while I was in Norfolk. He also introduced me to

Captain (Dr.) Kahn, who was at the Marine base in Quantico, Virginia. Bernhardt took me around and educated me about how things worked. When I got my orders to be assigned to the Marines, he asked me if that was what I wanted. I said 'No sir,' and he got my orders changed to serve at the Naval Hospital in Guam. I was very fortunate to run into Bernhardt."

John Wayne served four years in the Navy, went to college, and had a successful career in banking. Eventually, he retired from Fannie Mae, the Federal National Mortgage Association. He married three times over the years and had three children with his second wife, Judy. John Jr. is the oldest of the three, then Tim and Julie.

Misfortune befell Alice and John in 1962. Julia, Alice's younger sister, had not been lucky in her love life. She had a nine-year-old daughter, Pam, with one man she had married and divorced, and Brian, her six-year-old, with her second husband, whom she also divorced and with whom she had no contact. At the time, she was having an affair with another man and drinking excessively. In Julia's depressed state, she knew Pam could go live with her biological father. However, since Brian had no contact with his father, he should "go to heaven with her." John recalls what happened. "I remember the day I got the call when Alice's sister committed suicide. Pam called and was crying. She said, 'Mom took some poison and gave it to Brian, too.' Pam was told by her mother to watch TV and not go into the bedroom. But she sensed something was wrong, walked in, and then called us. I told her, 'Say no more—I'll be right there.' Alice and I got in the car and rushed over to their house. It was only a few minutes away, and we got there awful fast. When I got there, I felt for Julia's pulse and listened for a heartbeat, but there was none. I could tell she was gone, and Brian was hardly breathing. I picked him up, put him in the car, and rushed him over to the infirmary. I knew we had to get whatever Julia gave him out of his system, to give him a chance to survive. When I got him to the infirmary, there was a nurse but no doctor. The nurse had the necessary tools to wash him out, but she wasn't doing anything. I asked her, 'What are you waiting for?' She said we had to wait for the doctor. Brian wasn't breathing anymore, so I said, 'No, no,' and grabbed the tube to put down his throat to get him to throw up whatever he had in his stomach. Luckily, the doctor walked in, finished getting the tube down, and Brian threw it all up. The doctor didn't even have to do CPR (*Cardio-pulmonary Resuscitation*). Just getting the stuff out of his system, I think, was enough of a shock that it revived him. Anyway, I don't think he would have made it if Pam hadn't called. We wouldn't have had enough time to get him to the infirmary."

According to John, both he and Alice realized that Julia was living a troubled life and were shocked that she took her life—but, in retrospect, not totally surprised. I asked John what impact that had on Alice, and he said. "Alice was very strong. She was always calm and collected and dealt with whatever came her way. Sure, it hurt, but she took care of what needed to be done."

Afterward, Pam decided to go live with her biological father, and Brian asked to live with John and Alice. They were happy to have him and formally adopted Brian, who lived with them till he graduated from college. Brian has great memories of growing up with Alice and John. He said to me, "Dad was not one to ever say, 'I love you,' but I always knew he did. Mom would say, 'I love you,' but she didn't have to, either, because I knew she did. Their love and caring for me, as it would be for the grandchildren, were unconditional. Dad loved cars, and he taught me how to put them together and take them apart. Like everyone in the family, I have great memories of being on the lake with them, skiing every day, and spending every summer up there." Brian was referring to a place that Alice and John owned in Clear Lake, California.

Alice and Brian in 1967. (From the personal collection of Brian Unger)

Like he'd done with John Wayne, when Brian graduated, John pulled him over and told him, "Now that you've graduated, you will not come back to live with us again." Brian told me, "That scared me a bit, because I didn't know where life was going to take me." It would not be till decades later that John Wayne and Brian realized that John had told them both the same thing when they left home. Brian graduated from Sacramento State University, where he attended Platoon Leaders Course, started the Semper Fi Fraternity, and, on the last day of exams, was commissioned as a second lieutenant. On the same day, he was issued orders to report to The Basic School in Quantico, Virginia, where he graduated with honors and received a Regular Commission. He served with III Marine Air Wing, including time as Aide-de-Camp, and then with 3rd Bn/4th Marines, including the first joint training exercise between the Japanese Ground Self Defense Force and U.S. Marines at Camp Fuji, Japan. He finished his career as an Instructor, Chief of Student Support at The Basic School. He left active duty as a captain, transferring to the Reserves. Brian credits his dad with influencing him to serve in the Marines. After the Marines, Brian entered the corporate world, where he again rose through the ranks and eventually would successfully serve as president and/or chief operating officer for three different companies.

In 1981, Brian and his first wife, Elizabeth, were living in San Onofre, Camp Pendleton, California, along with their infant son, Brian Patrick. Brian and Liz were in the process of a divorce when Brian received orders to deploy to Okinawa. Brian asked John and Alice to raise Brian Patrick while he was overseas, to which they willingly and lovingly agreed. That arrangement continued for eight years as Brian's career continued with the Marines and beyond, to his first postmilitary career, when he met and married Jacki. Jacki had two daughters from a previous marriage, Rachel and Alison. When Brian Patrick joined the new family, the transition was turbulent. Brian Patrick lived for a time with Jacki and Brian but at times returned to live with John and Alice. Eventually, the two families came together and formed a bond that is in its third decade. Brian adopted Rachel and Alison based on the girls' desire to become "Unger-girls" and his love for them.

John and Alice continued to work at Mare Island, where John progressed from a Civil Service salary-grade-level of GS-5 to a GS-9 when he retired in 1977. John, like many of the ex-POWs, developed a heart condition that, for years, was treated primarily with nitroglycerin. John eventually needed surgery. At the age of seventy-three, he had a quadruple bypass. Alice, who had started as a keypuncher, worked at Mare Island till 1984 and retired as a Manager, level GS-13. Alice was ahead of her time as a female, having a long and successful career.

Granny Julia passed away in 1992. Born in 1898 in Aua, American Samoa, she was considered a princess as the firstborn of the Unutao family. She had been a great single mother to her children and had taken care of John after the war to ensure he recovered his health. Granny helped with John Wayne and Brian's upbringing as Alice and John were employed full-time. She passed away after suffering from dementia. In her last years, Julie Ikeya, John Wayne's daughter, and Alice had been Granny's primary caregivers. Granny had been living in a mobile home not too far from Alice and John. John purchased the home for her so she could have her own place. When she passed away, John and Alice took the home and placed it on the lot in Clear Lake.

Waterskiing was a favorite pastime of the Ungers. John Wayne recalls an incident with his dad. "Dad loved to ski but had never jump-started from a dock. My Uncle Leon and I did it all the time. One day, Dad wanted to show us that he could do whatever we could do. We explained what he had to do but not as well as we should have. Mom was driving the boat, and, as the rope was uncoiling on the dock, Dad yelled for her to 'Hit it!' Alice took off and was going so fast that Dad went into the air without the skis. He never let go of the rope, and it was a nasty landing. Leon and I were laughing on the dock. Even though he was in pretty good shape at the time, he never tried a jump-start again. That was at Lake Berryessa, before we had the place in Clear Lake." More than one hundred miles north of Vallejo, Clear Lake would become a favorite getaway spot for the entire family for decades.

Alice with John Wayne's Children Julie, John, and Tim. (From the personal collection of Julie Ikeya)

For several years, John Wayne's children and, subsequently, Brian Patrick spent entire summers at Clear Lake with Alice and John. Tim Unger described what it was like at the lake. "We had a daily routine.

We'd go skiing in the morning, come in for lunch, have some quiet time, and go out skiing again or fishing in the afternoon. Grandpa had his happy hour every day, when he enjoyed his whiskey, and then it was dinnertime. We repeated that every day except Sunday. Sunday was for the family to go to church together and enjoy a great dinner cooked by Grandma. Grandma was still working, so she'd come up only on weekends. The rest of the time we'd spend with Grandpa. On Sundays, we'd be sitting outside the place, looking at the lake, and Grandpa always said, 'Look at those whitecaps. Can't ski on a day like this, anyway.'" John Wayne added, "Alice slept in the porch with all the kids to protect them. I don't know what she would have done if something really bad had happened, like a bear or a mountain lion attacking them. She just felt it was her duty to always protect the kids."

Alice and John with the great-grandchildren on John Wayne's side of the family. (From the personal collection of Julie Ikeya)

Years later, when the place on the lake became too much work for John and Alice, John Wayne bought it from him and moved there permanently after his retirement. With the money he got from selling the lake property, John bought an RV (Recreational Vehicle). The RV became the place for family to spend time with John and Alice all over California. A testament to John's tenacity is that his last RV was a 2006 Fleetwood Flair 33 that he bought new, at eighty-five years old! The RV was also how the next generation, their great-grandchildren, enjoyed time with Alice and John—"on the road."

Tim described a couple of experiences with John that he will never forget. "Grandpa had purchased a dinghy to go fishing and just play around. One day, my older brother John and I were out on the lake hot-dogging and doing doughnuts in the water, and the motor partially detached from the boat. I remember running up the hill to the house, dreading telling grandpa that I had messed up the boat. I have such respect for him, I never wanted to disappoint him. I always wanted him to be proud of me. All the while, my brother John was razzing me about how much trouble I was in. When I told grandpa about the dinghy, he asked me, 'Is the motor still there?' I said 'Yes,' and all he said was, 'Fine—let's go fix it.' He didn't get mad or raise his voice. There were other times like that, and he was always calm and collected. Grandpa taught us how to shoot, ski, and fish. He loved to teach. One time, he really scared me. I was thirteen, and my brother John was fourteen, and we had been out on the boat. When we got up to the house, grandpa started having chest pains, and both he and grandma were looking for the nitroglycerin pills but couldn't find them. Grandma told John and me to go back to the boat to see if we could find his medication. All the while, Gramps was laid out on the couch, something we had never seen before. Grandma gave us the keys to Gramps' Cadillac. A gold

1973 Sedan de Ville that Gramps took immaculate care of. My brother drove, and I rode shotgun. Neither of us had ever driven a car before. We drove down to the dock, worried to death about Gramps and scared that someone would see us boys driving a car and we'd get in trouble. We ran to the boat and searched, finding the medicine under a seat in the boat. We ran back to the car and drove back to the trailer. Grandpa would be okay, but it really scared us to see him in such pain."

Tim also spoke with love and admiration about Alice. "Grandma was the matriarch of the family. She was always there for the grandkids. My parents divorced when I was seven, and she made sure we got lots of love and attention. Christmas Day was a microcosm of what the kids meant to our grandparents. The living room would be coated with gifts. Everyone got plenty of them, and John and Alice would sit and watch till all of us opened all our gifts before they opened their own. A big meal would follow, and it made for a special day. After Grandma retired from civil service, she went to work as a bookkeeper at St. Vincent's Ferrer while I and my siblings went to school there. She also worked there when my brother John's kids and Brian Patrick attended school there. She would go out and get us lunch from a fast-food location from time to time. When she did, she would also get a lunch for one of our friends. We didn't have lunch with her every day, but we saw her every day when we stopped by her office. She always had treats to share with us. She wanted to be close to us and eat lunch with us every day. She helped pay for tuition for some families who couldn't afford it. If you had to define love, that was Grandma."

Tim shared another story about John that is still fresh in his mind. "My grandparents had gone to a few of the Wake Defender reunions. However, eventually they stopped going because most of the reunions were held in the Midwest, and John did not like to travel outside of California. In December of 2001, the reunion was held in California, and Grandpa decided to attend. I think it had been more than a couple of decades since he had been to a reunion. He asked my dad, my brother, and me to accompany him and Alice. Though Grandpa had started talking to us more about the war by then, we thought it would be an opportunity to hear from some of the guys he served with.

"At the event, there was a room where the group met to socialize and have drinks before the ceremony. We could tell Grandpa was nervous. Maybe the thought of seeing all those old faces would bring back painful memories. He reached out and took my grandma's hand as we walked into the room. You could tell Grandma knew Gramps was nervous. She held his hand, but not a word was spoken. As we entered the room, one Marine looked at him, said, 'Doc,' and started to cry. He told Grandpa how happy he was to see him and that he'd thought he was dead. The Marine was one of the guys who Grandpa had cared for and saved his life. The Marine then looked at me and my brother John, who had also been a Marine, and asked who we were. When we told him we were his grandchildren, he and other Marines who had joined us told us, 'You guys don't buy drinks tonight. The drinks are on us.' I also recall several guys coming up to Grandpa and hugging him and thanking him for sacrificing himself to help them. The sheer joy that they showed at recognizing he was alive was something to behold. It was a night I'll never forget." The keynote speaker at that reunion was Retired Brigadier General John F. Kinney. Kinney had been one of the twelve pilots who fought so valiantly at Wake.

Brian's son, Brian Patrick, lived with Alice and John longer than any of the grandchildren. For the earliest part of his life and then again during his formative years as a teen. Alice and John were more his parents than grandparents. He spoke about growing up with his grandparents. "Grandpa always had routines. For example, at the lake, the daily routine was ski, eat, nap, ski or fish, whiskey before dinner, and then dinner." It was the same routine Tim and his siblings had experienced years earlier. Brian Patrick continued, "We had a couple of big dogs that Grandpa kept nice and fat. I think they each weighed one hundred pounds. He didn't want them to go hungry."

Eating was still an obsession with John. In a disability claim in 1996, Alice wrote the following about John:

He has an obsession about food. Swears he will never go hungry again. When he eats too much, he says, "I'm also eating for tomorrow. He dislikes to waste food. Children are made to clean their plates and gets upset with me if he thinks I'm wasting food. Even after his heart surgery and being told to go on a strict diet, his eating habits have not changed much. He still eats for tomorrow and will not deny himself any food he wants.

Brian Patrick described another aspect of his obsession. "The freezer at the house was always packed with food, and he had a big cabinet in the garage. It was about ten by twelve feet and was stacked with canned goods and K-rations." I asked John why he'd kept all the K-rations, some that were decades old. He responded, "You never know what tomorrow is going to bring, and I wanted to be prepared to take care of the family if something bad happened. When the Navy started getting rid of the K-rations, I'd bring boxes home. I also kept morphine in the garage." I asked John, "Did you miss having that stuff when you moved to the assisted-living facility?" He said, "No, but today I carry a one hundred dollar bill in my pocket every day, in case of an emergency."

Brian Patrick continued sharing his perspectives about Alice and John. "Grandpa and Grandma had a profound influence in making me the man I am today. My first memories of Gramps' stories as a boy and throughout his life (including wartime) were always humbling. I had asked Grandpa what it was like being in the war. In his normal, calming voice, he shared how he 'was doing his job.' I'd ask him a bunch of questions about being a prisoner, and he would gracefully close the discussion by saying that he witnessed people being beaten and how he would do his best to help them, even by stealing medical supplies when he could. He'd also say, 'I didn't have it as bad as others.' Though he downplayed what he did in the war, the scars stayed with him. After his heart surgery in 1993, I went to visit him and Grandma. At the time, the two of them were sleeping in separate rooms but never too far for Grandma to be able to hear him. A couple of nights during that visit Grandpa screamed in his sleep in a way that I can only describe as sheer agony. Probably, it was a combination of the drugs he was taking to recuperate and nightmares about the war. Grandma would go into his room and calmly comfort him till it passed."

"Grandma and Grandpa had a profound influence on me regarding morals and values. The greatest gifts Gramps gave me were strength and patience. Strength with faith in God and strength to do right by family. Grandpa, to me, is the most patient and unconditionally loving person I've known. In my lifetime. Gramps lost his temper with me only twice—and deservedly so. He taught me many life lessons."

Brian Patrick shared one of those lessons. "I was seventeen and driving around in an old Mazda pickup truck that ran just fine, but I fell in love with a Mustang Cobra. I found one on the Internet that I could afford and asked Gramps if I could buy it. He tried to coach me that the insurance on the Mustang would be more expensive, and when I turned eighteen he was expecting that I pay the full amount. I insisted on buying the car, so he drove me to the place where I picked it up. When we got there, I guess I hadn't done my research as well as I should have, because the car was manual transmission and I knew how to drive only an automatic. I bought the car anyway and asked Gramps if he would drive it back home. He calmly looked at me and said, 'No, it's your car—you drive it.' Two hours later and after a lot of grinding of gears, I learned another lesson on humility and patience.

"There is not a day that goes by that I don't stop and think, 'What would Grandpa do?' Whether it be in daily life, with my wife (Kendra), or at work, I am constantly reminded of a man who, long before I was even born, endured the unthinkable. My worst day would have been a good day for Grandpa during the war. It gives me a sense of peace and helps me to be the best I can be and act in a way that would be worthy of grandpa's praise. Gramps always says, 'Take each day, each moment, a step at a time. Life can change in an instant. Value and appreciate what you have every moment.'"

John on his ninety-fifth birthday with his family, including Brian (back row 5th from the left), Brian Patrick (next to Brian on his left), and Jacki (in front of them). (From the personal collection of Jacki Unger)

Julie Ikeya, John Wayne's daughter, shared her perspective about her grandparents. "Grandma was the rock of the family. She took care of us and Grandpa. She was a great role model for us. She got the family together and kept it together. She loved her independence and that she had her own career. She always valued having family close rather than material things. Grandma had simple principles: work hard, and take care of the family. She was also very protective of us. Any new family members like husbands and wives had to prove themselves worthy of her. She was not warm and fuzzy to them at first. They had to prove to her that they were good and responsible people. But, once you proved yourself, she loved you like her own. She and Grandpa loved each other very much and took care of each other."

Julie, like Tim, spoke about Alice's impact on the kids who attended Saint Vincent Ferrer. "Half the kids there affectionally called her 'Grandma.' Some people called her 'The doughnut lady' because she would bring in doughnuts for kids all the time. She also bought clothes for kids who couldn't afford it."

Julie felt a very strong bond with Alice. "While Grandpa was not one to say, 'I love you,' Alice was the opposite." Julie told me, "Grandma taught me about unconditional love—always giving and expecting nothing in return. Grandma would hold my hand and say, 'I love you,' I would say, 'I love you,' and she would say, 'I love you more.'"

Julie played a special role in her grandparents' lives. Julie was married a short time and had her oldest daughter, Michelle. She then remarried to a Japanese man named Alan Ikeya. Alan was, of course, put through the test by Alice to gauge whether he was a good person, but his ethnicity was never an issue with her or John. As Julie said, "Alan being Japanese never came up. It was never an issue. It was also great that all my girls (Michelle, Ally, Molly, and

Maddie) lived close to my grandparents, who watched them grow up and adored them."

Alice retired in 2006 from Saint Vincent Ferrer at the age of eighty-four. Shortly after, she began to experience signs of dementia. Julie lived near her grandparents in Vallejo and took on the primary responsibility for helping John with Alice's care. However, Alice's condition continued to deteriorate. Julie explained. "Grandpa tried to take care of Grandma as much as he could, but seeing them almost every day, I could tell it was getting too much for him. At the same time, he was very proud and didn't like strangers doing things for them. I tried hiring several people to come in and help, and Grandpa would either fire them or he'd pull them into the living room to watch TV or tell stories, but they weren't helping with Grandma. A good friend of ours who lived down the street from them called me one day and said that they saw Alice wandering by herself down the street. Other things like that were beginning to happen regularly. The day she was formally diagnosed with Alzheimer's was a very long one. We had just returned to the house, and Grandpa went down the hall and literally passed out, hitting the floor hard. I decided then and there that they couldn't be by themselves any more. I called Brian and Jacki, and we all agreed that we had to get them into an assisted-living facility." Julie added, "It was a gift to have been able to help."

After living in Vallejo for more than 50 years, Alice and John moved to an assisted-living facility in Lafayette, California, about 25 miles south. John continued to try to do everything in his power to assist in Alice's care. Julie said, "To the very end, Grandma recognized Grandpa and called out for him. They would hold hands and just love each other." Alice spent most of her day in a unit that specialized in memory care. Tim explained John's routine: "Grandma would be upstairs in the memory-care unit all day, and at the end of the day, Grandpa would put on his sport coat and meet Alice at the elevator. Grandpa told me, 'Alice took care of me all those years, especially after the war. It's my turn now to take care of her.'"

God took Alice to heaven on February 22, 2014, almost three years after she and John moved to the assisted-living facility. Julie, Alan, and their oldest daughter, Michelle, were with John and Alice her last couple of days. The night she passed, John told Alice, "It's been a good life, honey, and if I had to do it all over again, I would not change a thing." In a moment of lucidity and love, Alice told John, "I wish you could come with me." With tears in his eyes, John responded, "I wish I could, too." He hugged her, and then Alice passed from this world but not from his heart.

Alan Ikeya was asked to deliver Alice's eulogy, in which he shared his personal perspective. "I came from the outside, a friend of Julie's. Meeting you (Alice) for the first time was intimidating. I can't lie, for you were so wonderfully protective of your family. But in no time, you embraced me—you literally embraced me. For anyone who has experienced a Grandma Alice hug knows . . . it's like no other. A bear hug— with a hearty slap or two in the back—that gave you a level of comfort, acceptance, and love that is impossible to put into words. Friends, if you ever want someone to feel good, give them a Grandma Alice hug!"

EPILOGUE

"To find that better way."

Of all the brave military men who served at Wake, I believe that only four, including John, are still living. There were seven Corpsmen on Wake Island. Their job, as John reminded me many times, was to take care of the sick, the wounded, and the dying, and anything else that was necessary to support the Marines. They executed their duties with distinction at Wake—and in the prison camps. Some, like John, continued to serve after the war. Of the seven Corpsmen, only John is still living. He is the last Corpsman from the group that helped in the defense of Wake Island.

John turned ninety-eight years young a few months ago and is enjoying life in Palm Coast, Florida. Alice's absence tears at his heart every day, but the memories of their life together help soothe the pain. John Wayne is now seventy-seven years old and lives in California. He and John are in contact on a regular basis. John lives near Brian and Jacki Unger, and she visits him almost every day. When she can't visit, she makes sure there is always someone close by, in case John needs anything. Jacki schedules doctor's appointments for John and makes sure that he is doing all he needs to do to stay healthy. John communicates with his grandchildren regularly, by phone or e-mail.

Brian Patrick, who resides in Florida, visits whenever he can. Recently, Brian Patrick took Grandpa shopping for an ice box. Previously, John had to go downstairs in the nursing home to get ice for his bourbon. Now he has ice readily available in his room for his predinner drink. John always asks his grandchildren about the great-grandchildren and is on top of all that goes on in their lives. It's a special joy for him when they come to visit. He still attends church every Sunday and enjoys going out to dinner with family. He also enjoys spending some afternoons at Jacki and Brian's, enjoying the Intercoastal Waterway and joining them on an occasional boat ride. John still tries to exercise every day.

John did not see his grandmother Anna again after he left Austria. She died when he was in his teens. John's brother Bill, also served during World War II. He was a "Tail Gunner" on a bomber crew that attacked Germany. He survived the war and lived till he was almost 92, passing away in 2013.

What John experienced during the war and the adjustment after it is so abstract and surreal to most people that they can't grasp what it was like for him and Alice. That, along with the anxiety about his experiences, caused John to shut down and not talk about it for decades. Eventually, he started sharing bits and pieces with his family. As his grandson Brian Patrick described it, "It was like peeling an onion. He wouldn't offer anything more than what I asked him, so I had to keep coming up with more questions."

Personally, I'm humbled and privileged that he spent so many hours with me and my wife, Randi, sharing his war experiences and stories about Alice and his family. In the course of writing this book, I asked John some very difficult, and often personal, questions. He never flinched. No question was too tough for the former Chief Corpsman. He shared everything he could recall.

One of my concerns about John at ninety-eight years old was his ability to withstand long hours of interviews. Specifically, I was concerned about wearing him out. I quickly learned that his endurance was just fine—the truth is, he wore me out. Time and again, I would ask him if he was okay or if he needed to take a break. His response was always the same: "I'm fine. Let's keep going." He was also very patient with me and an absolute gentleman. After hours of listening to recordings of

My wife Randi and me with John, on Memorial Day of 2018, after another round of interviews.

interviews and reviewing multiple documents, I'd get confused about some things. I'd call John and say, "John, this is what I'm going to write. Is that right?" He'd never tell me I was wrong. Instead, he would ask me, "Why would you say that?" It was his gentle way of saying, "No, Juan, it's wrong."

As we were concluding the interviews, I asked John what gave him the most pride about the war. He didn't hesitate to tell me: "I was proud I was a Corpsman and any time I could do some good. Helping the guys get better. Whether it was an illness or an injury, it was good to be able to help. That, and I made it; I survived." I asked him what his best memories were of the war years, and he said, "Getting letters from Alice and being the primary guy the doctors counted on to get medicine for the men. The Red Cross packages were really good to get." Then, his playfulness kicked in again, and he added, "At Wake, I always felt good after the bombs stopped."

Regarding his family, he considers his seventy-four years of marriage to Alice the best of all blessings. In a newspaper article in 2007 that appeared in the *Vallejo Times-Herald*, John was asked about the war and POW life. In an excerpt from that article, he talked about his postwar life and Alice. *Unger said he came back from the war a changed man. He was hard to put up with. He had trouble sleeping, suffered nightmares, and preferred to be alone. Eventually, Unger said he came out of it. "The wife never asked me what happened," he said. "She just let it go. Now it's been so long it's more like, 'Did I really do this or read it in a book?' . . . I think I've just had a good life," he said. "I was just so lucky to get out like I did. The wife says it's because she took good care of me."*[1]

His children, grandchildren, and great-grandchildren are a godsend to John. And he deeply values all the people who helped him and Alice throughout the years. He told me countless times, "I've been pretty lucky, you know." Finally, he is especially proud of helping to save Brian's life and seeing him grow into a successful Captain in the Marines and then, an executive in the corporate world.

The last question I asked John was what he wanted his legacy to be. Again, there was no hesitation at all. He said, "I hope my family respects me and that they recognize that I tried to do the best I could for them." I'm confident, based on talking to his sons and grandchildren, that his legacy is secure.

John has a shadow box in his apartment, with numerous medals he received for his military service. Among the medals is a crucifix. According to his grandson Tim, "It speaks to the importance of Grandpa's faith in God." To Tim's point, I found it interesting that, among the things

John is most proud of, or has brought him the most happiness, he did not refer to the medals or any other formal recognitions bestowed on him. Instead, he referred to his blessings, his love of family, and to his opportunity to help others.

To use John's words about the importance of God and family, below is how he ended a speech he was asked to deliver at a Memorial Day celebration in 2006. He spoke about his fellow servicemen and the war experience, and then he said:

> *"In conclusion, God, duty, honor, and country will always remain as our noblest calling.*
>
> *Now, I would like to give my heartfelt thanks to my wonderful wife Alice, for without her loving devotion, I would not be who I am today. Here also is my son John and his wife, Jane, my oldest grandson John and his wife, Jennifer, and their two children. Granddaughter Julie with her husband Alan and their children. Also present is my youngest grandson, Brian, who lived with us for most of his life. Absent are my other son Brian and wife Jacki and my grandson Tim and his wife Diane.*
>
> *If only I had enough words to express the constant support I have received from them. I am truly blessed, grateful, and proud of them all.*
>
> *Thank you and may the Lord bless us all."*

Alice and John were among the women and men that we know as the "Greatest Generation." But as he would most likely say it, "We were just men and women doing our jobs." Whatever that job might be, or whatever sacrifice it required. As I reflect on John's story and countless others like him, I fear that too many of us today have forgotten what the

"Greatest Generation" fought for in World War II, and what countless other servicemen and women have fought for since. May we never forget that, throughout our history, Americans have almost exclusively fought to stop fascists and megalomaniacs like Tojo and Hitler. They fought, to make our world a better place. May we never forget the sacrifices of all our POWs and those who paid the ultimate price. May we never forget that patriotism matters and devotion to our country matters.

It is also concerning that so many in our society today do not embrace the values of men and women like John and Alice. May we never forget the importance of the family unit and the sanctity of marriage—for better or worse and in sickness and in health. And may we never forget that tomorrow is promised to no one, and it matters how we live each day. It is, I believe, important that, like Alice and John, each of us tries to do the best we can for our families and for our country, every day.

On September 29, 2000, President George W. Bush provided his perspective about John's generation, in a letter to the surviving members of Wake. The letter read, in part:

> We as a nation are blessed with many things. Chief among them is peace. But we must never forget that it is our veterans who are responsible for securing that peace. General Douglas MacArthur once said that no one knows the true cost of peace like a soldier, for it's the soldier who "must suffer and bear the deepest wounds and scars of war."
>
> Your heroism at Wake Island and your many sacrifices during World War II allowed freedom and democracy to triumph over tyranny and oppression, and I thank you. The legacy of your generation is a history lesson for us and for future generations

that teaches: With freedom comes responsibility to live a life of decency and compassion and to earn this priceless inheritance of freedom that America's veterans have won for us.

Laura joins me in sending our prayers and best wishes to each of you.

Sincerely
George W. Bush

I'll conclude this labor of love with an excerpt from a poem by Alexander Pope, an eighteenth-century poet. It's titled, *"The Universal Prayer."* The poem, fittingly, appeared on the July 1984 edition of the *Wake Island Wig-Wag*. To me, it speaks of men like John, who lived through unspeakable cruelty, yet maintained an open mind about the goodness of people. It speaks about men and women like John and Alice, who valued the power of learning from others, and the beauty of forgiveness. Finally, I believe it speaks to the strength of unconditional love—the kind of love that Alice and John had for each other and for their family.

> *Teach me to feel another's woe,*
> *To right the fault I see:*
> *That mercy I to others show,*
> *That mercy show to me.*
>
> *If I am right, thy grace impart,*
> *Still in the right to stay;*
> *If I am wrong, O teach my heart*
> *To find that better way.*[2]

Alice and John fell in love, started a family, and together, overcame inconceivable challenges, throughout their time together. Through their love and commitment to each other, and to their family, they created an enduring legacy. Together . . . they found that better way.

★　　★　　★

ACKNOWLEDGMENTS

First and foremost, my heartfelt thanks to John for allowing me to share his life story. He has become a special friend and a big part of our lives. A heartfelt thanks also to Jacki and Brian Unger. Brian for asking me to write the book and helping me with the military content and Jacki for being incredibly flexible and supportive about all the requests I had during the course of this project.

A big thanks to Brian Patrick Unger who provided multiple documents about John's life and took the time to answer many of my questions. A special thanks to Julie Ikeya, who responded to numerous requests from me including providing beautiful pictures of Alice, her siblings and the Great Grandchildren.

My gratitude to John Wayne Unger, Jim Kelly and Tim Unger, for their perspectives and insight about life with Alice and John. My gratitude also to Katie Rasdorf who was invaluable for her research of the National Archives.

A huge thanks to Michele, Ronda, Frank and the entire team at 1106 Design, for once again sharing their expertise and helping this book become a reality.

I want to thank by beautiful daughter Michael Cowen for her insight about the book. She took time from her busy career and being a great Mom to our Granddaughter Elise to offer suggestions. Also, my deep gratitude to my son in law Eric Cowen and my son Kyle who provided key perspectives on the work.

Finally, thank you to my loving wife of 42 years, Randi, who worked with me every step of the way. She was the first to edit my work and make helpful suggestions. She also helped with every interview and with the research. Most important, she tolerated my pleasant disposition after some very long days of writing. She has, and always will be, my inspiration. Thank you darling. I love you so much it hurts.

★ ★ ★

NOTES

Chapter 1: "Those are bombs."

1. Lat.long.net, *Wake Island, U.S,* Web, June 6, 2018

2. Timeanddate.com, *Com/WorldClock/Distances,* June 6, 2018

3. Colonel James P. S. Devereux USMC, *The Story of Wake Island,* An Ace Book, by arrangement with J.B. Lippincott Company, Paperback Edition, 1947, p. 33

4. John Wukovits, *Pacific Alamo: The Battle for Wake Island,* New American Library, a division of Penguin Group, July 2003, p. 47

5. Devereux, *The Story of Wake Island,* p. 11

6. Devereux, *The Story of Wake Island,* p. 34

7. Devereux, *The Story of Wake Island,* p. 37

8. Wukovits, *Pacific Alamo: The Battle for Wake Island,* p. 57

9. Wukovits, *Pacific Alamo: The Battle for Wake Island,* p. 262

10. Wukovits, *Pacific Alamo: The Battle for Wake Island,* p. 41

11. Wukovits, *Pacific Alamo: The Battle for Wake Island,* p. 61

12. Devereux, *The Story of Wake Island,* p. 39

13. Devereux, *The Story of Wake Island,* p. 45

14. Wukovits, *Pacific Alamo: The Battle for Wake Island, p. 56*

15. Devereux, *The Story of Wake Island,* pp. 42-43

16. Devereux, *The Story of Wake Island,* p. 42

17. Devereux, *The Story of Wake Island,* p. 39

18. Devereux, *The Story of Wake Island,* p. 42

19. Wukovits, *Pacific Alamo: The Battle for Wake Island,* p. 64

20. Wukovits, *Pacific Alamo: The Battle for Wake Island,* p. 65

21. Wukovits, *Pacific Alamo: The Battle for Wake Island,* p. 66

22. Craig Shirley, *December 1941: 31 days That Changed America and Saved the World,* Nelson Books, 2013, p. 151

23. Shirley, *December 1941: 31 Days That Changed America And Saved the World,* p. 150

24. *Lynne Olson, Those Angry Days: Roosevelt, Lindbergh, and America's Fight over World War II,* Random House, Inc., p. 429

25. *Ourdocuments.gov, Transcript of Joint Address to Congress Leading to a Declaration of War Against Japan (1941),* Transcription courtesy of the Franklin D. Roosevelt Presidential Library and Museum, June 8, 2018

26. History.com, *December 8: This Day in History:* 1941, Jeanette Rankin Casts Sole Vote Against WW II, History.com Staff, Web, July 10, 2018

Chapter 2: "John, you should not do that ever again."

1. History.com, *Treaty of Versailles,* David Kaiser, *The Reader's Companion to Military History.* Edited by Robert Cowley and Geoffrey Parker, Houghton Mifflin Harcourt Publishing Company, 1996, Web, June 8, 2018

2. Donald L. Miller, *The Story of World War II,* Simon & Schuster Paperbacks, 2001, pp. 20-21

3. Iris Chang, *The Rape of Nanking: The Forgotten Holocaust of World War II,* The Penguin Group, 1997, pp. 3-4

4. Britannica.com, Encyclopedia Britannica, *Axis Powers: World War II,* By the Editors of Encyclopedia Britannica, Web, June 8, 2018

5. Max Hastings, *Retribution: The Battle for Japan 1944-45,* Alfred A. Knoff, 2007, p. 193

Chapter 3: "I was nineteen and invincible."

1. Htstl.org, *Detailed Early History,* Most Holy Trinity (MTH) Catholic Church, Web, June 22, 2018

2. William J. Bennett, *America: The Last Best Hope: Volume II: From a World at War to the Triumph of Freedom,* Thomas Nelson Inc., 2007, pp. 96-97

3. Bennett *America: The Last Best Hope: Volume II: From a World at War to the Triumph of Freedom,* p. 116

4. Olson, *Those Angry Days: Roosevelt, Lindbergh, and America's Fight Over World War II, 1939-1941,* p. 436

5. Miller, *The Story of World War II,* pp. 23-25

6. Miller, *The Story of World War II,* p. 28

7. Olson, *Those Angry Days: Roosevelt, Lindbergh, and America's Fight Over World War II, 1939-1941,* p. 436

8. The Atlantic, *The Debate Behind U.S Intervention in World War II:* Article based on the book: *1940 FDR, Willkie, Lindbergh,*

Hitler-the Election Amid the Storm, By Susan Dunn, July 8, 2013, Web, June 19, 2018

Chapter 4: "I just had this feeling you know, she was so pretty."

1. Discovermareisland.com/history, *Mare Island: A Brief History of Mare Island,* By Lennar, 2016, Web, June 25, 2018

2. Britannica.com, Encyclopedia Britannica, *Dunkirk Evacuation: WW II,* By the Editors of Encyclopedia Britannica, Updated May 19, 2018, Web, June 25, 2018

3. Walter Lord, *The Miracle of Dunkirk,* The Viking Press, 1982, p. 275

4. Lord, *The Miracle of Dunkirk,* p. 58

5. Lord, *The Miracle of Dunkirk,* p. 272

6. History.army.mil/books, *The Alaska Defense Command – US Army Center of Military History,* By Stetson Conn, Rose C. Engelman and Byron Fairchild, May 24, 1962, page created *30 May 2002, Web, June 25, 2018.* MARINES: THE OFFICIAL WEBSITE OF THE UNITED STATES MARINE CORPS, *Marine Corps Installations West: HISTORY OF THE MARINES IN THE WEST,* Web, June 25, 2018

Chapter 5: "There was a time I loved the sea."

1. Olson, *Those Angry Days: Roosevelt, Lindbergh, and America's Fight Over World War II, 1939-1941,* p. 409

2. Miller, *The Story of World War II,* p. 6

3. Devereux, *The Story of Wake Island,* p. 15

4. Navsource.org, *Nav Source Naval History; Online, Amphibious Photo Archive, USS William P. Biddle (APA-8), ex USS William P. Biddle (APA-15) (1941-1943)*, By Gary P. Priolo, last updated February 23, 2018, Web, June 28, 2018

Chapter 6: "Always Faithful."

1. Britannica.com, Encyclopedia Britannica, *Johnston Atoll: United States Territory, Pacific Ocean,* By the Editors of Encyclopedia Britannica, Web, June 29, 2018

2. Britannica.com, *Midway Islands: United States Territory, Pacific Ocean,* Web, July 2, 2018

3. Wukovits, *Pacific Alamo: The Battle for Wake Island,* p. 16

4. Devereux, *The Story of Wake Island,* p. 11

5. Devereux, *The Story of Wake Island,* p. 13

6. Donald L. Miller, *D-Days in The Pacific: Guadalcanal, Tarawa, Saipan, Iwo Jima, Okinawa,* Simon & Schuster Paperback Edition, 2005, pp. 7-8

Chapter 7: "I miss your kisses something awful."

1. Historyofwar.org, *USS Portland (CA-33), Articles and Weapons* By Richard J, November 11, 2014, Web, July 4, 2018

2. History.com., "Watch Roosevelt's 'Somber' Independence Day Speech from 1941," By Allison McNearny, July 2, 2018, Web July 4, 2018

3. History.com., "Watch Roosevelt's 'Somber' Independence Day Speech from 1941," By Allison McNearny, Web July 4, 2018

4. Miller, *D-Days in The Pacific: Guadalcanal, Tarawa, Saipan, Iwo Jima, Okinawa,* 2005, p. 9

5. Miller, *D-Days in The Pacific: Guadalcanal, Tarawa, Saipan, Iwo Jima, Okinawa,* 2005, p. 9

6. Miller, *D-Days in The Pacific: Guadalcanal, Tarawa, Saipan, Iwo Jima, Okinawa,* 2005, p. 10

7. William Taylor, *Rescued by Mao: World War II, Wake Island, and My Remarkable Escape to Freedom Across Mainland China,* Silverleaf Press, May 2007, p. 44

8. Navsource.Org, *NavSource Online: Service Ship Photo Archive: USS Castor (AKS-1),* By Gary. P. Priolo, Last updated September 26, 2015, Web, July 9, 2018

9. Devereux, *The Story of Wake Island,* p. 16

10. Devereux, *The Story of Wake Island,* p. 28

11. Devereux, *The Story of Wake Island,* p. 30

12. Olson, *Those Angry Days: Roosevelt, Lindbergh, and America's Fight Over World War II, 1939-1941,* p. 423

Chapter 8: "It was my job."

1. Gordon W. Prange, with Donald M. Goldstein and Katherine V. Dillon, *At Dawn We Slept: The Untold Story of Pearl Harbor,* the Penguin Group, Penguin Putnam Inc., Paperback Edition, 1981. p. 539

2. Prange, Goldstein and Dillon, *At Dawn We Slept: The Untold Story of Pearl Harbor,* p. 513

3. History.com, *History Stories: 5 Facts About Pearl Harbor and USS Arizona,* by Barbara Maranzani, December 2011, Web, July 7, 2018

4. Prange, Goldstein and Dillon, *At Dawn We Slept: The Untold Story of Pearl Harbor,* p. 588

5. Devereux, *The Story of Wake Island,* p. 57

6. Devereux, *The Story of Wake Island,* p. 59

7. Wukovits, *Pacific Alamo: The Battle for Wake Island,* p. 69

8. Devereux, *The Story of Wake Island,* p. 60

9. Wukovits, *Pacific Alamo: The Battle for Wake Island,* p. 70

10. Devereux, *The Story of Wake Island,* pp. 61-62

11. Wukovits, *Pacific Alamo: The Battle for Wake Island, p. 73*

12. Wukovits, *Pacific Alamo: The Battle for Wake Island, p. 75*

13. Devereux, *The Story of Wake Island,* p. 65

14. Devereux, *The Story of Wake Island,* p. 66

15. Wukovits, *Pacific Alamo: The Battle for Wake Island,* pp. 80-81

16. Devereux, *The Story of Wake Island,* pp. 68-70

17. Devereux, *The Story of Wake Island,* pp. 71-72

18. Wukovits, *Pacific Alamo: The Battle for Wake Island,* p. 89

19. Wukovits, *Pacific Alamo: The Battle for Wake Island,* pp. 89-90

20. Wukovits, *Pacific Alamo: The Battle for Wake Island,* p. 90

21. Wukovits, *Pacific Alamo: The Battle for Wake Island,* pp. 91-92

22. Devereux, *The Story of Wake Island,* p. 77

23. Devereux, *The Story of Wake Island,* pp. 79-80

24. Bill Sloan, *Given Up for Dead: America's Heroic Stand at Wake Island,* Bantam Dell, 2003, p. 384

25. Devereux, *The Story of Wake Island,* p. 78

Chapter 9: "Keep running, Doc!"

1. Wukovits, *Pacific Alamo: The Battle for Wake Island,* pp. 97-98

2. Devereux, *The Story of Wake Island,* p. 86

3. Wukovits, *Pacific Alamo: The Battle for Wake Island,* p. 111

4. Wukovits, *Pacific Alamo: The Battle for Wake Island,* p. 112

5. Wukovits, *Pacific Alamo: The Battle for Wake Island,* p. 114

6. Devereux, *The Story of Wake Island,* p. 87

7. Devereux, *The Story of Wake Island,* p. 94

8. Devereux, *The Story of Wake Island,* p. 93

9. Devereux, *The Story of Wake Island,* p. 97

10. Wukovits, *Pacific Alamo: The Battle for Wake Island,* p. 118

11. Wukovits, *Pacific Alamo: The Battle for Wake Island,* p. 123

12. Prange, Goldstein and Dillon, *At Dawn We Slept: The Untold Story of Pearl Harbor,* p. 577

13. Wukovits, *Pacific Alamo: The Battle for Wake Island,* p. 124

14. Devereux, *The Story of Wake Island,* p. 112

15. Wukovits, *Pacific Alamo: The Battle for Wake Island,* pp. 125-126

16. Wukovits, *Pacific Alamo: The Battle for Wake Island,* p. 129

17. Devereux, *The Story of Wake Island,* p. 120

18. Devereux, *The Story of Wake Island,* p. 122

19. Devereux, *The Story of Wake Island,* p. 122

20. Wukovits, *Pacific Alamo: The Battle for Wake Island,* p. 135

21. Wukovits, *Pacific Alamo: The Battle for Wake Island,* p. 132

22. Prange, Goldstein and Dillon, *At Dawn We Slept: The Untold Story of Pearl Harbor,* p. 576

Chapter 10: "Bullets were flying everywhere."

1. Devereux, *The Story of Wake Island,* p. 129

2. Wukovits, *Pacific Alamo: The Battle for Wake Island,* p. 138

3. Devereux, *The Story of Wake Island,* p. 132

4. Devereux, *The Story of Wake Island,* pp. 132-133

5. Wukovits, *Pacific Alamo: The Battle for Wake Island,* p. 139

6. Devereux, *The Story of Wake Island,* p. 134

7. Devereux, *The Story of Wake Island,* pp. 134-135

8. Wukovits, *Pacific Alamo: The Battle for Wake Island,* p. 133

9. Wukovits, *Pacific Alamo: The Battle for Wake Island,* p. 133

10. Devereux, *The Story of Wake Island,* p. 137

11. Devereux, *The Story of Wake Island,* pp. 137-138

12. Devereux, *The Story of Wake Island,* pp. 141-142

13. Wukovits, *Pacific Alamo: The Battle for Wake Island,* p. 164

14. Wukovits, *Pacific Alamo: The Battle for Wake Island,* p. 166

15. Devereux, *The Story of Wake Island,* p. 154

16. Wukovits, *Pacific Alamo: The Battle for Wake Island,* p. 169

17. Wukovits, *Pacific Alamo: The Battle for Wake Island,* p. 171

18. Devereux, *The Story of Wake Island,* pp. 153-156

19. Wukovits, *Pacific Alamo: The Battle for Wake Island,* p. 171

20. Sloan, *Given up for Dead: America's Heroic Stand at Wake Island,* p. 249

21. Devereux, *The Story of Wake Island,* p. 157

22. Devereux, *The Story of Wake Island,* p. 162

23. Devereux, *The Story of Wake Island,* p. 158

24. Devereux, *The Story of Wake Island,* p. 168

25. Wukovits, *Pacific Alamo: The Battle for Wake Island,* p. 182

26. Devereux, *The Story of Wake Island,* p. 169

27. Wukovits, *Pacific Alamo: The Battle for Wake Island,* p. 184

28. Wukovits, *Pacific Alamo: The Battle for Wake Island,* p. 188

29. Prange, Goldstein and Dillon, *At Dawn We Slept: The Untold Story of Pearl Harbor,* p. 577

30. Devereux, *The Story of Wake Island,* p. 184

31. Sloan, *Given Up for Dead: America's Heroic Stand at Wake Island,* p. 384

32. Wukovits, *Pacific Alamo: The Battle for Wake Island,* p. 192

Chapter 11: "They would have dragged me on that plane and pushed me out over Midway."

1. Devereux, *The Story of Wake Island,* pp. 186-187

2. Devereux, *The Story of Wake Island,* p. 190

3. Wukovits, *Pacific Alamo: The Battle for Wake Island,* pp. 192-193

4. "To the Marines on Wake Islands," *The Washington Post,* December 24, 1941, p. 1

5. Historylink.org, *Women Workers in WW II,* Source: Susan M. Hartmann, *The Home Front and Beyond: American Women in the 1940s,* (Boston: Twayne Publishers, 1982), Web, July 19, 2018

6. History.com, *American Women in WWII, History.com Staff,* Web, July 19, 2018

7. Wukovits, *Pacific Alamo: The Battle for Wake Island,* p. 195

8. Taylor, *Rescued by Mao: World War II, Wake Island, and My Remarkable Escape to Freedom Across Mainland China,* p. 113

Chapter 12: "Our lives meant nothing to them."

1. WW2DB.com, World War Database, *Chuyo,* by C. Peter Chen, Lava Development LLC., Web, July 20, 2018

2. Prange, Goldstein and Dillon, *At Dawn We Slept: The Untold Story of Pearl Harbor,* p. 313

3. WW2DB.com, World War Database, *Chuyo,* by C. Peter Chen, Web, July 20, 2018

4. Invaluable.com, *The History of the Bushido Code,* Last Updated, December 13, 2017, Web, July 23, 2018

5. Hastings, *Retribution: The Battle for Japan 1944-45,* p. 54

6. Hastings, *Retribution: The Battle for Japan 1944-45,* p. 54

7. Chang, *The Rape of Nanking: The Forgotten Holocaust of World War II,* p. 20

8. Chet Cunningham, *Hell Wouldn't Stop: An Oral History of the Battle of Wake Island,* Carroll and Graff Publishers, 2002, pp. 240-241

9. Devereux, *The Story of Wake Island,* p. 197

10. Wukovits, *Pacific Alamo: The Battle for Wake Island*, p. 208

11. Miller, *The Story of World War II*, Simon & Schuster Paperbacks, 2001, pp. 104-111

12. Northchinamarines.com, *Prisoner of War Camps in Areas Other Than the Four Principal Islands of Japan: Woosung China*, Liaison and Research Branch American Prisoner of War Information Bureau, By Capt. James I. Norwood and Capt. Emily L. Shek, 31 July 1946, Web, July 26, 2018

Chapter 13: "Wow—did they beat me! I was so mad I didn't feel it."

1. Craig Nelson, *The First Heroes: The Extraordinary Story of the Doolittle Raid—America's First World War II Victory*, Viking Penguin, 2002, p. 9

2. Nelson, *The First Heroes: The Extraordinary Story of the Doolittle Raid—America's First World War II Victory*, pp. 32-33

3. Nelson, *The First Heroes: The Extraordinary Story of the Doolittle Raid—America's First World War II Victory*, p. 61

4. Nelson, *The First Heroes: The Extraordinary Story of the Doolittle Raid—America's First World War II Victory*, p. 233

5. Homeoftheheroes.com, *Doolittle's Tokyo Raiders*, C. Douglas Sterner with contributions by Carroll V. Glines, 1999-2014, Web, July 24, 2018

6. Northchinamarines.com, *Prisoner of War Camps in Areas Other Than the Four Principal Islands of Japan: Woosung China*, Liaison and Research Branch American Prisoner of War Information Bureau, By Capt. James I. Norwood and Capt. Emily L. Shek, 31 July 1946, Web, July 26, 2018

7. Cunningham, *Hell Wouldn't Stop: An Oral History of the Battle of Wake Island,* P. 197

8. Wukovits, *Pacific Alamo: The Battle for Wake Island,* p. 240

9. Devereux, *The Story of Wake Island,* pp. 205-206

10. Northchinamarines.com, *Prisoner of War Camps in Areas Other Than the Four Principal Islands of Japan: Woosung China, Norwood and Shek,* Web, July 26, 2018

11. Miller, *D-Days in The Pacific: Guadalcanal, Tarawa, Saipan, Iwo Jima, Okinawa,* 2005, p. 39

12. Walter Lord, *Incredible Victory,* Harper and Row, 1967, pp.79-80

13. Lord, *Incredible Victory,* p. 299

14. History.com, "Battle of Midway," By John Prados, Web, July 27, 2018

15. Hastings, *Retribution: The Battle for Japan 1944-45,* p. 38

16. Miller, *The Story of World War II,* p. 133

Chapter 14: "I tore it up and threw it in the latrine."

1. Cunningham, *Hell Wouldn't Stop: An Oral History of the Battle of Wake Island,* P. 189

2. Cunningham, *Hell Wouldn't Stop: An Oral History of the Battle of Wake Island,* P. 170

3. Wukovits, *Pacific Alamo: The Battle for Wake Island,* p. 225

4. Wukovits, *Pacific Alamo: The Battle for Wake Island,* p. 234

5. Wukovits, *Pacific Alamo: The Battle for Wake Island,* p. 236

6. Wukovits, *Pacific Alamo: The Battle for Wake Island,* pp. 235-237

7. John Wukovitz, *One Square Mile of Hell: The Battle for Tarawa*, New American Library, 2006, p. 217

8. Eyewitnesstohistory.com, "The Bloody Battle of Tarawa," 2003, Web, July 29, 2018

9. Wukovitz, *One Square Mile of Hell: The Battle for Tarawa*, pp. 217-218

10. Wukovitz, *One Square Mile of Hell: The Battle for Tarawa*, p. 256

11. Ian W. Toll, *The Conquering Tide: War in the Pacific Islands, 1942–1944*, W.W. Norton and Company, Inc., 2015, p. 314

12. Cunningham, *Hell Wouldn't Stop: An Oral History of the Battle of Wake Island*, p. 179

13. Michael Jones, *Leningrad: State of Siege*, Basic Books, 2008, p. 293

14. Stephen E. Ambrose, *D-Day: June 6, 1944: The Climactic Battle of World War II*, Simon and Schuster Paperbacks, 1994, p. 576

15. Ambrose, *D-Day: June 6, 1944: The Climactic Battle of World War II*, p.583

16. Jon Meacham, *Destiny and Power: The American Odyssey of George Herbert Walker Bush*, Random House, 2015, pp. 57-58

17. History.com, "Battle of Saipan," History.com Staff, 2009, Web, August 1, 2018

18. Harold J. Goldberg, *D-Day in the Pacific: The Battle of Saipan*, Indiana University Press, 2007, p. 200

19. Goldberg, *D-Day in the Pacific: The Battle of Saipan*, p. 210

20. Bill Sloan, *Brotherhood of Brothers: The Marines at Peleliu, 1944—The Bloodiest Battle of the Pacific War*, Simon and Schuster Paperbacks, 2005, p. 315

21. Sloan, *Brotherhood of Brothers: The Marines at Peleliu, 1944—The Bloodiest Battle of the Pacific War,* p. 350

Chapter 15: "Due to the atomic bomb, we surrender."

1. Hastings, *Retribution: The Battle for Japan 1944-45,* pp. 276-277

2. Hastings, *Retribution: The Battle for Japan 1944-45,* p. 277

3. Miller, *The Story of World War II,* p. 358

4. James Bradley with Ron Powers, *Flags of Our Fathers,* Bantam Books, 2000, p. 135

5. Bradley with Ron Powers, *Flags of Our Fathers,* p. 135

6. Eric Hammel, *Iwo Jima,* Zenith Press, 2006, p. 235

7. Encyclopedia.com, "The Liberation of the Philippines," The Oxford Companion of American Military History, Web, August 9, 2018

8. Miller, *D-Days in The Pacific: Guadalcanal, Tarawa, Saipan, Iwo Jima, Okinawa,* p. 201

9. WW2db.com, *Filipinos dead in WWII,* C. Peter Chen, Web, August 11, 2018

10. Miller, *D-Days in The Pacific: Guadalcanal, Tarawa, Saipan, Iwo Jima, Okinawa,* p. 311

11. Hastings, *Retribution: The Battle for Japan 1944-45,* p. 402

12. USS Indianapolis Survivors, Introduction by John G. Gromosiak, *Only 317 Survived: USS Indianapolis (CA-35), Real Experiences of the USS Indianapolis Survivors,* Printing Partners, Inc., 2002, pp. ix-x

13. Bennett *America: The Last Best Hope: Volume II: From a World at War to the Triumph of Freedom,* pp. 262-263

14. Miller, *The Story of World War II,* Simon & Schuster Paperbacks, 2001, pp. 607-608

15. Miller, *The Story of World War II,* Simon & Schuster Paperbacks, 2001, p. 608

16. Miller, *The Story of World War II,* Simon & Schuster Paperbacks, 2001, p. 614

17. *Hampton Sides, Ghost Soldiers: The Epic Account of World War II's Greatest Rescue Mission,* First Anchor Books Edition, May 2002 p. 12

18. Hastings, *Retribution: The Battle for Japan 1944-45,* p. 528

19. Hastings, *Retribution: The Battle for Japan 1944-45,* pp. 514-515

20. Miller, *The Story of World War II,* Simon & Schuster Paperbacks, 2001, p. 639

21. History.navy.mil, *U.S. Prisoners of War and Civilian American Citizens Captured and Interned by Japan in World War II: The Issue of Compensation by Japan, Congressional Research Service Report for Congress,* Gary K. Reynolds, Updated December 17, 2002, Web, August 11, 2018

Chapter 16: "Are you my daddy?"

1. Norman Gruenzer, *The Japanese Story: Postal History of American POWs: World War II, Korea Vietnam,* Packet #10, American EX-POW Inc., National Medical Research Comm., p. 46

2. History.navy.mil, *U.S. Prisoners of War and Civilian American Citizens Captured and Interned by Japan in World War II: The Issue of Compensation by Japan, Congressional Research Service Report for Congress,* Gary K. Reynolds, Updated December 17, 2002, Web, August 11, 2018

3. Wukovits, *Pacific Alamo: The Battle for Wake Island,* p. 263

4. Warhistoryonline.com, *Battle of Wake Island—All Those Who Surrendered Were Tortured, 98 Were Machine-Gunned,* By Elaine Smith, September 23, 2016, Web, August 1, 2018

5. History.com, *1948 Japanese War Criminals Hanged in Tokyo,* Web. August 11, 2018

6. Miller, *D-Days in The Pacific: Guadalcanal, Tarawa, Saipan, Iwo Jima, Okinawa,* p. 365

7. Nationalww2museum.org, *Research Starters: Worldwide Deaths in World War II,* Web, August 11, 2018

8. Hastings, *Retribution: The Battle for Japan 1944-45,* p. 541

9. Nationalww2museum.org, *Research Starters: Worldwide Deaths in World War II,* Web, August 11, 2018

10. Cunningham, *Hell Wouldn't Stop: An Oral History of the Battle of Wake Island,* P. 198

11. Cunningham, *Hell Wouldn't Stop: An Oral History of the Battle of Wake Island,* P. 159

12. Wukovits, *Pacific Alamo: The Battle for Wake Island,* pp. 249-250

13. Wukovits, *Pacific Alamo: The Battle for Wake Island,* p. 250

14. *The Japanese Story: Medical Department, United States Army, Internal Medicine in World War II, Vol. III, Infectious Diseases & General Medicine, Office of the Surgeon General, Department of the Army, Malnutrition in the Far East,* Packet #10, American EX-POW Inc., National Medical Research Comm., 1968., pp. 61-62

15. *The Japanese Story: Medical Department, Study of World War II Prisoners of War, H.R. 8848 S. 3903, Evidence of Permanent Physical & Mental Disabilities as a Result of Imprisonment or*

Internment, Replies from Physicians Formerly Prisoners of the Japanese Government, September 1950, p. 56

16. *The Japanese Story: Medical Department, Study of World War II Prisoners of War, H.R. 8848 S. 3903, Evidence of Permanent Physical & Mental Disabilities as a Result of Imprisonment or Internment, Replies from Physicians Formerly Prisoners of the Japanese Government,* September 1950, p. 58

17. Navsource.org, *USS Rescue (AH-18): NavSource Online: Service Ship Photo Archive,* Contributed by Don McGrogan BMCS, USN Ret, October 2017, Web, August 13, 2018

Chapter 17: "I hate to wake up, because you are not there."

1. VA.govopapublications, *VA History in Brief,* Department of Veterans Affairs, p. 15, Web, August 14, 2018

2. Historyofptsd.wordpress.com, *History of PTSD: Every man has his breaking point,* Web, August 14, 2018

3. Navsource.org. *USS General W. A. Mann (AP-112) (1943 - 1949)* Gary P. Priolo with contributions from Mike Smolinski, December, 2016, Web, August 17, 2018

Chapter 18: "I'm okay. It was a lizard."

1. Navsource.com, *USS Kenneth Whitting (AV-14),* Gary P. Priolo, Updated February 2016, Web, August 22, 2018

2. Maurice Isserman, *Korean War: Americans at War,* Facts on File Inc., 2003. pp. 15-25

3. *Kanpai-Japan.com, Genbaku Dome: The Remains of the Atomic Bombing of Hiroshima,* Updated June 2018, Web, August 22, 2018

4. Isserman, *Korean War: Americans at War,* p. 120

5. Isserman, *Korean War: Americans at War,* pp. 112-113

6. To-hawaii.com, *Punchbowl National Cemetery, Oahu,* 2016-2018, Web, August 23, 2018

7. Cem.va.gov, *VA National Cemetery Administration: National Memorial Cemetery of the Pacific,* Updated August 2018, Web, August 23, 2018

Chapter 19: "I wish you could come with me."

Epilogue: "To find that better way."

1. Dan Judge, "Years as a POW not forgotten," *Vallejo Times Herald,* August 25, 2007

2. *Wake Island Wig-Wag,* published by Franklin D. Gross, Volume 11, July 1984

★　★　★

ABOUT THE AUTHOR

Juan Carlos Marcos spent four decades in leadership roles in the corporate world retiring as Senior Vice President and Chief People Officer McDonald's U. S. *The Last Corpsman* is his second book. Previously he wrote *Warriors at the Helm: A Leader's Guide to Success in Business*. Born in Cuba, Juan immigrated to the U.S. in 1962. He holds a bachelor's degree in business from Northern Illinois University and a master's degree in business from the University of Wisconsin. Juan lives in Evergreen, Colorado, with his wife Randi.

Made in United States
North Haven, CT
17 December 2021